HE RUNS, SHE RUNS

HE RUNS, SHE RUNS

Why Gender Stereotypes Do Not

Harm Women Candidates

Deborah Jordan Brooks

PRINCETON UNIVERSITY PRESS

Princeton & Oxford

Copyright © 2013 by Princeton University Press
Published by Princeton University Press, 41 William Street,
Princeton, New Jersey 08540
In the United Kingdom: Princeton University Press, 6 Oxford Street,
Woodstock, Oxfordshire OX20 1TW

press.princeton.edu

Library of Congress Cataloging-in-Publication Data
Brooks, Deborah Jordan.
He runs, she runs : why gender stereotypes do not harm women candidates /
Deborah Jordan Brooks.
pages cm
Includes bibliographical references and index.
ISBN 978-0-691-15341-4 (hardcover : alk. paper) — ISBN 978-0-691-15342-1
(pbk. : alk. paper) 1. Women—Political activity—United States. 2. Women
political candidates—United States. 3. Political campaigns—United
States. I. Title.
HQ1236.5.U6B77 2013
320.082—dc23
2012045252

British Library Cataloging-in-Publication Data is available

This book has been composed in Sabon LT Std

Printed on acid-free paper ∞

Printed in the United States of America

1 3 5 7 9 10 8 6 4 2

To my daughters, Riley and Avery

MAY THEY DREAM BIG DREAMS

CONTENTS

TABLES

ACKNOWLEDGMENTS

An incredible group of people helped to make this book possible, and I am enormously grateful to all of them for their help. Very special thanks are due to Joe Bafumi, Jamie Druckman, Kim Fridkin, John Geer, Marc Hetherington, Mike Mastanduno, Chuck Myers, and Ben Valentino for their tremendous assistance at multiple stages of this project. Their support made this a much stronger book. I also owe many thanks to a wide range of people who provided feedback and assistance on specific pieces of this project. I appreciate the help of Lisa Baldez, Barbara Burrell, Alice Eagly, Linda Fowler, Danny Hayes, John Hibbing, Jen Lawless, Alan Gerber, Matt Green, Leonie Huddy, Richard Isomaki, Beth Jafari, Dean Lacy, Celinda Lake, Rick Matland, David Mayhew, Rose McDermott, Diana Mutz, Zoe Oxley, Deborah Prentice, Kira Sanbonmatsu, Brent Stranthman, Debbie Tegarden, Beth Theiss-Morse, and Dan Wirls at critical points during the process of writing this book. Additionally, I would like to thank all of the participants at the New Research on Gender and Political Psychology conference held at the Institute for Women's Leadership at the Eagleton Institute at Rutgers University in the spring of 2011 for extremely useful feedback on this project, along with the coordinators of the conference (Monica Schneider and Angie Bos) for organizing such a fantastic event.

This project most certainly would not have been possible without the creativity and dedication of Sam Luks and Ashley Grosse at YouGov (formerly named Polimetrix), along with the rest of their team of survey professionals who make it possible to undertake online survey work like this. I could not be more impressed by their ability to turn my research designs, no matter how complex, into rich, high-quality public opinion data. I deeply appreciate their partnership on this and so many of my projects.

Several research assistants deserve special recognition for their commitment to this book project. The book was not only improved because of their efforts, but working with such a truly great team of energetic and sharp Dartmouth undergraduates made the entire process more enjoyable along the way. Tremendous thanks are due to Michelle Chan, Katie Gonzalez, Julia Greenberg, Franziska Hertel, Hannah Katterman, and Despina Sideri for extended involvement with this project. I also greatly appreciate the assistance of Natalie Colinari, Ana Haggerty, Fermin Liu

Ku, Sam Marullo, Jenna Pfeffer, Caitlin Veator, and Amanda Wheelock at particular stages of this project.

This project would not have been possible without research funding from Dartmouth College. I am very grateful for that support, and to the deans at Dartmouth College for making it available to me. And every day, I appreciate Chris Gex and Gina Sekula for providing administrative support that allows me and all of the professors in the Government Department at Dartmouth to be productive on research.

While my former colleagues at the Gallup Organization did not directly assist on this book, the learning I received there about polling and managing complex research projects very much radiates throughout this book, as it has through all of my work. Many thanks to Jeff Jones, David Moore, Gale Muller, Frank Newport, and Lydia Saad, in particular, for the learning they provided to me during my half decade working there. In a similar manner, the early and continued mentorship of Alan Gerber, David Mayhew, and Dan Wirls permeates my work in countless ways.

Finally, I would like to deeply thank my best friend, favorite colleague, and husband, Steve Brooks, for being there at every step of this project. And I would like to thank my two daughters, Riley (currently nine years old) and Avery (currently six years old), for being amazing little future women who inspire me every day; this book is dedicated to them.

HE RUNS, SHE RUNS

CHAPTER 1

Introduction

"I'm no lady; I'm a member of Congress,
and I shall proceed accordingly."

—MARY THERESA NORTON,
U.S. HOUSE MEMBER FROM 1925–1951[1]

When Hillary Clinton ran in the 2008 Democratic presidential primaries, she seemed to have trouble connecting effectively with the public. After months of a campaign that emphasized her toughness and experience, she underperformed in the polls relative to her biggest competitors. While some observers argued that her strong emphasis on experience caused voters to think she was "trying too hard to be 'the smartest girl in the room,'" others maintained that the focus she had adopted was dictated by the politics of gender: although a male candidate like Barack Obama could be seen as credible without much past experience, a woman candidate would not be.[2] And while Clinton's chief strategist emphasized that she had to establish herself as a tough "father" figure for the country and not as the "first mama,"[3] she was frequently criticized for being angry, aggressive, and unfeminine and was called an "ice-queen" for her apparent lack of empathy.[4] As a journalist put it, "she presented herself as a person of strength and conviction, only to be rejected as cold-hearted and unfeminine—as a 'nutcracker.'"[5]

When Clinton's campaign then sought to soften her image through more intimate gatherings, more compassion-oriented discussions, and more personally emotive moments to increase her "likeability," that approach seemed to backfire as well. Her campaign started a Web site "TheHillaryIKnow

[1] "National Affairs: I'm No Lady," *Time Magazine*, March 20, 1950.

[2] Judith Timson, "From the Mouths of Critics: A Glaring Double Standard," *Globe and Mail*, February 26, 2008., February 26, 2008 Tuesday, Pg. L1.

[3] See Mark Penn's "Launch Strategy Thoughts" memo from December 21, 2006, http://www.theatlantic.com/politics/archive/2008/11/penns-launch-strategy-ideas-december-21-2006/37953.

[4] Leslie Jorgensen, "Ice Queen, Bitch, or Sentimental Pushover: Clinton Got It All," *Colorado Statesman*, September 5, 2008; Peter Nicholas, "Hillary Clinton Cold, Calculating? Not according to Bill," *Los Angeles Times*, December 12, 2007.

[5] Waleed Aly, "When It Comes to Being President, Is Sexism the Final Frontier?" *The Age* (Melbourne Australia), June 11, 2008.

.com" that presented videotaped testimonials by friends and supporters to highlight Hillary's caring and compassionate side.[6] As the New Hampshire primaries approached, Clinton's campaign featured stories of mothers of sick children in a series of emotional ads that were designed to portray her in a more caring light.[7] Clinton's effort to, as one media analyst described it, "run away from [her] tough, kind of bitchy image" ran into difficulties: no longer too unemotional, she was now pegged by some as being "weak" and a "cry baby."[8] As one journalist put it, "when she did show emotion by crying on the hustings, she was branded weak, or accused of playing cynically to the cameras."[9]

While Clinton attracted a devoted set of core supporters, she also had high unfavorable ratings. With conflicting advice ricocheting from pundits and consultants about how to present herself, she tried a variety of different approaches for connecting with primary voters. In the end, of course, more Democrats voted for Barack Obama, and she lost the Democratic nomination for president.

Hillary's loss was not the last chance for a woman to appear on a national ticket in 2008. When Sarah Palin was announced as the vice presidential candidate on the McCain ticket for the general election, commentators zeroed in on her low levels of previous experience. Knowledge gaffes in her infamous Charles Gibson and Katie Couric interviews did not help Palin's case on the credentials front, and some argued that the scrutiny of her experience was exacerbated because she was a woman.[10]

While campaigning, Palin proclaimed herself to be a "pit bull with lipstick" and tried to claim both toughness and compassion. Palin attempted to manage the balance between toughness and compassion in part by surrounding herself with her young family and discussing issues such as disability rights while talking tough about issues and her opponents. Like Clinton, Palin attracted a strong cohort of devoted followers while suffering very high unfavorable ratings; in other words, she, too, was a polarizing figure.

Many analysts chalked up the electoral failings of Clinton and Palin to good old-fashioned sexism. With headlines such as "How Sexism Killed Hillary's Dream," "This Smacks of Double Standards; Women Kept in

---

[6] Leslie Jorgensen, "Ice Queen, Bitch, or Sentimental Pushover: Clinton Got It All," *Colorado Statesman*, September 5, 2008; Jill Lawrence, "New Clinton Campaign Out to Show Her Likeability," *USA Today*, December 16, 2007, 4A.

[7] Lawrence and Rose 2010, 119.

[8] Timson, Judith, "From the Mouths of Critics: A Glaring Double Standard," *Globe and Mail*, February 26, 2008.

[9] Waleed Aly, "When It Comes to Being President, Is Sexism the Final Frontier?" *The Age* (Melbourne, Australia), June 11, 2008. The crying episode was widely thought to have hurt Clinton, until she unexpectedly won the New Hampshire primary, which generated some revisionist news stories about how crying actually helped her with voters.

[10] See, e.g., McGinley 2009, 721.

Place," and "The 'Bitch' and the 'Ditz': How the Year of the Woman Reinforced the Two Most Pernicious Sexist Stereotypes and Actually Set Women Back," commentators frequently reflected the conventional wisdom about women in politics: their credentials and campaign behavior are subjected to double standards that make it harder for them to win political office.

For many, the experience of Clinton and Palin clearly confirmed that the country is still not ready to elect a woman president. Others were more cautious in their assessments. For example, Anne Kornblut, journalist and author of *Notes from the Cracked Ceiling: Hillary Clinton, Sarah Palin, and What It Will Take for a Woman to Win*, sought to answer whether the country is ready to elect the first woman president by looking back over what she described as "a battlefield littered with gender-related detritus, with charges of sexism, the phrases 'she-devil' and 'pit bull with lipstick' and 'lipstick on a pig' and 'likable enough' and 'Caribou Barbie' and 'baby mama' scattered everywhere."[11] At various points in her book, Kornblut strongly implies that gender held back Clinton and Palin, but she ultimately demurs from directly making this causal claim owing in large part to the idiosyncrasies of the particular candidates and races in question.[12]

Kornblut's reluctance to tell a causal story about the role of gender in 2008 is both understandable and wise. When the campaigns of individual candidates falter, it is impossible to determine the degree to which any single factor—whether it be gender, race, ethnicity, a scandal, or something else entirely—produced the observed outcome with any reasonable level of analytical precision. Did Hillary Clinton and Sarah Palin fail in their electoral goals because of gender-related issues or because of other factors that pertained to them as individuals or to their respective races? Perhaps it was Palin's political inexperience, socioeconomic background, polarizing ideology, the inherent challenge of running as a Republican in 2008, John McCain's difficulty connecting with voters, his weakness on economic issues in combination with a rapidly declining economy, or yet another factor that hampered her, rather than her gender. Perhaps Clinton was hampered, not by gender, but by (Bill) Clinton fatigue, questionable campaign management and early spending decisions, exaggerations of her past history, the voters' desire for a fresh approach, Obama's ability to connect with younger voters, the Obama team's superior ground organization, or other such factors.

All races involve unique sets of candidates, candidate behaviors, partisan dynamics, and local and national circumstances that can contribute to an electoral outcome. This inherently constrains our ability to look at a given race—or even a given set of races—and draw meaningful conclusions about the role of candidates' gender. To produce firm answers about

[11] Kornblut 2009, 10.
[12] Kornblut 2009, 10.

the role of candidate gender in public opinion about campaigns, we need to be able to effectively isolate it. We need to know how gender affects public views overall—and how it interacts with candidate behavior—while holding constant all the other moving parts in a campaign.

In this book, I isolate two dynamics that many see as crucial barriers to the electoral success of women: gender stereotypes and gendered standards. Many have long suspected that the public makes special assumptions about, and applies special "rules" to, female candidates, and the experiences of Palin and Clinton in the 2008 election cycle led to an explosion of interest in this issue. According to the conventional wisdom, just as gender stereotypes have long caused women to be treated differently in the workplace and in society more generally, they also make it harder for women to win political office. This book provides the first systematic theoretical and empirical analysis of whether gender stereotypes and double standards do, in fact, hold back female candidates on the campaign trail.

My overall conclusion is an optimistic one: while my results show that gender stereotypes still do matter in various ways, the analysis is a striking refutation of the conventional wisdom about double standards in campaigns. I do not find any evidence that the public makes less favorable underlying assumptions about female candidates, nor do I find that the public has more challenging rules for the behavior of women on the campaign trail. My findings solve a puzzle that has vexed this field for decades: if stereotypes and double standards disproportionately hurt women candidates as the conventional wisdom posits, then how can we square this with findings that demonstrate that women receive vote shares that are comparable to those of similarly situated men?[13] If voters penalize women in politics for being women, women candidates should win their campaigns against men at relatively lower rates. They do not, which is entirely consistent with my overall finding regarding the insignificance of damaging gender stereotypes on the campaign trail.

The primary focus of my analysis is at the legislative level, where far more women run for office. Although this is a common pipeline for *future* presidential candidates, my study cannot definitively rule out that a glass ceiling may remain for women seeking the highest office of the land. That being said, what my findings do reveal is a clear pattern regarding the qualities of leadership and toughness that are typically seen as being especially critical at the executive level: the general public simply does not view women legislators as being less capable than men on traits cen-

---

[13] See, e.g., Tolleson-Rinehart and Josephson in Tolleson-Rinehart and Josephson 2000, 5; Erika Falk and Kathleen Hall Jamieson in Watson and Gordon 2003, 48; Burrell 1996, 55; Carroll 1994, 48; Lawless and Pearson 2008; Pearson 2010, 237; Palmer and Simon 2001, 62; Fox 2000, 232; 2010, 194; Darcy, Welch, and Clark 1994, 67 and 100; Seltzer, Newman, and Leighton 1997; Smith and Fox 2001.

tral to leadership and does not penalize women for acting in a tough and "unfeminine" manner. My study yields some suggestive findings that older individuals might hold different views with respect to women and the presidency; to the extent that this might be the case, the natural process of generational replacement may improve prospects for women at the presidential level in the United States. More generally, if women were significantly held back by gender stereotypes at the presidential level today, it would also be reasonable to expect to find at least some evidence of that dynamic at other levels, and yet my study finds none. In the end, my analysis is thus very encouraging for the long-term future of women in politics at all levels.

Why Candidate Gender Matters

Over the course of a dramatic century for women's rights, women have progressed from being disenfranchised before 1919 to a much-expanded role in the political sphere. Casting over half of the votes in the U.S., women today are a powerful force in terms of deciding who will be elected.[14] In fact, some in the media believe that the 2012 elections were defined largely by the power of women as voters, with headlines like, "Women take stock after historic vote," "How women ruled the 2012 election and where the GOP went wrong," and "How women won it." With a sizeable partisan gender gap in voting preferences in play, women were critical to putting Barack Obama back in the White House (had it been up to men, Mitt Romney would have been president), and were pivotal to a number of sub-presidential wins and losses, as well.

Female candidates have also made great strides. Until quite recently, women occupied a tiny percentage of Congress—a mere 2 percent of House seats and 1 percent of Senate seats in 1950, and just 4 percent of House seats and still 1 percent of Senate seats in 1980; moreover, many of these early women legislators were in office because they took the place of departed husbands, and not because they won competitive elections entirely on their own personal merits. Women are now far more likely to win office, and to do so without following on their departed husbands' coattails.[15] And yet the parity that has been achieved for female voters is still an elusive goal for female politicians. As of 1990, women held only 7 percent of House seats and 2 percent of Senate seats. Increases in 1992, the "Year of the Woman," bolstered those numbers (to

[14] Verba, Schlozman, and Brady 1995, 255.

[15] The Center for American Women and Politics at Rutgers University has produced a several useful resources regarding the change in the number of women in Congress over time; see, http://www.cawp.rutgers.edu/fast_facts/levels_of_office/Congress-CurrentFacts .php.

13 and 7 percent, respectively), but by 2011 women held 17 percent of House seats, 17 percent of Senate seats, and six governorships. In the current era, women hold roughly one-quarter of state legislative seats, with considerable variation between states.[16]

The 2012 elections increased the number of women in national office further, with a record number of both women House members (81) and women senators (20) sworn into office the following January.[17] Several states (Hawaii, Massachusetts, North Dakota, and Wisconsin) elected women Senators for the first time ever, while New Hampshire elected the first-ever all women congressional delegation, along with a woman governor to boot. Describing the 2012 results, Karen Tumulty of the *Washington Post* claimed that, "Twenty years after the election that was heralded as the 'year of the woman' comes another one that could be called that."[18]

While representing significant progress over a relatively short time, the ratios of female to male political leaders are still nowhere near gender parity at any level of American government. Vigorous debates could be undertaken concerning what the "correct" or "best" percentage of women in office should be: Should it be the percentage of women in the population? The percentage of women relative to men who work—or work full time—outside of the home? The relative percentage of women who are interested in politics? Regardless, most people would likely agree that, by any measure, there is a significant "parity problem" with respect to the descriptive representation of women, even in the current era.[19]

The descriptive underrepresentation of women in public office matters in part because it can lead to underrepresentation of women's concerns and opinions. Scholars have shown that women officeholders are better able to represent the preferences of women and are more likely to sponsor and vote for women-friendly policies.[20] Other scholars have demon-

---

[16] "Fact Sheet Archive," Facts, Rutgers: Center for American Women and Politics, http://www.cawp.rutgers.edu/fast_facts/resources/FactSheetArchive.php. Sanbonmatsu (2006) points out that substantial variation exists in the descriptive representation of women between states; merely 9% of South Carolina's state-level legislators are women versus 41% of Colorado's legislators, with the rest of the states arrayed fairly evenly along the continuum.

[17] Ashley Parker, "Day of Records and Firsts as 113th Congress Opens," *New York Times*, January 3, 2013. See also http://history.house.gov/Exhibitions-and-Publications/WIC/Historical-Data/Women-Representatives-and-Senators-by-Congress/.

[18] Karen Tumulty, "Female candidates make history, head for the Hill," *Washington Post*, November 8, 2012.

[19] I will be referring to the "parity problem" at different points in this book as shorthand for discussing the current percentage of women in office relative to men. See the Hunt Alternatives Fund's "Political Parity Project" Web site, http://www.politicalparity.org, for more information on this issue along with some practical actions that are being taken to increase the descriptive representation of women.

[20] See, e.g., Burrell 1994; Caizza 2004; Gerrity, Osborn, and Mendex 2007; Norton 1999; Swers 1998; Thomas 1991, 1994.

strated that women legislators more frequently give speeches on issues that are thought to be of greater concern to women, such as abortion, gender equity, food stamps, and flex time than were their predecessors.[21] Some scholars argue that the inclusion of more women in legislatures changes decision making by producing a more cooperative, inclusive, and less hierarchical legislative process.[22] Women with political power also empower other women in a symbolic sense by simply being in office: participation, efficacy, and political interest have been found to increase substantially among women when they are represented by women.[23] This effect reaches into future generations as well: David Campbell and Christina Wolbrecht found that adolescent girls had a higher level of planned political involvement when they were exposed to more highly visible women in office.[24]

Given that a marked gender disparity still exists and is likely to affect both the political behavior and the substantive representation of women, it is critical to fully investigate the potential causes of this parity problem.

Harmful Stereotypes and Double Standards as a Potential Explanation for the Parity Problem

The world abounds with information, and humans use a variety of simplification tools such as gender stereotypes in order to more efficiently (if not always accurately) process the regular onslaught of stimuli. Gender stereotypes are commonly used in everyday life; psychological research reveals that strong gender stereotypes are commonly applied to ordinary people, a finding that gives weight to the concern that female candidates may be hobbled by double standards. Studies have found that men are commonly thought to be more decisive, more assertive, more forceful, more ambitious, and less naïve and to have more leadership ability and business sense than women.[25] People also tend to hold strong beliefs about how men and women *should* act—for example, women are expected to be less assertive and forceful and more caring and compassionate—and men and women tend to be penalized heavily if they act con-

[21] See, e.g., Gerrity, Osborne, and Mendez 2007 and Pearson and Dancey 2011. The Pearson and Dancey article is especially interesting because it examines gender and partisanship, and finds that both Democratic and Republican women legislators were more likely than their male counterparts to discuss matters pertaining to women, and Republican women were more likely to discuss matters pertaining to women more than Democratic men in three out of the four Congresses they studied.

[22] See, e.g., Weikart et al. 2007.

[23] High-Pippert and Comer 1998; Atkeson and Carrillo 2007; Atkeson 2003.

[24] Campbell and Wolbrecht 2006.

[25] See, e.g., Lippa 2005; Deaux and La France 1998; Prentice and Carranza 2002; Williams and Best 1982.

trary to those gendered expectations.[26] Furthermore, the significance of gender stereotypes extends beyond normal interpersonal relations in everyday life: there is considerable evidence that female business leaders face a different—and, by and large, tougher—set of expectations about their qualifications and behavior than do their male peers.[27]

But what about the political realm? Do women running for office face tougher expectations by the public regarding their qualifications and behavior than male candidates do? If so, does that contribute to the parity problem? That is the underlying question this book systematically addresses. As a foundation for investigating this question empirically, we first need to understand whether the public makes differing baseline assumptions about male and female candidates—that is, whether people stereotype male and female candidates based on gender from the start.

That question—the matter of whether people use gender stereotypes to evaluate candidates without respect to a candidate's actual behavior or individual qualifications for office—has drawn the attention of many scholars, including Deborah Alexander, Kristi Andersen, Kathy Dolan, Erika Falk, Richard Fox, Kim Kahn (Kim Fridkin),[28] Leonie Huddy, Pat Kenney, Kate Kenski, David King, Jennifer Lawless, Rick Matland, Monica McDermott, and Kira Sanbonmatsu. Although there seems to be broad consensus among academics that the public adopts gender stereotypes in the evaluation of political candidates, the implications of those stereotypes for the election of women candidates are not clear.[29] The results of studies in the field range from the idea that baseline stereotypes are very harmful, on net, to the electoral prospects of female candidates to the view that positive stereotypes about women counterbalance any negative stereotypes; a study by Kahn even found that women candidates only benefit from positive stereotypes held by the public, once media coverage is held constant.[30] Directly comparing the results of those studies to one another in order to answer with confidence whether women candidates are harmed by gender stereotypes is difficult, however, as the stud-

---

[26] See, e.g., Prentice and Carranza 2002; Tyler and McCullough 2009; Rudman and Phelan 2008.

[27] For an outstanding review of findings in this area, see Eagly and Carli 2007.

[28] Note that "Kim Kahn" and "Kim Fridkin" are the same scholar, with her more recent work published under the name "Fridkin." Throughout this book, I refer to her work with the name she published with at the time.

[29] With the kind of characterization about the literature on gender stereotypes that is common in work about women candidates, Dolan, Deckman, and Swers state in their 2011 textbook that, "voters presume that female candidates possess certain feminine personality traits whereas men possess certain masculine traits. Female candidates are seen as more compassionate, moral, honest, and ethical than are men. Voters perceive men as tougher, better able to handle crises, more qualified, and more decisive than women" (143).

[30] Kahn 1994, 183.

ies rely on a wide range of methodologies (direct questions about views on candidate gender, views of real candidates, or experiments), different kinds of samples (local undergraduates, local temp-agency employees, or U.S. adults), and data collected in different eras.

The issue of when the studies were conducted is critical. Many of the studies still being cited as proof that women candidates have to battle the pernicious effects of gender stereotypes were conducted in the 1970s, 1980s, and early 1990s, when gender relations were at a very different stage in the social world and in the workplace. The public may have very different views about women and leadership today. In contrast, the data for the present book were collected in April 2009—that is, after the 2008 election, an election that may well have altered the way some people think about female candidates. Thus, this book provides a starting point for understanding gender stereotypes in the post-2008 era.

An examination of the baseline stereotypes that the public may apply to male and female candidates in the current era is only the first piece of this study. It is an important first step because it permits a dialogue with much of the previous literature on the topic and, more generally, because it provides a foundation for understanding how candidate gender affects public views about candidates before people start reacting to specific candidate behaviors or qualifications. The specific issue addressed here—whether women candidates are held to different standards for their qualifications or behavior that make it harder for them to win office relative to male candidates—has been neglected by the literature to date.

One of the goals of any political campaign is to consolidate existing positive opinions of the candidate held by the public while undermining any harmful ones by highlighting appealing information about him or her; this is all usually done while also trying to highlight any negative information about the opponent in order to encourage voters to view the opponent in a relatively more negative light. By concentrating primarily on the starting assumptions that the public might apply to candidates without systematically examining how such views might change in response to new information that they might get about a candidate during a campaign, the current literature on gender stereotypes cannot reach answers to many important questions. At present we know almost nothing about whether people react to the behavior of candidates through a gendered lens, nor has anyone studied whether people might have different standards for the qualifications of women to hold office. As such, we are leaving much of the story about how gender might enter into the public's evaluations of candidates almost entirely unexplored.

Some academics such as Kathleen Hall Jamieson and Deborah Tannen discuss the possibility of double standards—both frequently argue in media interviews that women candidates do face higher standards—but they are the exception rather than the rule: most scholars generally do not address the issue.[31] Although there have been a few attempts to analyze how people react to the individual characteristics or behaviors of male and female candidates (specifically, there have been a couple of tests of candidate gender and toughness, and a couple of tests regarding candidate gender and reactions to financial scandals or sex scandals),[32] no one has analyzed this dynamic across multiple characteristics or behaviors in order to provide a systematic portrait of how the public reacts to candidates in a way that allows us to understand whether the public might have more challenging standards for women candidates that might be contributing to the parity problem.

There is, nevertheless, a pervasive conventional wisdom in the public sphere about female candidates: they face tougher expectations about their qualifications and are penalized for certain behaviors more than their male counterparts. The conventional wisdom is regularly included in news headlines: "Women's 'Double Bind': Competence, Femininity Collide in Candidates' Paths"; "Rules of the Game Stacked against Women Candidates"; and "Stuck in Second: The Double Standard Is Alive and Well; It's Just More Nuanced." And the text of news articles is no less strident in advancing those kinds of assumptions.[33] Moreover,

---

[31] As just one example, Deborah Tannen maintained in 2007: "Our image of a politician, a leader, a manager, anyone in authority, is still at odds with our expectations of a woman. To the extent that a woman is feminine, she's seen as weak. To the extent that she puts it aside and is forceful, aggressive and decisive, she's not seen as a good woman" (cited in Ellen Goodman, "Rules of the Game Stacked against Women Candidates," Opinion section, *Daily Herald*, December 11, 2007). Kathleen Hall Jamieson stressed in one recent interview that female candidates "are supposed to be warm and accessible, because that's what's perceived to be gender-appropriate. But they also need to be tough and competent. The minute they appear that way, their warmth and accessibility are called into question" (quoted in Jocelyn Noveck, "Clinton's Task: Being Likable AND Tough," *USA Today*, January 10, 2008). To Jamieson's credit, she is the scholar to date to directly focus on gendered leadership standards across multiple dimensions. However, her book *Beyond the Double Bind: Women and Leadership* (1995), focuses primarily on case studies and does not systematically evaluate public attitudes.

[32] Huddy and Capelos (2002) and Smith, Powers, and Suarez (2005) study gender and scandals. Sapiro (1981–82), Leeper (1991), and Huddy and Terkildsen (1993a, 1993b) study candidate gender and toughness. In all cases, the studies examine a particular kind of behavior rather than multiple kinds of behaviors, and in most cases the studies are speaking to different issues than mine (using, e.g., entirely different kinds of dependent variables) and/or use different methodologies (i.e., no control groups from which to draw clear comparisons about the role of gender).

[33] See, e.g., "Women (candidates) are still held to a double standard, and they tend to buy into it themselves" (Kate Zernike, "She Just Might Be President Someday," Week in Review, *New York Times*, May 18, 2008) or, "You don't have to look too far to see what happens when women fail to adjust for the double standards and higher thresholds for female candidates" (Nicolle Wallace, "How Bachmann Is Outrunning Palin—and Hillary," Outlook section, *Washington Post*, August 7, 2011).

political consultants frequently invoke the conventional wisdom in public discussions about women candidates.[34]

The widespread silence of scholars on this topic means that the conventional wisdom in the media goes largely unchecked. As such, our collective "knowledge" about whether harmful double standards exist for female candidates primarily consists of speculative comments confirming the conventional wisdom that are made by political practitioners, pundits, and journalists.

Despite the fact that most of those headlines and observations likely come out of perfectly good intentions—at the very least, they all reflect the fact that suspected gender dynamics in campaigns can now be discussed openly rather than kept in the shadows, where they used to reside—there are reasons to believe that the perpetuation of the conventional wisdom may actually help to create negative outcomes for women in politics. If it is indeed true that women candidates face a tougher playing field with respect to winning over the public, it *should* be discussed widely because such discussion could itself help to level the playing field. But if there is not actually a biased playing field, a focus on how women are disadvantaged vis-à-vis the public might negatively influence how women run or keep them from ever trying to run for office and thus produce substantially more net harm than good for the progress of women in politics.

I argue that those misperceptions may very well have important effects on whether women choose to run for office, and how they go about running if they choose to do so. In particular, Lawless and Fox (2010) convincingly argue that the paucity of women running for office is caused, in part, by a lack of confidence on the part of potential women candidates that they have what it takes to win over the public. They also find that potential female candidates have pervasive concerns that women have to be much better than their male counterparts to have a chance at winning; specifically, they find that nearly nine out of ten potential women candidates believe that it is significantly harder for women than for men to win elections.[35] Lawless and Fox also find that women are less likely than men to be recruited by party leaders, or to be encouraged by friends, family, and colleagues, to run for office; it may very well be that some portion of this reluctance to recruit and encourage women derives from misperceptions that the American public is not ready to fully embrace female leadership. Furthermore, among those women who do decide to run for office, a belief that they start out a disadvantage may potentially have harmful effects on how they choose to run their campaigns; instead of

---

[34] Nearly all of the quotes by political consultants that I could find on the topic of candidate gender support this point, and many statements by made by consultants are included throughout this book.

[35] Lawless and Fox 2010, 124–26, 167. I return to these findings in greater detail in chapter 8.

proceeding with confidence, they may worry more than they should, police their own campaign behavior more than they should, and defer to advisers about how they should act more than they should (advisers who, themselves, may be relying on outdated or inaccurate conventional wisdom). A detailed evaluation of whether double standards exist for female candidates not only allows to better understand the role of women in society and how campaigns work but may also help to improve whether and how female politicians present themselves to the public.

Chapter Overview

Chapter 2 outlines the theoretical foundation of this book. It begins by addressing the critical issues of what gender stereotypes are, how they might be expected to affect male and female candidates, and how those stereotypes might interact with candidate behavior in order to produce different standards for candidates. I then outline two general theories that are systematically contrasted over the course of the book: the *double standards theory*, which posits that women face systematic barriers on the campaign trail (and is thus compatible with the conventional wisdom on this topic) and the *leaders-not-ladies theory*, the alternative framework I develop, which posits that female candidates will be judged on the basis of good leadership rather than on the basis of good femininity, and thus do not face higher standards. A particular theoretical contribution of this book is the clear separation of perspectives based on descriptive stereotypes (assumptions about how people *are*) from those based on prescriptive stereotypes (assumptions about how people *should* act or *should* be). While the importance of this distinction in the study of gender stereotypes in business and psychology has long been recognized, research on candidate gender has thus far focused on descriptive stereotypes only.

The underlying theories having been described, chapter 3 then provides an overview of the methodology used in this study. The empirical data derives from experiments that I conducted on a large, representative sample of U.S. adults. With the luxury of 3,000 respondents and six experiments in total, I am able to undertake a very broad assessment of how candidates' credentials and campaign behaviors influence public attitudes while holding everything else constant except gender. Holding constant all of the unique characteristics associated with a campaign makes it possible to isolate the specific dimensions of gender in question and derive generalizable conclusions. Experiments are, quite simply, the only way to systematically examine whether people hold male and female candidates to different standards.

Chapter 4 examines the baseline descriptive stereotypes that exist for male and female candidates in the current era. This analysis is necessary to determine whether gender stereotypes held by the public cause female candidates to start out at a relative disadvantage. I argue that inexperienced women may best be able to position themselves as outsiders and may therefore be more affected by stereotypes than more experienced candidates (who may be thought of as "insider politicians" and less distinctively as "men" or "women"). I find that gender stereotypes are virtually nonexistent for candidates with a great deal of past political experience. In contrast, some gender stereotypes are applied to inexperienced candidates; however, to the extent that there are any stereotypes, they are all only beneficial to women and thus provide inexperienced women with some specific advantages over inexperienced men. This analysis helps to shed some light on discrepancies in the existing literature regarding gender stereotypes and it also clears the decks of any notion that women politicians necessarily start at a disadvantage relative to their male counterparts vis-à-vis the public, at least in the modern era.

Even if female candidates do not face an inauspicious starting point because of gender stereotypes, certain kinds of behaviors during the campaign could still harm women more than men. Chapters 5–7 examine five different types of campaign behavior that have been posited as damaging women more than men. All of these behaviors were featured prominently in discussions of candidates' gender in the 2008 elections and in discussions of earlier campaigns as well.

Chapter 5 addresses emotional displays by candidates. Avoiding emotional displays has long been seen as a cardinal rule for female candidates. In this chapter, I examine the two emotional displays that are most prominent in discussions of the role of gender in real-world politics: crying and anger.[36] My overall finding is that there is no double standard for these behaviors: men and women are similarly penalized for both crying and anger. Candidates overall are heavily penalized for displays of anger but only minimally penalized for crying (largely because of a push-pull effect in which crying reduces perceptions of strength while increasing perceptions of honesty and caring-related attributes).

Chapter 6 addresses the key question of how the public reacts to candidates who act tough or seem to lack empathy. It has long been argued that women face a double bind: they have to prove that they are tough in order to be seen as leaders, but if they show toughness, they are disproportionately disliked because they are no longer acting in the caring and deferential manner expected of women. I find that female candidates do not, in fact, face a toughness-related double bind; on a couple of critical measures, women candidates actually *benefit* disproportionately by acting in a tough manner. With respect to the other behavior this chapter examines, many have long suspected that the public places a higher value

[36] Brooks 2011.

on empathy in female candidates and penalizes them more when they appear to lack it. I find that this concern is not valid: women and men are similarly penalized for acting in a nonempathetic manner.

Chapter 7 further grapples with the question of whether female candidates are held to higher standards on the campaign trail than are their male counterparts by examining a common type of candidate foible, the knowledge gaffe. Many candidacies have suffered greatly in recent electoral cycles owing largely to knowledge gaffes—arguably none more so than Rick Perry following his now-legendary "oops" moment in the 2011 Republican presidential primary debates. Examining gaffes is an ideal final testing ground for the question of whether female candidates are walking an especially difficult tightrope when they run for office. Again, I find that they are not: knowledge gaffes are very harmful but not disproportionately so to the candidacies of women.

Chapter 8 integrates my findings into a wider discussion of what we now know—and what still remains to be discovered—about the parity problem for women in politics. Accordingly, I move beyond the specific parameters of this study to examine the many other potential explanations for the gender imbalance among politicians. In addition to bringing aspects of my findings to bear on those questions, I also call readers' attention to promising opportunities for future research. I ultimately concur with the findings of Lawless and Fox that lower levels of recruitment of women candidates as well as lower ambition and confidence on the part of potential women candidates provide compelling explanations for explaining existing gender imbalances. I further argue that my findings have the potential to help to rectify a least part of the recruitment and confidence differentials that are holding women back from running for office.

In Chapter 9, I conclude the book with a discussion of why my study indicates we should be optimistic about the electoral prospects of women who decide to run for office and how more women can potentially be encouraged to run for office through wider recognition of the reasons for that optimism. I then examine whether this optimism was always warranted, or whether it might be a relatively new state of affairs. Through an analysis of generational differences in views of women candidates, I gain some leverage on whether the playing field for women candidates represents an improvement over time. I find some evidence of generational differences in views of women candidates at the presidential level. These results suggest that campaign dynamics may indeed be changing between generations, and thus that they may continue to improve for women at least partly through the process of generational replacement. Looking forward, I concur with those who argue that women have a very promising future in American politics.

CHAPTER 2

Theoretical Foundations

"So tell me, Barbara, when do you
have time to do your dishes?"

— FIRST QUESTION POSED TO BARBARA BOXER AT A CAMPAIGN
EVENT FOR HER 1971 RUN FOR COUNTY SUPERVISOR[1]

When Barbara Boxer first ran for office in 1971, gender stereotypes and
gendered expectations seemed to be part of the playing field to her. During one of her first races, her neighbor replied to her pitch by saying:
"Barbara, I don't think you should do this. Your kids are young and it
doesn't seem right." In response, Boxer remembers:

> I convinced myself that had I gone over to my next door neighbor's
> house to tell her I was going to nursing school she would have cheered.
> But because I was trying for a job traditionally held by men, even
> though the men in local government had families and even outside
> jobs, I simply had to expect this kind of prejudice . . . there were days
> when I thought I had broken through, days when no one asked me
> how old my children were or what my husband thought of my candi-
> dacy. But then the prejudice would return.[2]

She notes further that "in the '50s, it became almost unpatriotic to hold
down a decent-paying job if you were a woman . . . to those women and
men who had lived through the '50s, I seemed a complete rebel; I was not
to be trusted; I was not the kind of woman I should have been." She goes
on to attribute her eventual loss as county supervisor, in part, to that kind
of shock and discomfort at the idea of a woman in politics.[3]

Senator Boxer is certainly not the only woman candidate who has reported that she was subject to sexist comments, demeaning stereotypes,
and/or gendered expectations from opponents and voters during earlier
eras. A particularly colorful example involves the race between Congresswoman Helen Gahagan Douglas and Richard Nixon in the 1950 general

[1] Boxer 1994, 85.
[2] Boxer 1994, 83–84.
[3] Boxer 1994, 75.

election for a California seat in the U.S. Senate. The race between "Tricky Dick" and the "Pink Lady" was a bitter and highly gendered one. According to Sally Denton, a biographer of Douglas writing for the *New York Times*, "Nixon injected gender into the dialogue at every opportunity," including attacks he made that Douglas was "pink right down to her underwear," and strong innuendo he used to imply that Douglas was involved in a sexual relationship with President Truman.[4] Denton reports that the fact Nixon raised this innuendo "fostered little, if any, outrage."[5]

Overtly sexist comments and attacks by the public and opponents have seemed to decline in prevalence over time, however; for example, Boxer herself eloquently discusses in her autobiography how vastly improved the 1990s were for female candidates with respect to voter expectations as compared to earlier times in politics (Boxer's characterization is discussed in more detail in the concluding chapter of the book).[6] Sexist comments and attacks clearly have not disappeared entirely, however: as just one example, Hillary Clinton faced two male hecklers chanting "Iron my shirt!" at a campaign event on the day before the 2008 New Hampshire presidential primary. But in contrast to earlier times, when sexist statements made by the public may have been either ignored or used to disparage the female candidate further, the incident was actively dissected and critiqued by the media and voters; in the end, the effects of the attack were probably not negative (some say that the effects were beneficial), and Clinton went on to win the New Hampshire primary the next day.[7] While such overtly sexist comments by voters appear to be relatively infrequent, at least as compared to earlier decades, it does not necessarily mean that people do not still harbor stereotypes and normative expectations of female candidates that undermine their electoral prospects.

[4] Sally Denton, "A Long History of Sexism in Politics," *Los Angeles Times*, December 22, 2009.

[5] Sally Denton, "A Long History of Sexism in Politics," *Los Angeles Times*, December 22, 2009.

[6] Boxer 1994.

[7] Rather than ignore the heckling and move on, as might have been the likely response by female candidates several years ago, Clinton confronted their comments head on: "Ah, the remnants of sexism—alive and well. . . . As I think has been abundantly demonstrated, I am also running to break through the highest and hardest glass ceiling." Later at the event, Clinton joked about the situation during the question and answer period, saying, "If there's anyone left in the auditorium who wants to learn how to iron a shirt, I'll talk about that" ("Clinton Responds to Seemingly Sexist Shouts," *USA Today*, January 7, 2008). Instead of hurting Clinton, the incident is thought by some to have helped her with many voters, but proving that assertion in this instance will never be possible with available data (consider, e.g., the inextricable effect of Clinton's emotional moment, which had occurred earlier that same day). As discussed in chapter 9, there is some recent experimental evidence which indicates that Clinton's direct response of labeling these remarks as being sexist is the best approach to take.

Within the business world, a transition from overt sexism and associated leadership barriers to more subtle gender barriers has prompted a move away from the "glass ceiling" terminology that was long prevalent. According to Alice Eagly and Linda Carli, what was once a "concrete wall" for women's progress as business leaders eventually morphed into a "glass ceiling."[8] However, they argue that the glass ceiling has now been shattered by enough examples of successful women business leaders in recent years that the term is no longer appropriate: instead, they argue that women now face a "labyrinth" to leadership positions and success. Eagly and Carli maintain that "paths to the top exist, and some women find them. The successful routes can be difficult to discover, however."[9]

Do public attitudes lead to a similar labyrinth to leadership and success for women in the political sphere? The conventional wisdom suggests that gender stereotypes and gendered normative expectations among the public still hold women back in politics, perhaps not as much as they once did, but in a powerfully detrimental way nonetheless. In this chapter, I delineate two general theories (the "double standards theory" and the "leaders-not-ladies theory") that have opposing predictions regarding whether gender stereotypes and higher standards are now likely to harm female politicians. To properly understand these two theories, it is first necessary to carefully explore gender stereotypes as a theoretical concept.

What Are Gender Stereotypes, and Why Are They Important?

Stereotypes can be defined as "cognitive structures that contain the perceiver's knowledge, beliefs, and expectations about human groups."[10] Mark Peffley and John Hurwitz liken stereotypes to Walter Lippmann's 1922 description of "pictures in the head," which allow "cognitive misers with limited motivation and mental capacities to process ambiguous information more efficiently."[11] In other words, stereotypes allow people to quickly and efficiently—if not always accurately—make assumptions about the likely characteristics and behavior of people.

Stereotypes are commonly applied to a range of different groups. However, gender stereotypes are unique in several respects. As Alice Eagly and Steven Karau point out, gender tends to produce especially powerful and pervasive stereotypes: "Not only is sex the personal characteristic that provides the strongest basis of categorizing people, even when compared with

---

[8] Eagly and Carli 2007, 6. For more discussion of the end of the glass ceiling, see p. 183.
[9] Eagly and Carli 2007, 6; also see p. 183.
[10] Hamilton and Trolier 1986, 133.
[11] Peffley and Hurwitz 1997, 377.

race, age, and occupation . . . but also stereotypes about women and men are easily and automatically activated."[12] Moreover, business scholar Amy Cuddy argues that regular exposure to men and women allows people to feel especially entitled to and comfortable with gender-based attitudes: "Contact [with men and women] hasn't undermined these stereotypes, and it might even strengthen them. Many people don't believe seeing women as kind or soft is a stereotype. They're not even going to question it, because they think it's a good thing."[13]

Within the broad definition of stereotypes presented above, further refinement is necessary to discuss gender stereotypes with any level of precision. In particular, it is critical to consider descriptive stereotypes (i.e., the matter of how people "*do*" act—or, more precisely, are assumed to act) separately from prescriptive stereotypes (i.e., the matter of how people "*should*" act).[14] People regularly rely upon descriptive stereotypes about traits they assume other individuals will have based on skin color, ethnic origin, gender, socioeconomic class, and other possible groupings; this is especially the case when they are given little information about an individual other than group membership.[15] Common descriptive gender stereotypes include assumptions that women are more "communal" than men (i.e., more sensitive, nurturing, empathetic, compassionate, honest, affectionate, helpful, etc.), while men are more "agentic" than women (i.e., more confident, competitive, ambitious, dominant, independent, forceful, leader-like, etc.).[16] Descriptive stereotypes are the "baseline stereotypes" and "starting assumptions" I have been referring to until this point and have been the focus of nearly all of the work on gender stereotypes and politics to date.

In contrast, prescriptive stereotypes are the normative beliefs that men and women should (or should not) act in particular ways.[17] In other

[12] Eagly and Karau 2002, 574.

[13] Drake Bennett, "Black Man vs. White Woman: Hillary Clinton Contends with Gender Stereotypes, and Barack Obama with Racial Ones. Which Bias Runs Deeper in the American Psyche? The Answer Does Not Bode Well for Clinton," *Boston Globe*, February 17, 2008.

[14] See, e.g., Burgess and Borgida 1999 and Prentice and Carranza 2002, 2003. Note that there is variety in the usage of this terminology within the literature; Cialdini and Trost (1998) and Eagly and Karau (2002) use the term "descriptive norms" instead of "descriptive stereotypes" and "injunctive norms" instead of "prescriptive stereotypes." The terms are also sometimes interchangeably called "prescriptive expectations"or "prescriptions." The flip side of a prescription is a proscription—that is, the way someone should not be/act; however, "prescription" is frequently used as the catchall term to describe both negative and positive normative expectations and will generally be used as such throughout this book.

[15] See, e.g., Locksley et al. 1980 and Locksley, Hepburn, and Ortiz 1982.

[16] Eagly and Karau 2002, 574.

[17] See, e.g., Brugess and Borgida 1999; Eagly and Carli 2007; Heilman 2001; Spence and Helmreich 1978.

words, not only do people believe that women are more likely to have communal traits than men, but they also commonly believe that women *should* have communal traits and sometimes also believe that men *should not* have (some) communal traits. Similarly, people not only hold descriptive stereotypes that men are more likely to possess agentic traits than women but also tend to believe that men *should* possess agentic traits and that women *should not* possess them.

According to Prentice and Carranza, violations of gender proscriptions and prescriptions tend to involve substantial social sanctions, at least with reference to ordinary people: "Thus, when women fail to be warm, friendly, and well groomed, or worse, show signs of being aggressive, forceful, and arrogant, they receive social censure. Similarly, when men fail to be self-reliant, decisive, and rational, or worse, manifest signs of being melodramatic, naïve, and superstitious, they too are punished."[18] One of the ways in which they and others argue that "gender deviants" are punished is through negative evaluations.[19] The psychology literature does not examine politicians, per se, but one could reasonably extend the same logic to the political realm to expect that deviation from a harmful descriptive stereotype may allow a candidate to successfully differentiate (i.e., "individuate" or "distance") himself or herself from that harmful stereotype, while at the same time violating any associated prescriptive stereotypes could still potentially harm the candidate's prospects for election. In this regard, a very common argument (one I evaluate empirically in chapter 6) is that a female candidate who acts tough may successfully differentiate herself from a descriptive gender stereotype that she is too weak, but she then is likely to be penalized for failing to be feminine and communal when she displays this more "male" characteristic.

In contrast to descriptive stereotypes, prescriptive stereotypes have received relatively less attention within political science for several reasons. One reason is that prescriptions seem to be at least somewhat less prevalent in racial and ethnic contexts than in gender contexts (in the modern era, at least), and because much of the political science research on stereotypes focuses on race and ethnicity, it makes sense that most researchers who study stereotypes are primarily oriented toward examining descriptive stereotypes. Furthermore, prescriptions are mainly relevant within the political realm when one is examining not just the baseline assumptions that people make about male and female politicians that might be made from the start (such as "she won't be tough enough to stand up to the terrorists") but rather how the public reacts to new information about an individual politician. As was mentioned in chapter 1,

[18] Prentice and Carranza 2003, 272.

[19] Prentice and Carranza 2003; Costrich et al. 1975; Tepper, Brown, and Hunt 1993; Rudman and Glick 1999.

research to date on candidate gender stereotypes has neglected the latter issue, with nearly all studies concentrating only on baseline assumptions (whether female candidates are assumed by the public to be weaker, more compassionate, and so on). Some of the studies examine perceptions of actual leaders, and many study hypothetical candidates, but in almost all cases, the focus has been solely on examining the descriptive stereotypes that people apply to male and female politicians prior to learning new information about them, rather than on examining the degree to which the public wants male and female candidates to act in a certain, gendered manner, and how they might be penalized for not doing so. And in the handful of exceptions to that characterization, the analyses have focused on a single kind of candidate behavior (either toughness or scandals) rather than on building general theories and undertaking systematic empirical analyses across a wide range of different types of candidate characteristics and behaviors.[20]

This oversight in the literature has unnecessarily limited our understanding of how gender stereotypes operate in politics. Given that the main function of campaigns is for candidates to define themselves and to redefine their opponents—and given that women are frequently told by their advisers and the media that they have to follow certain gendered "rules" and be especially careful in terms of how they get defined in light of gender stereotypes—it is vital to study the possible role of prescriptive stereotypes in order to properly understand the role of candidate gender in politics. Specifically, it is crucial to determine whether behavior by a candidate that confirms or disconfirms a descriptive gender stereotype will be disproportionately rewarded or punished by the public on the basis of prescriptive stereotypes. Developing theories regarding how the public might be expected to react to different types of candidate behavior or characteristics on the basis of gender is the goal of the remainder of this chapter.

The Double Standards Theory

The conventional wisdom in the public sphere has long held that women in politics are handicapped by negative descriptive stereotypes that the

[20] Specifically, Huddy and Capelos (2002) and Smith, Powers, and Suarez (2005) study candidate gender and scandals. As will be discussed in chapter 6, Sapiro (1981–82), Leeper (1991), and Huddy and Terkildsen (1993a, 1993b) study candidate gender and toughness, but in each case the study designs were not able to speak to the question about how the public penalizes candidates overall for engaging in those behaviors (Huddy and Terkildsen were focused on a different kind of dependent variable and Sapiro and Leeper do not separately consider normative expectations and descriptive stereotypes).

public attaches to women in politics. In addition to positing that the public will assume that women will be worse leaders than their male counterparts from the start of a campaign, the conventional wisdom also assumes that women are at a disadvantage because they face different, higher standards regarding their qualifications and behavior on the campaign trail as compared to their male counterparts.

The theorists, in this case, have been an amalgam of pundits, candidates, and consultants who have engaged in their theorizing largely in newspapers, on the Internet, and on television sets (a handful of academics, most notably Deborah Tannen and Kathleen Hall Jamieson, have also contributed to this narrative in publications that are directed toward the public sphere). Without intending to do so, they have constituted a remarkably uniform voice with a clear belief that female candidates will fare poorly with the public compared with their male counterparts across a wide series of different campaign situations.[21]

In contrast to that dominant view in the world of applied politics, those scholars doing research on this general topic have been somewhat more divided regarding the question of whether gender stereotypes work to the net detriment of women candidates, while most have demurred from addressing the question of different normative beliefs and double standards entirely. Without systematic empirical analysis, the conventional wisdom in the public sphere will continue to stand unchallenged. Moreover, given its foundation in the world at large rather than in the halls of academe, the conventional wisdom lacks a clear theoretical framework that will allow us to fully understand the nature of the question at issue before it can be taken on empirically. We need a comprehensive theory that can be used to derive predictions across multiple different campaign behaviors to be tested accordingly; only then can we meaningfully assess the accuracy of the conventional wisdom.

THE FIVE COMPONENTS OF THE DOUBLE STANDARDS THEORY

At first glance, the conventional wisdom in the public sphere seems rather simple: women are at a disadvantage in the electoral arena due to gender stereotypes held by the public. But what are the underlying theoretical reasons why this might be the case? The current literature does not explicitly delineate the theoretical foundations for the range of mechanisms

---

[21] It should be noted that many of the same analysts would also posit that female candidates will be treated in a different—and harmful—manner by the media. That is an important question, but it is separate from the matter at the core of this study. Here, I am considering whether the public itself holds female candidates to different standards than male candidates. I return to a discussion of the possible role of the media in chapter 8.

regarding how female candidates are disadvantaged by public expectations of candidates, nor does anyone stitch together those mechanisms into a cohesive theoretical package. Below I convert the informal articulation of the conventional wisdom into a general theory—termed "double standards theory"—by specifying the underlying theoretical basis for the five mechanisms through which women can potentially be disadvantaged by public attitudes in campaigns.[22]

1. Female candidates start out at a disadvantage with voters due to descriptive gender stereotypes.

The first component of the double standards theory is an assumption that female candidates start out at a relative disadvantage on agentic traits that are critical to perceptions of high-quality leaders. In this view, even when equally qualified for office in an objective sense, women candidates will be assumed to be less capable leaders by the public.

The idea that, first, men and women are stereotyped in a gendered manner according to how they are perceived to typically act and, second, that overall perceptions of people can be helped or harmed on the basis of these stereotypes will be called the *descriptive stereotype perspective* throughout this book. With reference to the baseline gender stereotypes that people have about candidates, the descriptive stereotype perspective would predict that women will be simultaneously helped and hurt by stereotypes. Barring information to the contrary (or perhaps still even after information to the contrary), women candidates will be stereotyped as better on communal traits (e.g., caring, compassion, honesty) and men candidates will be stereotyped as better on agentic traits (e.g., leadership, authority, gets things done, toughness).[23]

---

[22] These five items are not perfectly distinct; in some cases, they relate so closely to one another that it could be reasonably argued that this should really be combined into a list of three or four items or, conversely, expanded into six or seven. I grouped ideas together where feasible, and separated them when I felt they required individual attention.

[23] Occasionally political scientists have drawn on gender schema theory to describe a similar set of assumptions to that of the descriptive stereotype perspective (e.g., Sanbonmatsu 2002; Chang and Hitchon 2004). While schemata are different from stereotypes (they represent overall cognitive belief structures rather than isolated expectations), the predictions derived about the existence of baseline assumptions about how male and female candidates would behave are quite similar to those of the descriptive stereotype perspective. Schema theory becomes unclear, though, in its predictions regarding how people will react to schema-consistent versus schema-inconsistent information. Studies (all nonpolitical in nature) are divided on whether schema consistent information will be remembered better or worse than schema inconsistent information (see Flannery and Walles 2003 and Rojahn and Pettigrew 1992 for descriptions of the mix of findings). Because of this mix of results, and because this research primarily focuses on predicting recall rather than affect for an individual, schema theory is not especially useful for discussing how behavioral double standards will affect candidates.

If the public imposed an equal number of negative stereotypes on men and women that were of equal significance for electoral performance, then the dynamic might be interesting, but it would not be especially pressing: men will be assumed to be better on some traits, women will be assumed to be better on others, and therefore neither men nor women will have an advantage when it comes time for people to vote. However, the conventional wisdom also implicitly assumes that "male" (agentic) traits will loom larger than "female" (communal) traits in the minds of voters when voting for candidates, perhaps especially at higher levels of office and perhaps especially in the post-9/11 era in which security concerns are heightened.[24] In their recent textbook, *Women and Politics*, Dolan, Deckman, and Swers claim with certainty that "if both (male and female) sets of personality characteristics were valued equally, female candidates would be on relatively equal footing with male candidates. But voters value masculine traits over feminine traits."[25]

However, evidence to support this assumption is actually quite mixed: there is some evidence suggesting that although public assessments of a candidate's communal traits (like empathy) are a significant predictor of candidate preference, they tend to be less important than evaluations of many other traits associated with leadership.[26] Yet traits typically considered to be descriptive strengths for women such as "honesty," along with others that may be less gendered, such as "competence," have been found to drive overall leadership evaluations more than traits like "strong leader" or "gets things done."[27]

Thus, there is actually no strong basis for assuming that if gender stereotypes are prevalently used by the public, then the net effect will necessarily favor male leaders. Regardless, the conventional wisdom in the public sphere posits that although women candidates might have some relative advantages over male candidates in the minds of voters, they will ultimately be at a net disadvantage vis-à-vis the public due to the power of negative stereotypes about women leaders.

2. The confirmation of negative stereotypes will be especially damaging for women candidates.

The second theoretical component of the double standards theory is that confirmation of negative stereotypes about women based on actual behavior will be especially damaging for a woman's candidacy. For exam-

---

[24] Lawless 2004.

[25] Dolan, Deckman, and Swers 2011, 143.

[26] See Funk 1999, 702, for a summary of findings on the topic; see also, e.g., Kinder 1986 and Miller, Wattenberg, and Manchuk 1986 for analyses that reach the conclusion that empathy is less important to overall evaluations than other candidate traits.

[27] See Funk 1999; also see Rudman and Glick 2001 regarding "competence."

ple, strength and toughness are commonly thought to be critical traits for candidates as well as being the traits that might be most problematic for women in terms of how they are viewed by the public; therefore, any behavior that demonstrates weakness will tend to produce a substantial penalty for women candidates and involve relatively little penalty for their male counterparts. As one example, the act of crying in public should therefore be more of a problem for female candidates than for male candidates.

Attribution theory provides one explanation for why that kind of dynamic might occur. It is predicated on the idea that stereotypes provide expectations about an individual's behavior and therefore affect the causal attributions that people make about that behavior. Unexpected behavior—that is, counter-stereotypical behavior—tends to cause people to attribute the behavior to a particular situation (i.e., they make a situational attribution by believing a behavior was caused by a temporary condition). In contrast, expected or stereotypical behavior tends to get attributed to an individual's core personality (i.e., people make a dispositional attribution by believing that the behavior is due to relatively permanent internal causes).[28] Much of the psychological research focuses on causal attributions for the success or failure of an individual: for example, whereas the success of Caucasians and men is more often attributed to dispositional causes (e.g., intelligence, ability), scholars have found that the success of African Americans and women is more frequently attributed to situational factors (e.g., an easy task, luck, or their level of effort).[29] Note that the logic is that women or blacks are assumed to be less successful at a task, and so when they do succeed, it is not due to the positive nature of their core personality; rather, it is most likely just a temporary aberration for that individual. This kind of processing allows people to maintain stereotypes even after observing many examples of stereotype-inconsistent behavior.

The measure of interest to attribution theorists tends to be the nature of the attributions themselves, whereas political scientists focus on overall assessments, such as candidate preference, candidate affect, likely effectiveness in office, or vote preference. However, it seems reasonable to extend the logic of attribution research to posit that dispositional attributions for a behavior (i.e., a belief that a behavior is indicative of a person's persistent personality strengths or deficits) will be more predictive of overall evaluations of a candidate than behavior that is attributed to temporary causes like the difficulty of the situation. Along these lines,

[28] See, e.g., Barrett and Bliss-Moreau 2009; Jackson, Sullivan, and Hodge 1993; Heilman 1983; Nieva and Gutek 1980.

[29] Deaux and Emswiller, 1974; Ilgen and Youtz, 1986; O'Leary and Hansen 1984; Yarkin, Town, and Wallston, 1982.

the expectation is that a behavior that conflicts with a descriptive stereotype of an individual (e.g., a female candidate who acts tough or nonempathetically) will be relatively unimportant to the overall evaluation of the candidate as compared to behavior that is consistent with the descriptive stereotype (e.g., a female candidate who cries). In this view, a male candidate who cries must have had something important to cry about and will therefore not be penalized much, whereas a female candidate who cries is emotionally unstable and would therefore be deemed an unsuitable leader. It should be noted that, although attribution theory does help provide stronger theoretical foundations for the conventional wisdom, a perfect overlap does not exist: the predictions emerging from attribution theory only sometimes coincide with those from double standards theory.[30]

3. Female candidates will be punished if they don't act like ladies.

The third component of the double standards theory is that female candidates will be penalized for violating prescriptions associated with femininity. The term *prescriptive stereotype perspective* will be used throughout this book to distinguish the general argument that men and women are subject to gendered normative beliefs about how they should and should not act and are penalized heavily for violating those beliefs. Note that the prescriptive stereotype perspective does not in any way rule out the existence of descriptive stereotypes or consequences flowing from them; it simply posits that prescriptive stereotypes will also play a powerful role in terms of determining reactions to the behavior or characteristics of men and women.

As applied to candidates, the core logic of the prescriptive stereotype perspective is that female candidates are expected to conform to the prescriptive stereotypes associated with women; that is, they should be caring, compassionate, empathetic, honest, and so on. At the same time, women should refrain from being tough, uncaring, angry, dominant, and so on. In this respect, Marie Wilson, president of the White House Project—a nonpartisan organization focused on getting women elected to higher office—argues that "the conventional wisdom for women running for executive office is that she must be tough, but not too tough, smart, but not too smart, assertive but not aggressive and feminine but not girly."[31]

The key point is that a female candidate who violates gender prescriptions risks the ire of the observers—for example, a nonempathetic woman

---

[30] As I discuss in chapter 5, attribution theory and double standards theory make a similar prediction regarding crying but predict entirely different dynamics regarding anger.

[31] Ellen Sorokin, "Female Candidates Face Uphill Push; Study Says Women Seeking Executive Office Seen as Soft," *Washington Times*, November 14, 2002.

will be penalized more than a nonempathetic man, an angry woman will be penalized more than an angry man, and so on. As with attribution theory, the prescriptive stereotype perspective does not align perfectly with the double standards theory across all behaviors;[32] the theories do, however, align in their predictions regarding how people react to male and female candidates across some of the behaviors that are examined in this study.

4. Female candidates will be punished if they don't act like ladies, but they will also be punished if they don't act like leaders.

The fourth component of double standards theory shares with the third component an assumption that female candidates have to act in a feminine manner; however, it goes on to posit that prescriptions of feminine behavior inherently conflict with the prescriptions associated with good leadership, which puts female candidates in an unsolvable dilemma. In particular, the prescription that women should act in a communal manner rather than in a tough and dominant manner inherently conflicts with prescriptions for leaders to be capable of tough behavior. In contrast to behaviors like anger, crying, or lack of empathy, which are all negatively prescribed (i.e., they are "proscribed") for leadership, toughness is a behavior that can be useful for leadership and is likely to be expected by voters. The conflict between the communal prescriptions of femininity and the agentic prescriptions of leadership therefore puts female candidates at a disadvantage because to succeed on one front will be to necessarily fail on the other front. Regardless of how she chooses to act, a woman candidate will be at a disadvantage relative to a male counterpart, who can conform to both male and leadership prescriptions with the same agentic behavior.

The relevant stereotype theory pertaining to this dynamic is the role congruity theory of prejudice developed by Alice Eagly and Steven Karau.[33] They argue that "a potential for prejudice exists when social perceivers hold a stereotype about a social group that is incongruent with the attributes that are thought to be required for success in certain classes of social roles."[34] Role congruity theory melds the descriptive stereotype that women are less likely to be perceived to have leadership characteristics with the prescriptive stereotype (and associated backlash for violating it) that women are not supposed to have "agentic" traits (i.e., leadership and strength-related traits). According to Eagly and Karau, "women

---

[32] For example, it is not clear that there are gender prescriptions for knowledge, such as "women should not be smart"; therefore there would not be an expectation that this dynamic would be in play regarding knowledge gaffes or the like.

[33] Eagly and Karau 2002.

[34] Eagly and Karau 2002, 574.

leaders' choices are thus constrained by threats from two directions: Conforming to their gender role would produce a failure to meet the requirements of their leader role, and conforming to their leader role would produce a failure to meet the requirements of their gender role."[35]

In short, the theory stipulates that a woman is in a no-win situation when agency is required: even if a woman could successfully differentiate herself from a descriptive stereotype—for example, she can prove that she is assertive—she will still be penalized for violating the proscriptive stereotype that women should be deferential and communal. Given that agency is often required in political settings, role congruity theory would predict that female candidates will be at an inherent disadvantage in the political sphere. In this regard, a 2002 White House Project report compiled by a bipartisan team of pollsters, media, and general political consultants concluded: "Women candidates, especially for executive office, are often judged differently and more harshly than male candidates. A challenging double standard exists for women, especially on the dimension of effectiveness and strength.... Voters start out with more questions about effectiveness, toughness, and proven records for women than for men and are much more judgmental about presentation on this dimension."[36]

Thus, on the matter of agency-related traits like toughness that may be beneficial (or at least not negative) for male leadership, the conventional wisdom and role congruity theory make the same overlapping prediction: barring other information, female candidates will be descriptively stereotyped as being less tough than male candidates, which will put women at an electoral disadvantage. Yet once a woman tries to establish that she is tough, the presumption is that she will be penalized for not being feminine enough. As Gloria Steinem maintained in 1979, "If you are assertive and aggressive enough to do the job you're unfeminine and therefore unacceptable; if you're not aggressive you can't do the job—and in either case, goodbye."[37]

5. Female candidates will tend to be held to higher standards than male candidates.

The fifth component of the double standards theory quite simply posits that women will be held to a higher standard than their male counter-

---

[35] Eagly and Karau 2002, 576.

[36] The White House Project 2002, 9. They arrived at these conclusions based on a study of actual candidate ads and on an experiment they conducted in which candidate clothing and backgrounds were varied from formal to informal. They found that it was more important for female candidates to use formal settings and appearances.

[37] As quoted in Leslie Bennetts, "On Aggression in Politics: Are Women Judged by a Double Standard," *New York Times*, February 12, 1979.

parts and will be penalized if they do not live up to that standard. In this view, female candidates simply have to be "better": although a man can slip up on occasion, any mistake by a woman will be used as evidence of her unsuitability for leadership, and she will be punished disproportionately as a result.

This potentially could occur even if we find that there are no descriptive stereotypes that put women at a disadvantage a priori. The logic of that would be that support for women candidates may be present initially, but more tenuous. Women may be granted an equal level of support at the start of a campaign as a function of a more open-minded era, but perhaps owing to "outsider" status in political leadership or perhaps because of a legacy of discrimination, if a woman demonstrates incompetence during a campaign, support for her candidacy may be more swiftly and decisively withdrawn than if she had been a man. Bad behavior could thus trigger latent feelings that women are not really up to the task of governance. In other words, when initially probed for feelings about a female candidate, people could potentially express support; but when an imperfection is pointed out, latent concerns about women in politics could then emerge and compound a negative reaction to the behavior in question.

As a function of outsider status or latent concerns about women being up to the task of politics, it is also conceivable that women could be held to a higher standard of qualification by voters; for example, a woman may need to have more experience in politics than a comparable man to be viewed as promising leadership material. Thus, women with considerable political experience might be able to avoid detrimental gender stereotypes, while their less experienced sisters will be thwarted by it.

Perhaps gendered aspects of specific behaviors could especially activate otherwise-latent stereotypes. Studies within psychology have found that simply reminding people about the existence of gender stereotypes (even those that exclusively paint women in a positive light) can generate more traditional views about women.[38] With extension to the questions at hand, it is plausible that some kinds of campaign behaviors (e.g., crying, which is thought of as a feminine behavior) could cause people to apply gendered double standards to candidates who display those behaviors, even if those same people would not have not engaged in gender stereotyping in the absence of behavioral cues with strong gender associations.[39]

The bottom line prediction is that women candidates will be penalized by the public for any imperfections they happen to display far more than their male counterparts will be.

[38] Jost and Kay (2005) found that simply exposing people to stereotypes about women serves to increase their acceptance of traditional views regarding gender relations (i.e., respondents showed less concern about the division of labor between men and women, the current structure of gender roles, etc.).

[39] See chapter 5 for more discussion of crying as a behavior.

Taking Stock of the Double Standards Theory

My articulation of the double standards theory moves past the general assumptions and case-specific predictions that currently form the basis for the conventional wisdom on this topic and provides the theoretical foundation for a set of predictions about how we would expect the public to judge male and female candidates in general. The double standards theory predicts that female candidates will be penalized more than comparable male candidates for lacking political experience, for lacking empathy, for crying, for getting angry, for acting tough, or for slipping up by getting caught in a knowledge gaffe, and it could potentially extend to a range of other behaviors beyond those as well. By articulating a theory of double standards for female candidates, and by linking that theory to a set of more specific theories and perspectives from the business and psychology fields, we move an important step closer toward being able to effectively evaluate how candidate gender influences public perceptions.

My goal in articulating the double standards theory is clarity, not advocacy, however. In the next section, I delineate an alternative theory that I find more compelling—one that predicts that female candidates occupy a largely equitable playing field with respect to the public, at least in the current era.

The Leaders-Not-Ladies Theory

On the basis of discussions about women candidates in the public sphere, one would never guess that the conventional wisdom about higher double standards for female candidates might be wrong. Assumptions and declarations about the tougher political environment for women in politics are rampant, while discussion of any alternative understanding is essentially absent. Yet there are strong theoretical reasons to expect that female candidates may not face detrimental stereotypes and double standards in politics today. With a nod to the quote by Representative Mary Theresa Norton that began this book—"I'm no lady; I'm a member of Congress, and I shall proceed accordingly."—my "leaders-not-ladies theory" of public opinion about political leadership postulates that women politicians will be evaluated by the public more as politicians than as women. In this view, we would not expect female candidates to start out at a disadvantage relative to male candidates, and we would also expect them to be held to similar standards of behavior. In short, women politicians will be held to the standards of good leadership rather than to the standards of good femininity.

There are three overarching theoretical reasons why I expect this to be the case. First, to the extent that stereotypes play a role, there are reasons to believe that women candidates will be stereotyped according to beliefs about politicians more than beliefs about women. Second, there are strong reasons to think that information about the behavior of candidates will be evaluated in a relatively objective and nongendered manner. Third, there are far more women in politics than in previous eras; for the matter at hand, this is significant because gender stereotypes and penalties tend to thrive in arenas where women leaders are unusual—that is, where women are tokens—and tend to diminish in arenas where they constitute a higher proportion of leaders.

1. Women candidates will be evaluated on entirely different grounds compared to ordinary women.

The prevalence of gender stereotypes that are applied to ordinary men and women in the world at large is undeniable. However, there are important reasons to believe that women candidates will be evaluated on very different grounds compared to their nonpolitical sisters and that they may not be evaluated in terms of traditional feminine norms much, if at all.

Studies have found that people who differ from group stereotypes are often evaluated on a completely different basis from that of the rest of the group; in particular, people who violate stereotypes often end up classified within a "subtype" and are often subject to very different types of assumptions as a result. Kunda and Oleson describe the process of subtyping as the "fencing off" of particular members of a group who are different from a group stereotype.[40] Subtypes can be long-lasting—existing as a subcategory into which future people meeting those characteristics can be quickly fit—and can involve entirely different evaluations from what might otherwise be generated from the overall stereotype or stereotypes that would otherwise apply.[41] Through the mechanism of subtyping, people can maintain their global stereotypes, even in the presence of counter-stereotypical information about particular individuals.[42] In other words, subtyping allows people to retain stereotypes of a general group (e.g., women) while selectively not applying many, or even any, of the stereotypes associated with the overall group to people who also belong to a more specific, nonconforming subset of a general group.

Moreover, multiple group stereotypes are often at play. Beyond "women" and "politician," multiple stereotypes can potentially generate "sub"-subtypes (e.g., race, region of origin, ethnicity, partisanship, and

[40] Kunda and Oleson 1995, 565.
[41] Kunda and Oleson 1995, 565.
[42] Kunda and Oleson 1995; Webber and Crocker 1983. Stereotypes are most likely to be maintained especially if membership of the subtyped group is relatively small; as the subtyped group becomes larger, it has more potential to challenge the global stereotype.

socioeconomic status). Rather than simply being put in a mental "woman candidate" category, many women might instead be placed in a separate category for "black woman politician," "rich woman politician," "working-class woman local politician," and so on. Multiple stereotypes often compete with one another for dominance,[43] and studies have demonstrated that stereotypes with more consistent predictive power tend to be more powerful in determining views of an individual. For example, Irman (2006) finds that stereotypes associated with "career woman" override stereotypes associated with the more global category of "woman," and she argues that it is because "career woman" is far more useful for predicting the actions of individuals. Considered from that perspective, "candidate" (or "U.S. House candidate" or "mayoral candidate") is likely to be far more specific and predictive of behavior than "woman," and we should therefore expect "candidate" to have relatively more power in determining public views of a woman candidate. By extension, it may also be that, through a combination of selection effects and socialization, leaders who have served in office are more consistently similar to one another than first-time candidates, who may show considerably more variation; as such, it may be that women officeholders will be evaluated according to even less feminine standards than women candidates.

Thus, despite the prevalence of stereotypes that are applied to ordinary women, it is reasonable to expect that political women—women who regularly violate all sorts of traditional feminine stereotypes in the course of any given day—may not be evaluated according to traditional standards of femininity much at all. Furthermore, there are also good reasons to believe that any individual woman candidate may be evaluated as much, or more, according to her own individual traits and behaviors, rather than by the standards for any given group.

2. Information about candidates beyond group membership will tend to minimize the power of stereotypes.

When forming opinions about an individual, people are typically confronted with multiple types of information besides gender. This is certainly the case with respect to campaigns: while American voters tend to possess far less information than scholars would normatively prefer they have about candidates, they do tend to be exposed to at least some information about a given candidate besides candidate gender, at least in all but the lowest-profile elections. Many people may know, for example, if

[43] Kunda and Thagard (1996, 290–91), for example, show how a stereotypical association of "Black" and "aggressive" can be overturned by simply describing a black individual as well-dressed, thus quickly overriding a stereotype of "ghetto Black" with a subtype stereotype of "Black businessman" and dramatically lowering perceptions of aggression.

the candidate has held public office before, or his or her party affiliation, educational background, vocational background, or geographic origin. This is significant in light of the finding from the psychological literature that stereotypes dissipate or even disappear in the presence of even fairly minimal individuating information.[44] As people learn information about someone, that person becomes an individual more than a member of a stereotyped group and, as a result, is then evaluated as much, or even more, by individual rather than group-based standards.

Behavior rests at the core of any discussion about double standards, and research shows that information about an individual's behavior can be especially powerful at overriding stereotypes. Ziva Kunda and Paul Thagard argue that evidence about behavior is much more powerful than general stereotypes when determining assessments of an individual's traits, and they point to a large body of studies (confirmed with a meta-analysis) that show that the average effect size for behavior-based information about an individual is substantially larger than the average effect size typically obtained for group-based stereotypes.[45]

Studies have also shown that information about behavior is particularly effective at overriding stereotypes when information about the behavior is relatively unambiguous. For example, Ziva Kunda and Bonnie Sherman-Williams found that people applied stereotypes to evaluations of behavior when a person was ambiguously described as acting aggressively but not when an actual situation (i.e., hitting a neighbor or spanking a child) was described, even just with a brief reference. In other words, undefined "aggressiveness" by a woman was assumed to be less aggressive in objective terms than undefined "aggressiveness" by a man, but once an actual situation involving aggressive behavior was described, people no longer applied gender stereotypes to their understanding of the situation.[46] Because candidate behavior is often described in specific, unambiguous terms, the finding that unambiguous behavior-based individuating information overrides stereotypes suggests that female candidates may not face different standards than men do for their behavior.

With some of the only work that touches on this idea in the political sphere, Leonie Huddy and Nayda Terkildsen confirm this dynamic and find evidence that information about a candidate's behavior overrides gender stereotypes.[47] They do not focus on the kind of dependent variable that would be necessary to directly address the conventional wisdom, but

[44] E.g., Locksley et al. 1980 and Locksley, Hepburn, and Ortiz 1982.

[45] See Kunda and Thagard 1996, 292, for a review.

[46] Kunda and Williams 1993.

[47] Huddy and Terkildsen 1993b. They use a combination of described traits and implied behaviors as their treatment (i.e., the candidate with "male" characteristics was described as being intelligent, tough, articulate, and ambitious and as having strong leadership and

their study suggests that the public is more likely to judge a candidate by objective standards of behavior rather than according to gender stereotypes.[48]

It may be that information about a candidate's behavior entirely over-rides otherwise applicable subtypes and associated stereotypes, or it may be that such information about an individual merges with a subtype to form an impression about that individual. The "parallel processing" model developed by Ziva Kunda and Paul Thagard proposes that stereotypes will be dominant in the absence of specific information about an individual (i.e., if voters on a survey are asked if women candidates, in general, tend to be "tough" or "compassionate"), but that if specific information about an individual is processed before impressions are entirely formed, both sources of information will be factored into an overall evaluation of an individual.[49] In some of the only other work on these matters that has been conducted within politics, Leonie Huddy and Theresa Capelos examine candidate gender in the context of the parallel processing model and conclude that it performs well in explaining their findings regarding a candidate involved in a financial scandal.[50]

3. The higher proportion of women in politics in recent decades may minimize the use of gender stereotypes by the public.

Double standards and gender stereotypes may have harmed women politicians in previous eras, but it is not clear that we should expect that to still be the case given that the proportion of women in politics is far higher now than in previous eras. In articulating their role congruity theory that posits that women leaders will be at an inherent disadvantage, Eagly and Karau outline conditions under which the challenges would be substantially lessened. In this regard, a key condition to which they point is that workplaces with low ratios of women will be more problematic for female leaders than those with a more equitable gender balance.[51] Studies have indeed shown that women are more successful both at obtaining leadership positions and in being equitably evaluated in business

---

administrative skills), so this effect might potentially be even stronger with a direct description of actual behavior rather than with the implied behavior they used.

[48] Huddy and Terkildsen (1993a, 1993b) do not focus on overall rewards or punishments for candidates in their studies; rather, they focus on whether describing a candidate as being (essentially) tough versus communal affects whether candidates are seen as being better on certain types of issues (e.g., handling the military versus caring for the elderly).

[49] Kunda and Thagard 1996; also see Kunda 1999.

[50] Huddy and Capelos (2002) test how people reacted to a fictional male or female candidate's involvement in a financial scandal. They find a mix of results (stereotypes on some dimensions, and similar ratings on others) and concluded that their results are consistent with Kunda's parallel processing model.

[51] Eagly and Karau 2002.

leadership roles when the ratio of women to men increases.[52] The increase does not even have to be dramatic; some studies have found that an upward movement to just 15 percent women in a particular organization can greatly improve the leadership prospects for women there.[53] The reasons for this are multiple, including the fact that when there are more women as leaders in an organization, people have a wide array of examples of actual women leaders to call to mind. Individual female leaders are less likely to be regarded as tokens, and they are less likely to be treated by others in a gendered manner, when they are surrounded by a critical mass of other women.

By extending that logic to legislative politics, it is conceivable that women political leaders may face less prejudice when they are operating in legislative bodies that have higher ratios of women. As women occupy more positions of leadership in U.S. legislative bodies, successful leadership may get defined by others—colleagues, financial backers, and the public—in less exclusively masculine terms; over time, this could reduce the disjuncture between being a successful woman and being a successful political leader that is postulated by role congruity theory.[54] Many analysts point to the 1992 elections as being a watershed moment for female candidates because so many women openly celebrated their gender for the first time.[55] Instead of trying to minimize gender as a liability, "Moms in tennis shoes" were running in—and winning—elections in substantial numbers. This may have helped to dissipate any stereotypes that had been associated with women candidates in earlier eras.

CONSIDERING LEVEL OF OFFICE

Are there any offices for which women will be at a relative disadvantage? Some scholars have suggested that level of office might help to determine the prospects for women candidates, particularly at the executive level.[56]

While the first two components of the leaders-not-ladies theory identify reasons why double standards for women should be minimized at all

---

[52] See, e.g., reviews by Ely 1995; Eagly and Karau 2002; Rudman and Phelan 2008.

[53] See Ely 1994 and Kanter 1977a, 1977b.

[54] A recent meta-analysis of all of the findings on the topic of gender stereotypes in nonpolitical organizations by Koenig et al. (2011) finds indirect support for this dynamic by revealing that beliefs pertaining to leadership have become significantly more androgynous over time; they conclude that the conception of leadership has changed to incorporate more communal strengths and argue that this broader conception of leadership may result from the greater exposure of people to women leaders.

[55] Kunin 1994, 205.

[56] See, e.g., Dolan 1997; Huddy and Terkildson 1993a; Kahn 1994; Rosenwasser and Dean 1989; Smith, Paul, and Paul 2007.

levels of government, that is not the case for the third component of the theory. It primarily suggests reasons for why double standards should be minimized in offices that have been populated by women before. In leadership situations in which women are sufficiently unusual that they are viewed as tokens, they may be more likely to be viewed by the public with an emphasis on gender. Hillary Clinton, Sarah Palin, Elizabeth Dole, Geraldine Ferraro, Patricia Schroeder, and other women have helped people to picture a woman in a presidential or vice presidential position, but the public has not seen a woman function in that capacity yet. That fact may conceivably highlight the role of gender in the minds of the public and push people toward applying stereotypes associated with "ladies" rather than "leaders" when evaluating those candidates. Similar logic might apply to the gubernatorial level as well, at least in states where women have not previously served at the governor (or perhaps lieutenant governor) level.

On the other hand, the success for women at lower levels of leadership presumably helps to establish that women can lead, perhaps even at higher levels. With respect to the presidency, the fact that women have gained entry to key foreign policy positions in the executive branch in recent decades (e.g., three out of the past four secretaries of state have been women) might have helped to establish that women are competent in the foreign policy domain. And with respect to governorships, even if a woman has not won the governorship in a particular state before, Americans might have been exposed to enough news about high-profile women governors from other states that female gubernatorial candidates will just not seem especially unusual.

Beyond any possible effects of token status, might women simply do better with the public in some kinds of office than others? For example, some scholars have suggested that women might do better in offices that emphasize matters that are seen as traditional strengths for women (say, governorships, with their relatively greater focus on issues such as education) versus legislative positions (where foreign policy, the economy, and so on tend to dominate more of the agenda). Given that I do not hypothesize that gender will play a role in candidate evaluations such that men and women will be assumed to have different strengths, I do not expect that kind of dynamic will exist, at least in the current day. Moreover, the most comprehensive research that has been conducted on this matter did not find that the public regarded gubernatorial and Senate women differently, even in the late 1980s and 1990s. Kim Kahn found that whether a woman was running for a Senate seat or gubernatorial position mattered with reference to how she fared with public opinion; however, Kahn found that the source of the difference resides with media bias, which varies by office level, rather than with the public itself.[57] As such, I do not see any reason to think that women candidates will enjoy any particular advantage or disadvantage with respect to different types of office, aside from the possibility that in leadership situations where women are still extremely rare, gender could conceivably have at least somewhat of an effect on candidate evaluations.

CONSIDERING THE LIMITS OF COMPARISON TO THE BUSINESS WORLD

I have discussed parallels between business and political leadership because the business and organization literatures contain the bulk of the research on gender stereotypes and double standards. That being said, it is critical to acknowledge important differences between the domains because the business and organization findings may well be more limited in their applicability to political leadership than they appear to be at first glance. There are two key reasons this may be the case.

First, the population of interest in the nonpolitical studies tends to be business managers and (less often) rank-and-file business people, rather than the public at large, as is the case for public opinion about political leaders. Very often, the samples for business and organization studies tend to consist of business school students. In virtually all cases, the population selected is going to be far more elite, far more male, and far less diverse in background than a cross section of the American public. That could produce differences in the degree to which people evaluate leaders with gendered standards.

Second, a growing segment of the literature on organizations has been devoted to examining the subject of social distance between leaders, and it may help to explain a greater receptivity to women political leaders than to women business leaders.[58] Social distance may change expecta-

---

[57] Interestingly, Kahn (1994, 183) found that, controlling for media coverage differences, the public did tend to use gender stereotypes in its evaluations of candidates, but only in a manner that benefited women candidates relative to their male counterparts. At the same time, Kahn found differences in media coverage that are disproportionately unfavorable to women candidates on critical measures for Senate races and found fewer problematic coverage differences in gubernatorial races. The combined result (factoring in different levels of media bias) was a relative disadvantage for women Senate candidates as compared to their male counterparts, while the results were more mixed, and largely more favorable, for women gubernatorial candidates (179–81).

[58] See, e.g., Boas Shamir 1995; Antonakis and Atwater 2002; Neufeld, Wan, and Fang 2010. Note that distance typically refers in the literature to physical distance, psychosocial distance, and/or hierarchical or cross-functional leadership (see Antonakis and Atwater, 680–81). Thanks are due to Alice Eagly for suggesting to me that this dynamic may be a likely explanation for differences in business and politics.

tions of appropriate leadership behavior; in most business settings, executives and managers or managers and their subordinates are more socially proximate to one another than politicians are from the average American;[59] as such, greater social distance may afford women politicians more leeway in terms of breaking any rules that ordinary women are expected to live by.[60] The promise of regular interactions with a socially proximate, nontraditional woman in the workplace may prove to be uncomfortable to some people in a way that representation by a socially distant, nontraditional politician woman may not be.

Finally, the ascendance of women as political leaders in recent years has been far more rapid than within the business world. If one considers U.S. legislators to be roughly equivalent to corporate CEOs in terms of status, then the gender imbalance is over six times greater in the business world than in U.S. national politics: in 2011, 17 percent of members of the U.S. House and Senate were female, whereas only 2.8 percent of CEOs of Fortune 1000 companies were women. As a result, the average member of the public is likely to have far more exposure to executive-level political leadership by women than the average worker has to executive-level business leadership by women. As such, gender stereotypes and prescriptions may now be relatively less salient in the political realm than in the business realm owing to relatively more equitable gender representation in the former as compared to the latter.

As such, we need to draw on the impressive body of research on gender and leadership that has formed within the business and organization fields, but we cannot assume that we will find the same labyrinth for women in politics that women in nonpolitical leadership roles must navigate in order to succeed in their roles.

Taking Stock of the Leaders-Not-Ladies Theory

The bottom line is that there are many reasons to doubt that female candidates are now subject to or held back by harmful double standards and gender stereotypes by the public overall. In today's era, there is a strong theoretical basis for expecting that women candidates will be assumed to

[59] Antonakis and Atwater (2002, 674) specifically criticize political scientists for studying "distal leaders" (i.e., far-removed leaders), while applying business leadership theories that have been developed for explaining "proximal leaders," which better characterizes the business leaders who are generally being evaluated by peers or subordinates just one or two tiers down the leadership hierarchy.

[60] For example, see Averill 1997; LaFrance and Hecht 1999, 2000; Hess, Adams, and Kleck 2005, which find that high-status or high-dominance individuals are less subject to stereotypical expectations than low-status or low-dominance individuals.

have the characteristics of "leaders" more than the characteristics of feminine "ladies." Leaders always face enormous challenges while running for office in the quest to win over the public, but my expectation is that higher standards for female candidates are not among them.

This line of reasoning does not mean that female candidates will not be penalized for their behavior on the campaign trail, of course. For example, women may still get penalized for acting angry because political leaders are prescriptively expected to maintain their composure; however, the key point is that they will not get penalized *more* than male candidates who do so. The general prediction from the leaders-not-ladies theory is thus that female and male candidates will face similar assessments by the public in response to their actions, at least at the legislative level, where a critical mass of women has served in recent years.

To posit that overall women politicians will be treated by the public more as leaders than as ladies is not to predict that absolutely no one in the public holds gender stereotypes and double standards; even in the absence of an overall effect of gendered stereotypes and standards for women candidates, it is undoubtedly true that at least some people hold views of candidates that either favor or disfavor female candidates primarily because of gender. It is also not to say that there might not be some special dynamics at the presidential level for women. Rather, it is to predict that most people in the current era will evaluate legislative candidates on the basis of matters other than gender. That is the focus of this book because it is critical to understanding the prospects for women in the electoral arena.

CHAPTER 3

How to Study Gender Stereotype Usage and Double Standards in Campaigns

> The many advances in interviewing technology present social science with the potential to introduce some of its most important hypotheses to virtual laboratories scattered nationwide. Whether they are evaluating theoretical hypotheses, examining the robustness of laboratory findings, or testing empirical hypotheses of other varieties, scientists' abilities to experiment on large and diverse subject pools now enable them to address important social and behavioral phenomena with greater effectiveness and efficiency.
>
> — DIANA MUTZ, *Population-Based Survey Experiments*[1]

If the goal of this book were simply to assess whether people hold candidate gender stereotypes to which they were willing to openly admit, the process would be relatively straightforward: people on a standard national survey could be asked whether male or female candidates would be more likely to possess various strengths or weakness. Alternatively, if the goal was to assess whether people perceive real male and female candidates to be different, I could achieve that by asking people their views of current-day politicians on a national survey and then compare the responses for male and female politicians while trying to control for a list of other factors that might also contribute to the observed differences. But many other scholars have examined those questions before. The questions at the core of this book are different, and neither of these methodologies is sufficient for answering them.

The starting point for my analysis is to establish the degree to which people actively apply gender stereotypes to candidates. While other scholars have examined this issue in the past, it is important to do so again in a more recent era using a geographically and demographically representative sample. I then need to undertake something that departs from the existing literature: I need to assess whether people react differently to the behavior of male and female candidates who are otherwise the same. This

[1] Mutz 2011, 4–5.

matter has been touched on only sporadically in previous work and has never been systematically studied across a range of different behaviors. In the first section of this chapter, I address the trade-offs involved with a variety of different methodologies for evaluating these questions and show why the best method is to undertake a Goldberg-paradigm approach with an experimental analysis of fictional candidates using a broadly representative sample of adults from across the United States.

In the remainder of the chapter, I describe the specifics of the experiments that were used for this study to avoid redundancies in the chapters to come. The overall experimental design, the nature of the sample, the dependent variables, the general analytical techniques I employ, and various other features of the methodology that I use are presented here.

Assessing Methodological Options for Studying Candidate Stereotypes

Although previous work on candidate gender stereotypes has neglected the question of how people react to candidate characteristics or behavior, there are various ways in which descriptive candidate gender stereotypes have been studied in the past. Each approach has its own advantages and disadvantages, and the major options are analyzed here so that the value of the methodology utilized throughout this book is clear.

Generic Gender Survey Questions

A common approach taken to study gender stereotypes is to simply ask survey respondents whether a male candidate or female candidate would be better. Specifically, many studies ask questions along the lines of "Would a male or female candidate be better at [insert a certain issue]?" or "Would a male or female politician be more likely to [insert a certain trait]?"[2] In fact, a great deal of our knowledge as a field about candidate gender stereotypes is based on this approach.[3]

---

[2] For example, Sanbonmatsu and Dolan (2009, 487) ask, "Which Congressional Representative do you think would be more likely to support abortion being legal in all circumstances—a Democrat who is a man, a Democrat who is a woman, or would they be equally likely?" Respondents who chose "man" or "woman" were asked a follow-up question about the extent to which a man or woman would be better, and they repeat the series across other issues. In another example, Kenski and Falk (2004) ask, "Thinking about the national issue that is most important to you, all other things being equal, would a male or a female president do a better job handling that issue?" Lawless (2004) assessed the degree of respondent agreement with questions such as, "Men are better at handling military crises," "Men are better at protecting the United States from future attacks," and willingness to vote for a qualified, party-nominated woman presidential candidate.

[3] See, e.g., Dolan 1997; Sanbonmatsu and Dolan 2009; Dolan and Sanbonmatsu 2009;

However, the generic survey question approach cannot capture the views of anyone who does not feel that it is acceptable (internally or socially) to admit to having gender stereotypes, even if they might actually apply such stereotypes to candidates when they go to the polls. Any assumption that people will openly admit to gender stereotypes does not hold up under scrutiny. Using an innovative "list experiment" in which the presence of social desirability bias (that is, the tendency of people to provide socially acceptable answers to survey interviewers) can essentially be eliminated, Matthew Streb, Barbara Burrell, Brian Frederick, and Michael Genovese recently found evidence that indicates that gender survey questions are heavily influenced by social desirability effects. As such, their findings cast considerable doubt on any findings in the literature that have been based on analysis of generic gender survey questions.[4]

Even if respondents were willing to admit to *holding* gender stereotypes about candidates, generic gender survey questions are not designed to tell us whether people actively *use* stereotypes when evaluating candidates. When people actually choose a candidate in an election, gender may not be at the forefront of their minds; in fact, it may not enter into their decision at all. But people who are posed with generic candidate questions are primed with just two pieces of information about candidates—gender and political position—and then are told to use that information to make a judgment. As noted previously, the findings within the psychology literature strongly suggest that people are significantly more likely to use stereotypes when they are given little information other than group membership (especially when the usage of the stereotype is not widely sanctioned socially), whereas stereotype usage will tend to be muted when respondents are provided with some—perhaps any—other information about the candidate.[5] Mary Anderson, Christopher Lewis, and Charlie Baird (2011) utilize a clever experimental design to test this dynamic in the political world by exposing respondents to different levels of information about candidates; they find that even the mention of a single-issue position can eliminate the appearance of gender affinity effects (i.e., a finding that women prefer women candidates). Generic gender survey questions focus a respondent's attention almost exclusively, and quite unrealistically, on gender, and that will tend to increase reliance on gender stereotypes in an entirely artificial manner. In this respect, Kira Sanbonmatsu argues that providing an array of information about a candidate rather than just gender is important so that respondents have the opportunity to attribute their choices to something other than gender,

Dolan 2010; Falk and Kenski 2006; Gillespie and Spohn 1987; Kenski and Falk 2004; Lawless 2004; Rosenthal 1995; Sanbonmatsu and Dolan 2009.

[4] Streb et al. 2008.

[5] See, e.g., Kunda 1999; Kunda and Sherman-Williams 1993; Kunda and Thagard 1996, 292–93; Locksley et al. 1980; Locksleyl, Hepburn, and Ortiz 1982.

because that is always an option available to voters when evaluating candidates in the real world.[6]

The bottom line is that there are reasons to believe that generic gender questions are both *underestimating* the presence of sexism in politics (owing to personal and social desirability effects) and *overestimating* it (by generally providing respondents with no information beyond job description and gender, whereas voters in the real world tend to have at least a little more information about a given candidate at their disposal).

If we want to know whether people actually use gender stereotypes in the course of evaluating candidates, we need a different method. Specifically, we need to know whether people rely on candidate gender in their evaluations when they are provided with a realistic array of political information about a candidate, and how they act when the intent of the study is hidden from them. Generic gender questions cannot achieve either of those goals and therefore cannot speak to the kinds of questions that are central to this book.

STUDIES OF REAL CANDIDATES

Some studies about candidate gender stereotypes examine assessments by the public of actual candidates or sitting public officials. The advantage of studying real political actors is clear: such analyses inherently have the highest possible level of external validity because they are studying perceptions of actual politicians. Studies of real candidates also allow researchers to speak directly to the political climate of the time, by characterizing public impressions of politicians who are actually on the campaign trail or serving in office. There have been many studies that examine public perceptions of real candidates to draw conclusions about the existence of gender stereotypes; I briefly discuss two of the most recent studies here—Fridkin and Kenney (2009) and Banwart (2010)—in order to address the current state of that literature, and to highlight the challenges generally associated with these kinds of approaches with respect to understanding whether the public holds gender stereotypes about candidates that hurt women electorally.[7]

[6] Sanbonmatsu 2002, 28. As such, in her 2002 article, Sanbonmatsu wisely triangulates her findings based on generic gender questions with an experimental analysis.

[7] For other examples, see Alexander and Andersen 1993 (candidates in three male vs. female races); Dolan 2004 (different types of races); Hansen and Otero 2007 (perceptions of Hillary Clinton vs. 2004 presidential candidates); Hayes 2011 (perceptions of members of Congress in 2006); Herrnson, Lay, and Stokes, 2003 (U.S. House and state legislative candidates who ran for office in 1996–98); Koch 2002 (perceptions of U.S. House candidates in 1994–98); Koch 2000 (perceptions of U.S. Senate candidates in 1988–92); McDermott 1997 (U.S. House races in 1986–94); Paul and Smith 2008 (Ohio voters views in 2006 of likely 2008 presidential primary candidates).

Kim Fridkin and Pat Kenney (2009) conducted an impressive analysis of public views about U.S. senators, involving 1,045 respondents and twenty-one Senate races (all of the 2006 races in which an incumbent was running). Their analysis revealed that when compared to their male colleagues, sitting female senators are not at a disadvantage with respect to public opinion. Instead, they found that women politicians benefit from positive gender stereotypes regarding communal characteristics and related policies (honesty, caring nature, ability to handle health-care issues) while not being perceived as less successful on agentic measures than male candidates.

Using a very different approach, Mary Christine Banwart (2010) relied upon the selection of three ads created by each of four candidates—two male and two female—in two U.S. House races; undergraduates then watched those ads and assessed the candidates. On the basis of those findings, Banwart concluded that a range of traditional stereotypes about male and female candidates are still alive and well, albeit with a few nontraditional caveats. Without using the same ads for the male and female candidates, however, it is not possible to sort out whether the preferences expressed by respondents reflect actual differences between the candidates, actual differences between the ads, or gender stereotypes.[8]

Ultimately, no study of real candidates can be used to determine whether gender bias in the public keeps women from winning campaigns. Given the prevalence of the conventional wisdom regarding special rules about how women politicians have to act (e.g., be extra compassionate but not too emotional, be tough but not too tough) in order to avoid alienating a fickle public, there are many reasons to expect that female politicians may push themselves to act quite differently than male politicians. Candidates may very well be wrong in those perceptions—ascertaining that matter is the role of this book—but there is ample evidence that those perceptions among candidates and their advisers do exist. Thus, the different views that people hold about male and female candidates may be, at least in some cases, accurate reflections of how the candidates themselves choose to behave.[9] Moreover, if the public does, in

[8] For example, perhaps the two women who were selected for the study happened to emphasize communal traits in the ads that were included in the study, or perhaps they were exceptionally warm and compassionate women, and naturally radiated that in photos and videos that the candidates chose to include in their ads. Perhaps the male candidates happened to decide to emphasize or naturally radiated agentic traits in their ads. Without controls and manipulations in the study that would allow candidate gender to be isolated, we cannot know.

[9] See, for example, Anzia and Berry (2011), who find evidence that women who are elected work harder than their male counterparts once in office. To the extent that is true, an examination of gender stereotypes held by the public about elected officials should be expected to result in disproportionately higher scores for women politicians.

fact, hold gendered standards for male and female candidates, there could be important selection effects in place: female candidates who do not readily conform to "the rules" for women candidates and acceptably differentiate themselves from male candidates may never make it to office or even past the primary election level. As such, studies of real candidates cannot allow us to separate out *actual* differences between male and female candidates from differences that are *perceived* but do not actually exist.

Those are all problems associated with using real candidates to test for the existence of inaccurate baseline stereotypes about candidates; trying to test for gendered reactions to the behavior of real candidates would add even more layers of problems into the mix. Candidates frequently get themselves into trouble with various types of suboptimal behavior, with outbursts of tears, anger, inappropriate comments, inaccurate comments, and the like; however, scholars virtually never have benchmark public opinion data on that candidate immediately before an incident takes place.[10] More importantly, comparable male and female candidates would never realistically engage in the exact same behavior at comparable points in time.

In the end, while studies of real candidates can potentially inform us about perceived differences between current-day male and female candidates and therefore have an important place in the literature, that methodology cannot address the kinds of questions about gender stereotypes and harmful double standards that are central to this book.

THE GOLDBERG PARADIGM: STUDIES OF FICTIONAL CANDIDATES

The use of fictional candidates is a third approach for studying candidate gender stereotypes, especially in experimental studies. There are necessarily some compromises to external validity with such an experiment—after all, the candidates are not real—but using this method does allow everything to be carefully controlled and isolated. Respondents are given information about a particular (male or female) candidate, often within the context of a newspaper article, radio story, or other such device, and are asked to express their views on that candidate. The use of fictional candidates rather than real candidates holds actual candidate quality constant, which is critical for establishing that different public reactions to male and female candidates reflect perceptions of, rather than actual,

[10] This is certainly true in low-profile races but also tends to be true in high-profile, highly polled races as well. See, e.g., Newport on why polls cannot reveal how Hillary Clinton's "emotional moment" in the New Hampshire presidential primaries affected public opinion (*Gallup Poll Online*, January 8, 2008, http://www.gallup.com/poll/103663/PostNH-Explaining-Unexpected.aspx).

differences in candidate quality. Since gender is not revealed as the topic of study, respondents are far more likely to reveal their true beliefs. Moreover, as recommended in the earlier quote by Sanbonmatsu, respondents are likely to react to candidate gender much as they would in the voting booth; they might factor it in, or they might not, because as in real campaigns, they can be presented with an array of candidate characteristics other than gender.[11]

The experimental approach of alternating gender for respondents by using different names and pronouns to see how gender affects public opinion is sufficiently common within the business and psychology literatures that it has its own term: the Goldberg paradigm. In 1968 Philip Goldberg undertook an experiment in which students evaluated articles written by a fictional man or fictional woman in order to be able to isolate the effects of gender. In subsequent decades, scholars have very frequently applied this methodology to a variety of questions pertaining to gender in multiple fields; for example, on just the specific matter of job applicant gender and job applications, a 2000 meta-analysis of the business literature found forty-nine articles and dissertations that used the Goldberg paradigm approach.[12]

Ultimately, the Goldberg paradigm design is a very good option for studying the baseline descriptive stereotypes of candidates: it can provide a realistic amount of information about candidates to respondents, it avoids issues associated with stereotypes versus actual differences in real male and female candidates, and it allows for the identification of the kinds of stereotypes that are actively applied solely because of a candidates' gender. Yet, for addressing the fundamental puzzle at the heart of this book—whether the public holds higher standards for the characteristics and behavior of male and female candidates—using fictional candidates is more than simply a very good methodological option; it is, quite simply, the only option. With a Goldberg paradigm design, candidate gender and candidate characteristics and behavior can be carefully manipulated within a scenario that is otherwise held exactly constant. In comparison, recall that the behavior of real candidates and the context in which it occurs is too idiosyncratic to attempt direct comparisons of a given action by a man and a woman. And a generic gender question approach would not yield us anything of use for studying these dynamics.

Although isolating the effects of behavior or qualifications on voters is simply not possible with any methodology other than the Goldberg-paradigm approach, the use of fictional candidates is not without its own

---

[11] Sanbonmatsu 2002, 28.

[12] Davidson and Burke 2000. See discussion of the use of the Goldberg paradigm in business in Eagly and Karau 2002, 582.

limitations. Obviously, the dynamic nature of campaigns cannot be fully captured within an experiment. A real campaign entails not just what candidates say and do but also includes various other dynamics such as the media's reaction to candidates and responses by the opponent's campaign. What we can determine using this methodology is whether the public applies disproportionate penalties for female candidates across a range of different behaviors when everything else is held constant. We can assess the underlying reaction that people have to various kinds of situations that have been hypothesized to produce gender bias for candidates. If women face a playing field very different vis-à-vis the public from what men face in the quest for political office, we should see evidence of it using this methodology.

How I Study Gender Stereotypes and Double Standards

My analysis consists of a set of six Golberg paradigm-style experiments that were included on a survey administered to three thousand U.S. adults by YouGov, a leading Internet-based survey provider.[13] After discussing important details regarding the online survey, I describe the overall experimental design.

The Timing of the Survey

The study was conducted from April 17–29, 2009. As the survey was conducted more than five months after the conclusion of the 2008 campaign and much longer after the heat of the 2007 presidential primaries, the timing of this study minimizes any concerns there might be about potential panel fatigue during election-time interviewing. It was also a realistic time to read about a candidate's announcement of a 2010 election bid, and a very good opportunity to capture views in the post-2008 era.

There is no "perfect" era for any type of scholarship, and in no way am I suggesting that there is some sort of magical finality to the spring of 2009. There is not. As with all research, later examinations of these phenomena would be wise and interesting, and future replication is the highest compliment to any research. But capturing a baseline understanding of gender stereotypes in the post-2008 era is an important step given the enormous changes that arguably have been experienced by women inside and outside of politics in recent years.

---

[13] YouGov is the new name for Polimetrix, which also for a time was called YouGov/Polimetrix.

The Sample

Until recently, it was not feasible to use geographically and demographically representative samples of respondents for most experiments. Although studies of stereotypes about actual candidates and of preferences to generic male vs. female candidates or politicians typically used random digit dial national samples of U.S. adults, those studies were not experiments: they often were not hiding the intent of the study, and they never systematically varied characteristics of the candidates. In contrast, any study that required understanding of long verbal passages—components of nearly all experiments—was simply not feasible over the telephone.

Much of the published gender stereotype research to date that uses fictional candidates is based on convenience samples of undergraduates at the universities at which the researchers were employed.[14] Because there may be a relationship between stereotype usage, age, and education levels, some studies have tried to broaden their samples by using geographically proximate adults instead of undergraduates.[15] A key potential problem associated with the use of geographically limited samples for gender research, however, is that research has shown that gender stereotypes can vary significantly geographically. Specifically, Richard Fox and Eric Smith studied the matter and found no bias against female political candidates among undergraduates at the University of California at Santa Barbara but found bias against female candidates at the University of Wyoming.[16] Those findings suggest that geographic representation is relevant to sampling for studies on gender stereotypes, at least for any study that wants to characterize the views of the national public. In terms of previous research, I know of only one published study to date that used a national sample for an experiment about how the public responds to fictional male and female candidates.[17]

It is primarily with the recent onset of online surveys that researchers have gained the ability to obtain geographically and demographically representative samples while being able to utilize the kinds of stimuli that

[14] See, e.g., Elkstrand and Eckert 1981; Huddy and Terkildsen 1993a, 1993b; Leeper 1991; Rosenwasser and Dean 1989; Ogletree et al. 1992; Rosenwasser and Seal 1988; Rosenwasser et al. 1987; Riggle et al. 1997; Sapiro 1981–82; Smith, Paul, and Paul 2007.

[15] See, Huddy and Capelos 2002 (residents of Suffolk county, Long Island, for one study; undergraduates for another study); Kahn 1996 (adults from Ann Arbor and Phoenix). McDermott 1998 (Los Angeles adults); Sanbonmatsu 2002 (Ohio adults); Thompson and Steckerider 1997 (adults from the Westchester area of Los Angeles).

[16] Fox and Smith 1998.

[17] King and Matland (2003) embedded an experiment on a national telephone poll sponsored by the Republican Network to Elect Women in order to examine the relationship between partisanship, gender, and vote choice.

scholars typically need to run experiments. Studies by Berrens et al. and Sanders et al have demonstrated that the samples used in online surveys—especially those weighted carefully to reflect the U.S. population as closely as possible, even if they are restricted to only users with access to the Internet—can meet or exceed the quality of traditional telephone surveys.[18] It should be noted that in drawing their conclusions, the Berrens et al. and Sanders et al. studies specifically studied YouGov, the online survey supplier used for the present study.

YouGov uses a technique called "sample matching" to generate a nationally representative sample.[19] Volunteers register at a Web site to join a panel of respondents who take both political and nonpolitical surveys. Modest incentives are provided for participation on the panel. Since 2004 YouGov has developed a panel of more than 2 million Americans, the population from which random samples for particular surveys are drawn. The core of this sampling process is the YouGov "target matrix," a combination of local, state, and national voter lists as well as other consumer databases that represent the American population overall. The firm draws a representative sample by matching characteristics of individuals from the panel to the characteristics determined by the target matrix, and the data are weighted on the back end to reflect the population at large.

A subset of the YouGov total panel was invited to participate in this study, and 39.6 percent of those invited respondents completed the survey, which represents a very good survey response rate. The demographic characteristics of the sample are comparable to those used by the U.S. Census Bureau, the typical standard by which sample demographic representativeness is judged (see table 3.1).[20]

---

[18] Berrens et al. 2003 and Sanders et al. 2007. It should also be noted that the quality of telephone surveys has declined since the early 2000s due to the dramatic rise of caller-ID and cell-phone only households, especially among younger populations.

[19] See Rivers 2006 for a description of sample matching.

[20] I hesitate to add that I engaged in the common practice of conducting randomization checks, and no significant differences between the demographics I present in table 3.1 were found between the experiment cells. My hesitation stems not from that result—obviously, that would be the result one would hope for with a randomization check—but rather from Diana Mutz's (2011, 126) important admonition to experimentalists that the entire premise of conducting randomization checks is wrong: "This practice is simply misguided. The statistical significance of a randomization check has no bearing on whether the imbalance matters to the analyses. Unless one suspects a technical problem, this practice is philosophically and statistically unsound, of no practical value, and potentially misleading. If a randomization 'fails' such a check, there is nothing one can or should do about this. Including a control variable because of a 'failed' randomization check does not adjust for the problem and only makes matter worse. Randomization checks reflect a lack of confidence in the power of random assignment to equalize measured and unmeasured variables across conditions, as well as a misunderstanding of what statistical tests take into account."

TABLE 3.1. Sample Demographics as Compared to Census Bureau Population Estimates for *He Runs, She Runs* Experiments

Respondents (Percentages)	Weighted Overall	Unweighted Overall	U.S. Census Overall
Female	51.7	51.7	50.9
Black	11.0	11.1	12.3
Some College or more	53.7	60.3	51.7
College Grad (4 yrs. +)	25.0	27.0	24.4
Age 65 or older	11.6	12.7	12.4

Note: The unweighted numbers represent the actual breakdown of the sample, while the weighted numbers represent the degree to which certain groups are represented in the analyses. Because all data are weighted in the analyses in this book, the weighted numbers are the most relevant point of comparison to the 2000 U.S. Census numbers.

Data were weighted in all of the analyses throughout this book in order to reflect the views of the public at large.[21] That being said, a look at table 3.1 indicates that the differences between the weighted and unweighted data and census estimates are quite modest, with the only substantial difference (just under seven percentage points) being the percentage of individuals who had at least some college.

Are YouGov samples perfectly random representations of the public? Of course not; no surveys or experiments are. Perfection is not the accurate benchmark. Telephone surveys are fighting increasingly low response rates in what may ultimately prove to be a losing battle.[22] Experiments conducted on convenience samples of undergraduates (the most common source of experimental samples in the pre-Internet era) limit the applicability of the results to eighteen- to twenty-two-year-olds if views might vary by generation, which may plausibly be the case for gender issues. Conducting experiments on local temporary agency employees not only tends to be hugely expensive for studies that require large samples but also limits the demographic representativeness of a

[21] I used a within-cell weighting design, with weights that were produced by YouGov so that each experimental cell reflects the population parameters. This is an approach that Mutz outlines as a wise option for population-based experiments (as compared to weights that are applied to the sample overall, as is the case for standard surveys). According to Mutz (2011, 120), "Either weighting scheme has the benefit of increasing generalizability to the full population. However, [as shown in an example] the side benefit of reducing noise due to uneven randomization is obtained through within-condition weighting, but not generally through full sample weighting."

[22] Asher 2012, 107–10.

sample, particularly geographically, which is a problem for studying views on gender. With YouGov, people need to have access to the Internet in order to participate, and not all people have that; they also have to decide to participate on the YouGov panel and to participate in a particular study. As can be seen on table 3.1, the unweighted demographics are quite close to expected population percentages, with the exception of education; however, weighting brings even that close to population norms. To be sure, demographics do not tell us everything about the representative nature of a sample, but these are good signs. In any case, the goal for an experiment (versus a regular survey) is to look at how views differ depending on which randomly assigned treatment an individual receives; as such, the real question is whether the experimental treatment is likely to interact markedly with any systematic skews in the sampling process that cannot be corrected through the process of weighting the data. In this case, a plausible story cannot be constructed to that effect for public responses to candidate gender. This sample is more than up to the task at hand.

The Experimental Design

In an administrative sense, this was one large experiment with sixteen conditions because it was conducted during the same specific time period and each individual within the sample was randomly assigned into different cells within the study. But analytically, this is a set of six separate experiments (see table 3.2 for a layout of the different experiments and cell sizes for each). The six experiments involve sixteen different cells in total (two experience conditions × candidate gender that are compared only to one another, plus one control group × candidate gender, and five different candidate behaviors × candidate gender).

Half of the respondents were randomly assigned to read a newspaper article about a fictional candidate named "Karen Bailey," and half read an article about "Kevin Bailey." The articles included the kind of standard information one would read about a candidate in a news story, and all information outside of the dimensions specifically tested in this experiment was held constant across candidates. Each respondent read one news article about a single candidate (Karen or Kevin Bailey) and had no way of discerning the focus of the study. To increase the external validity of the experimental treatment, each news article was attributed to a nationally recognized syndicated news service with a reputation for being unbiased.[23]

After reading the article, respondents then completed a series of questions about the candidate described in the article. Respondents were prevented from returning to the article because the goal was to capture their

---

[23] The source was not varied between respondents; everyone was exposed to an article by the same source.

TABLE 3.2. Experiment Conditions and Cell Sizes

	CHAPTER 4		CHAPTER 5		CHAPTER 6		CHAPTER 7	CONTROL GROUP (for Ch. 5-7 also analyzed separately in Ch. 4)
	EXPERIENCE - High	EXPERIENCE - Low	ANGER	CRYING	TOUGH	LACK OF EMPATHY	KNOWLEDGE GAFFE	
FEMALE CANDIDATE	COND #1 (N=191)	COND #3 (N=202)	COND #5 (N=185)	COND #7 (N=194)	COND #9 (N=188)	COND #11 (N=185)	COND #13 (N=185)	COND #15 (N=185)
MALE CANDIDATE	COND #2 (N=184)	COND #4 (N=184)	COND #6 (N=186)	COND #8 (N=190)	COND #10 (N=184)	COND #12 (N=186)	COND #14 (N=191)	COND #16 (N=180)
n=	375	386	371	384	372	371	376	365
Experiment n	761		736	749	737	736	741	

general impression about the candidate and not their opinion after reread-
ing the article in the context of specific questions. Respondents were then
diverted into a separate, unrelated experiment and afterward answered demographic questions and other questions about their own personal traits.
Throughout the survey, respondents were prevented from using the "page
back" function so they could not change previous answers. This is particularly critical because, once questions were given toward the end of the survey that implied that the experiment was about candidate gender or behavior, respondents could not go back to change their answers to the primary
questions of interest. After completing the survey, respondents were de-
briefed about the nature of the experiment.[24]

The experience experiment is structured in a way that is different from
the behavior-oriented experiments (i.e., those that respectively examine
anger, crying, toughness, lack of empathy, and knowledge gaffes). The
amount of past political experience for the candidate was varied between
a high level (ten years of political experience) and a low level (no political
experience), and all comparison occurs between those two groups (more
details on the design of this experience experiment will be discussed in
chapter 4, and the full text of each article can be reviewed in appendix 1).

The other experiments—the behavior-based experiments—all share a
common control group. The control groups (one for the female condition, one for the male condition) read a news article about Karen or
Kevin Bailey that did not contain information about the candidate's behavior and held political experience constant at an in-between level (the
candidate had completed one term in the U.S. House and was just starting his or her second term). Respondents in the specific behavior conditions each read the same exact article as the control group, but with the
addition of one or two paragraphs that describe two incidents of the behavior in question as well as a different headline and a different pull
quote that highlights the specific behavior in question (additional details
on these experiments are discussed in chapters 5–7).

A choice existed as to whether to use videotaped stimuli (video clips of
male and female politicians acting in different ways) or to describe the
behavior within a newspaper article. The latter was selected to enhance
internal validity by varying only gender and not any of the other potential factors such as overall attractiveness, strength of facial features, facial
expressions, tone of voice, and clothing that could have otherwise reduced internal validity if male and female actors had been featured in
photos or on video in the treatments.[25] Over 85 percent of respondents

---

[24] As part of the debrief, all respondents were told that "the candidates, their activities
and behaviors, and the news articles themselves were all fictional."

[25] For example, some studies have suggested that perceived attractiveness may have different effects for male and female leaders (e.g., Herrick, Mendez, Thomas, and Wilkerson
2012; Lewis and Bierly 1990; Sigelman, Sigelman, Thomas, and Ribich 1986; Sigelman, Si-

properly identified the gender of the candidates, which suggests that gender was effectively cued for respondents.[26]

The matter of partisanship—specifically, whether to explicitly cue partisanship for respondents or not—also needed to be carefully considered in the design of this study. Partisanship is a prominent feature of most general elections. Moreover, Danny Hayes argues that partisan stereotypes actually trump gender stereotypes for candidate traits; in other words, that stereotypes pertaining to matters such as Democrats being compassionate or Republicans being stronger leaders are more likely to determine public views of real candidates than candidate gender.[27] By that logic, some studies of gender stereotypes may be picking up stereotypes that would diminish in the presence of partisan cues. Yet, without the normal cacophony of events that unfold in a campaign over a matter of months, partisanship would be likely to loom unnaturally large in determining a respondent's responses within an experiment. Given that my theoretical expectation was that candidate gender stereotypes will not be as substantial as they are commonly believed to be, I needed to allow gender stereotypes and double standards to have a reasonable chance to emerge. Without clear theoretical expectations regarding different behavioral standards for Democratic women versus Republican women and Democratic men versus Republican men, the considerable costs involved with including partisanship (i.e., the complexities involved with layering in interactions between respondent partisanship and candidate partisanship such that four-way interactions would have to be untangled for even the most basic analyses, power limitations once cell sizes were effectively carved up by candidate and respondent partisanship, etc.) outweighed the possible benefits. As a result, partisanship was not specified in the experiments.

Although I did not explicitly cue partisanship in my experiments, I did not leave partisanship off the table entirely. I did ask for the respondent's perception of the candidate's partisanship and, at a separate time, for the respondent's own partisanship. This helps to address the matter of whether respondents are more likely to assume that female candidates

---

gelman, and Fowler 1987). While it is possible that people could have different reactions to viewing politicians act in a particular manner via video rather than reading about it in print, it seems less likely that people would systematically react differently to politicians of different genders via those different delivery mechanisms. As such, while this study uses print media within the experiment, it is reasonable to think that the gender differences it uncovers—the focus of this study—would not be dramatically different in the context of video.

[26] Manipulation checks never reach 100% correct (respondents sometimes register the wrong answer by mistake to a manipulation check survey question and/or have subconsciously processed the manipulation without being able to correctly identify the correct answer at a conscious level), and 85% is well within the comfort zone for a fine manipulation. Filtering respondents by correct candidate gender identification does affect the findings from this study; the full sample is used in the analyses shown in this book.

[27] Hayes 2011.

are Democrats—something that Koch and others have found as a stereotype for female candidates.[28] That relationship was not borne out in the data: people were not significantly more likely to project Democratic partisanship onto female candidates.[29]

I also created a "partisanship differential" variable to compare the distance between a person's own partisanship and the partisanship they guessed for the candidate. Unsurprisingly, I found that people who perceive a greater difference between themselves and the candidates in terms of partisanship are less likely to rate the candidate highly. This variable is somewhat problematic, however, in that people perceive greater partisan difference between themselves and the candidate when the candidate engages in the most negative behaviors.[30] But including the variable in the model has virtually no effect on the key relationship of interest (candidate gender * treatment condition) or on the main conclusions from this study. Perceived partisanship is ultimately best left out of the models, both for practical reasons (it has little effect and introduces an extra layer of interactions) and for theoretical reasons (the directional nature of the relationship between perceived partisanship and candidate ratings is unclear). In the end, although it would be interesting in future research to explore the role of partisanship further, I see little reason on the basis of the proxy I used to expect that it would meaningfully alter the key findings from this study.

Dependent Variables

The three key dependent variables in the experiment are referred to, collectively, as the "outcome measures": overall favorability, likely effectiveness in the Senate, and likely effectiveness as U.S. president about ten years from now.[31] I term them outcome measures because they are the variables in the study that most closely approximate the likely overall ef-

[28] Some scholars have found that people stereotype female candidates as being either more Democratic or more liberal than comparable male candidates. See, e.g., Huddy and Terkildsen 1993b; Koch 2000, 2002.

[29] The partisan guesses were nearly indistinguishable for Karen versus Kevin Bailey. Moreover, guesses at the partisanship of the candidates were distributed such that people were not more likely to guess that Candidate Bailey was a Republican or Democrat. Guesses tended toward the moderate range, with only about 1 out of 8 respondents guessing that the candidate was either a strong Republican or a strong Democrat, and the remainder guessing that he or she was either a weak Republican, Independent, or weak Democrat, in roughly equal percentages.

[30] This makes some sense and may be an interesting twist on "distancing" theory (people are distancing themselves from unsavory candidates in terms of partisanship).

[31] I opted against asking a direct "vote preference" question, which would be very artificial given that the announcement in the new story concerned a run for a primary more than a year away and because particular competitors were not mentioned in the article.

fect of qualifications or behavior on the candidate's chances of success. Favorability is included as an indication of satisfaction with the candidate in his or her current position in the House and contains an affective component lacking in the other two measures. Likely effectiveness in the Senate is a reasonable early indicator of likely vote preference. Likely presidential effectiveness is included because some scholars have hypothesized that female candidates are disadvantaged by gender stereotypes in their quest for executive office but not for legislative office.[32] This variable makes it possible to explore to some degree whether candidate qualifications or behavior might have a different effect on perceptions of effectiveness at different levels of office.

The outcome measures are clearly the most critical measures for assessing whether female candidates face higher standards in politics; however, they are not the only measures of interest. To the extent that candidate characteristics and behaviors might differentially affect the electoral prospects for male and female candidates, it is helpful to get a sense of the mechanisms through which those dynamics occur. In addition to examining the effects of candidate characteristics and behaviors on overall assessments about candidates, I therefore also examine whether public perceptions of a range of different traits and issue competencies are affected.

To this end, I include questions about respondents' perceptions of the candidate on different traits like honesty, intelligence, strength, and compassion. I also included perceived issue competencies in three areas: domestic programs (specifically, "strengthen programs like Social Security and Medicare"), the economy ("help to make America strong economically"), and ability to effectively handle an international crisis. Appendix 2 includes the wording for each of these questions, and different traits are discussed in more detail in relevant substantive chapters. Within any given chapter, only a subset of individual traits or issues may be of primary importance. Accordingly, I focus on the key variables of interest within the text of the chapters but then include a summary chart within the chapter and an associated appendix that includes the full range of results across all of the measures.

Finally, I also asked whether people attributed the cause of the candidate's behavior more to the "personal characteristics of the candidate" or to "the difficulty of the situation." That question was asked only of the respondents exposed to the behavior treatments (it was not relevant to the control group or experience treatments). These data allow me to test the predictions made by attribution theorists that stereotype-consistent behaviors will be attributed to the personal traits of an individual, whereas stereotype-inconsistent behaviors will be attributed to the situational factors.

[32] See, e.g., Smith, Paul, and Paul 2007; Dolan 1997; Huddy and Terkildsen 1993a.

ANALYTICAL TECHNIQUE

Analysis of variance (ANOVA) was used for the analysis of each experiment. A brief discussion of ANOVA is in order here to set the framework for the analyses that follow. When an analysis involves the examination of the effects of one or more categorical independent variables on a continuous dependent variable, ANOVA is ultimately just a type of regression. This is sometimes surprising to scholars who are often trained in one procedure and not the other. Rutherford points out that "separate analysis traditions evolved and encouraged the mistaken belief that regression and ANOVA constituted fundamentally different types of statistical analysis . . . ANOVA is a particular type of regression analysis that employs quantitative predictors to act as categorical predictors."[33] Results from the two procedures are displayed quite differently, however, and depending on the analysis in question, one procedure can yield interpretive benefits over the other; as a result, different fields tend toward different analytical techniques.

In psychology, ANOVA tends to be the procedure of choice because it handles interaction effects for categorical variables—the stock-in-trade of the experimental psychologist—in a very clear, intuitive manner. In contrast, political scientists generally tend to be trained in the use and interpretation of OLS regression rather than ANOVA: understandable because, until quite recently, relatively few political scientists engaged in experimental research. However, using regression to analyze results from experiments is unnecessarily cumbersome, particularly when more than one layer of interactions is involved. Diana Mutz, a leading experimentalist within political science, delineates in her book *Population-Based Survey Experiments* why ANOVA is typically preferable to regression for the presentation of most experimental data:

> In presentation as well as in analyses, investigators should present findings in as transparent and straightforward a manner as possible. For example, if an experimental design involves a 3 by 2 factorial design including interactions, then it makes little sense to present a complex regression equation full of dummy variables and their many interactions when a straightforward analysis of variance and table of means would be far easier to interpret. Although this choice will not affect the results in any way, it can easily affect readers' understanding of results when they are presented in a more complex fashion than need be.
>
> In my own field [political science], the "obsession with regression" as the one and only means of analyzing data produces some oddly complex presentations of relatively simple and straightforward find-

[33] Rutherford 2001, 3–5.

ings. I have nothing against regression, but it is not the only tool for analysis. Often an analysis of variance along with a display of means makes a far simpler and more understandable presentation, particularly when interactions are involved.[34]

Nearly every analysis in this book involves two-way or three-way interactions between categorical variables, and Mutz is correct that regression provides oddly and unnecessarily complex presentations for data that ultimately involve easily interpretable comparisons between group means. As a result, ANOVA is the procedure I use throughout this book.

All significance tests are conservatively based on two-tailed tests. I demarcate results that achieve significance of at least a .90 level of confidence, as is fairly common practice for experiments where any individual cell is relatively modest in size. Most importantly, I present all of the p-values for the two-tailed significance tests in the appendix so that readers can draw their own conclusions, and I often mention them where relevant in the text as well.

A note on control variables is in order. Political scientists are typically trained to use regression analysis with a long list of control variables in their models. The absence of control variables therefore tends to seem distressing to some because it appears that one is no longer "controlling" for other factors that may be related to the dependent variable. Even when one realizes that the nature of a controlled experiment eliminates the need for control variables through the process of randomly assigning participants to conditions, researchers who do not typically work with experimental data sometimes wonder why one would not simply "throw in" some control variables anyway for good measure. Mutz directly addresses this point, noting that "few population-based experiments actually benefit from such an approach. Because of the experimental protocol, temporal precedence and spurious correlation are not issues (other than the small probability of a random spurious correlation, quantified by the p-value). A significant empirical relationship between independent and dependent variables all but guarantees causal inference."[35] Additionally, she argues that what "scholars tend to misunderstand is that covariates are not always helpful or even benign influences. To haphazardly include a long list of covariates in your analysis of variance, or throw a batch of additional variables into your regression is not wise"; she further goes on to remind readers that "experimental inference is always valid with no covariates whatsoever."[36] As such, I do not routinely include covariates (or their categorical equivalents) in my models because they are not necessary. However, I do occasionally add an

[34] Mutz 2011, 127–28.
[35] Mutz 2011, 123.
[36] Mutz 2011, 124 and 126.

additional variable in a few very specific instances where theory would lead us to believe that a specific factor would interact with candidate gender in an important manner.

What This Methodological Approach Allows

By providing the opportunity to conduct experiments on geographically and demographically representative samples, the rise of online surveys has opened up avenues of inquiry that would not have been possible or worthwhile before this advent in technology. To date, there have not yet been any studies that take advantage of this new technology and employ national, representative samples with visual stimuli (e.g., newspaper articles) to analyze the degree to which people actively use gender in their assessments of candidates.[37] This study fills that gap with the set of six experiments that were just described.

The first step in the analysis is to assess the descriptive stereotypes in place for male and female candidates across a range of different attributes. By comparing public reactions to low- and high-experience candidates, I am able to compare the descriptive gender stereotypes that are applied to men and women at different stages of their political careers. Once those descriptive stereotypes are established, I am then in position to assess whether engaging in certain behaviors affects public perceptions of male and female candidates differently. Using a control group allows for the effect of the behavior on public opinion to be isolated: without a control group, one could not be certain that differences observed for male and female candidates who engage in a behavior did not actually reflect baseline differences between male and female candidates in general (i.e., descriptive stereotypes).

The bottom line of most of my findings is that the public does not have different standards for female candidates than it does for their male counterparts. But an exclusive focus on that finding downplays the richness of the dynamics occurring beneath the surface for male and female candidates, and for candidates overall. Setting gender aside, the effects of candidate behavior on public perceptions has only rarely been studied. While it is not the primary focus of this book, there is also much to be learned from these experiments about how the public reacts to the behavior and characteristics of candidates overall.

[37] As mentioned earlier, King and Matland (2003) were the first scholars to study gender stereotypes that I am aware of to use a nationally representative sample; they were highly limited, however, in the kind of experimental treatment they could use because it had to be delivered over the telephone and therefore had to be extremely concise and only verbally stated.

Descriptive Candidate Gender Stereotypes and the Role of Candidate Experience

"We've come a long way from the time I first ran for state
representative in 1974 and had a bumper sticker that said,
'People for Morella.' . . . My son came in and said his friends
wanted to know what dad is running for."

—U.S. HOUSE MEMBER CONSTANCE MORELLA[1]

When Geraldine Ferraro ran as the Democratic vice presidential nominee in 1984, gender was front-and-center in the campaign. As the first-ever female vice presidential nominee for a major party, it was an historic campaign for women by definition. Ferraro recounts that the novelty of being a woman on a national ticket had some important advantages; most notably, her campaign stops "drew huge crowds. The Secret Service told me that we had the largest crowds they'd seen since JFK. But many of those people came to bring their daughters to see the first woman nominated for a national office. I would see these men in the audience with their little girls on their shoulders, saying, 'You got to see the first woman nominated. This is historic.'"[2]

At the same time, Ferraro details that the novelty of her gender also led to various challenges and difficulties. Some of these were minor, such as the fact that she felt she could not wear pants even when campaigning: "At the time I ran, there were no women in political leadership, so people had nothing to compare me to. I didn't ever wear pants, and the reason I didn't was that I didn't want people to think I was trying to be a man."[3] However, she argues other constraints associated with her gender were much more significant—notably, the extra media scrutiny she felt she received regarding whether she was tough enough to be president. As Fer-

---

[1] Richard L. Berke, "The 1992 Campaign: Women; With Outsiders In, Female Candidates Come Forward," *New York Times*, April 30, 1992.

[2] Pat Wingert, "Gender on the Trail: Geraldine Ferraro on Palin, Clinton and the Campaign Ahead," *Newsweek*, September 15, 2008.

[3] As Ferraro notes in Pat Wingert, "Gender on the Trail: Geraldine Ferraro on Palin, Clinton and the Campaign ahead," *Newsweek*, September 15, 2008.

raro recounts, "Ted Koppel and 'Meet the Press' and 'Face the Nation' . . .
felt like they had to give me a foreign policy exam, and ask me if I was
strong enough to push the button. These were questions they never asked
men. But in 1984, I couldn't say, 'Stop it,' because I couldn't look like I
was whining or upset about it."[4] Certainly, Ferraro was correct that no
man would ever have been asked the following question that was directed at her on *Meet the Press*: "Do you think that in any way that the
Soviets might be tempted to try to take advantage of you simply because
you are a woman?"[5]

Ferraro's historic run occurred more than twenty five years ago, and
much has changed in the interim regarding the role of women in politics. Women have clearly moved beyond being token figures in American
politics: in recent years, we have seen the ascension of women into various congressional leadership positions, governorships, party leadership
posts, agency head positions, high profile cabinet positions, and a variety of other positions of political power. What was once an overtly hostile environment for women appears to have become more welcoming in
many respects, a development that can be traced in part to the role that
Ferraro and other women have prominently played in U.S. electoral politics over the past twenty-five years. Ferraro herself recently underscored
this dynamic:

> I've been saying for 24 years that women's candidacies—I'm not talk-
> ing about me, specifically, or Hillary or Governor Palin—but women's
> candidacies have a larger effect. They are like tossing a pebble into a
> lake, because of all the ripples that go out from there. . . . That was the
> impact of the '84 campaign, and they still go on. . . . The fact that Hill-
> ary conducted herself so well during her campaign has to help Palin as
> well. It has to, and she doesn't have to win to have an impact. Every
> time a woman runs, women win."[6]

Although we have nothing close to gender parity, we have clearly
moved beyond the era where seeing a woman candidate is surprising.
That being said, it does not necessarily follow that women do not still
face enormous challenges due to their gender in the current era. While
asserting that the environment for women candidates has improved since
1984, Ferraro also argued in 2008 that Hillary Clinton's nomination
campaign was undermined by sexism. Ferraro's charges of sexism did not

---

    [4] Pat Wingert, "Gender on the Trail: Geraldine Ferraro on Palin, Clinton and the Cam-
paign Ahead," *Newsweek*, September 15, 2008.
    [5] Jamieson 1995, 107.
    [6] Pat Wingert, "Gender on the Trail: Geraldine Ferraro on Palin, Clinton and the Cam-
paign Ahead," *Newsweek*, September 15, 2008.

concern the public at large but instead was focused first and foremost on the media and, to a lesser degree, on the Obama campaign.[7] What about the public itself? Before they even start campaigning, do female candidates suffer from disproportionate negative stereotypes among the public as compared to male candidates? For example, holding everything else constant, would a female candidate be regarded by the public as being inherently less tough than a similarly positioned male candidate? At the same time, do women benefit from any disproportionate positive stereotypes—for example, that they are more caring than male candidates?

Political science has devoted a great deal of research to these two questions and, by and large, the answers have been yes to both of them.[8] Many scholars find that female candidates are assumed from the start to be less effective than male candidates on a variety of agentic traits. With respect to communal traits, women candidates have often been found to hold the advantage. Before examining whether people react differently to particular characteristics or behavior of male and female candidates, an important starting place for this book is addressing those past findings about descriptive stereotypes—that is, the baseline assumptions that people make about male and female candidates—on their own terms in order to determine whether female candidates now begin campaigns at an inherent disadvantage. We cannot assume that those findings are necessarily still accurate in the current era given that many of them were collected in earlier periods when female politicians held more of a token status within politics. As noted previously, the psychology and business literatures have found that token status increases the application of stereotypes; an increase in the proportion of women running for and holding office would thus be expected to diminish those stereotypes. For this reason alone, it is important to reassess these issues using the most recent data.

The second goal of this chapter is to examine whether baseline gender stereotypes remain static as candidates shift from being political neophytes to experienced politicians. A variety of stereotypes—positive and negative—may be applied to established "politicians," and it is possible that the stereotypes for inexperienced candidates may be quite different; those for the latter may be closer to those of "male" and "female," while stereotypes for "female politicians" may correspond to the stereotypes associated with politicians, for better or for worse. The previous literature has not identified the characteristic of political experience to be a

[7] Geraldine Ferraro, "Healing the Wounds of Democrats' Sexism," *Boston Globe*, May 30, 2008.

[8] Kim Kahn (1994, 1996) and Fridkin and Kenney (2009) are exceptions to this, as they did not find negative stereotypes about women. They only found stereotypes that helped women relative to men.

potential source of divergent stereotypes for female candidates, so it has not grappled with this matter directly. Some studies focus on incumbent politicians, while others focus on challengers; others simply do not specify whether the candidate in question has past political experience. It is now critical to carefully examine candidate experience when we analyze descriptive candidate stereotypes in order to better determine the degree to which female politicians will be stereotyped more as "leaders" than as "ladies."

Thus far, the discussion has focused on the importance of identifying the baseline assumptions—the descriptive stereotypes—that people make about male and female candidates. But the analysis of experience also leads us directly to the core question of whether female candidates face a double standard. The fifth component of the double standards theory posits that women candidates simply have to be better, and experience is seen as being potentially very significant in this regard. For example, the issue of whether Hillary Clinton and Barack Obama were held to different standards regarding experience is one that was prominently discussed in the 2008 presidential elections. Along these lines, Martha Burk, president of the National Council of Women's Organizations, argued in 2008: "If [Barack Obama] were female, with his credentials, age, and track record, I don't think he'd be anywhere near the presidency of the United States."[9] Dee Dee Myers, the former press secretary for President Bill Clinton, reflected the same sentiment when she argued, "No woman with Obama's résumé could run. No woman could have gotten out of the gate."[10] And the issue of inexperience has arisen for many other female candidates before that as well. Despite decades of experience in unelected party politics, Nancy Pelosi faced accusations about her inexperience in her first congressional campaign (a particular set of attacks focused on the idea of her being a "dilettante").[11] This chapter gets to the heart of the vital question of whether women have to be more experienced than men to be perceived as being credible and produces some interesting and provocative findings.

The chapter is organized as follows. I first identify what the previous literature has found regarding candidate stereotypes. I then discuss the

[9] Susan Milligan, "Clinton's Struggle Vexes Feminists: To Some, Her Skills Losing Out to Style," *Boston Globe*, February 19, 2008.

[10] Kate Zernike, "She Just Might Be President Someday," Week in Review, *New York Times*, May 18, 2008.

[11] Pelosi 2008, 79. She reports in her memoirs, however, that the attacks did not work as intended because "many people seemed confused by the word. Some seemed to think that it somehow meant 'debutante.' I looked pretty old, they thought, to be a debutante! It backfired on my opponents, because the response from many voters was, 'Is that the worst they can come up with?"

importance of factoring candidate experience into the study of gender stereotypes and how doing so raises a series of empirical questions that have so far been unaddressed. When I turn to analyze my data, I first analyze gender stereotypes for inexperienced candidates. I find that some gender stereotypes do exist for inexperienced candidates but that they help women relative to men. These results are then contrasted to those regarding experienced politicians to see if the latter group is similarly subject to significant gender stereotypes. In fact, I find that experienced politicians are not subject to gender stereotypes for the most part. I then seek to determine exactly how political experience and gender interact. I conclude the chapter by examining some additional data that suggest that gender stereotypes may fade rather quickly as candidates are transformed into leaders.

Ultimately, the analysis from this chapter strikes a blow at the basic tenet of double standards theory: at least with reference to experience, women candidates are not held to a higher standard than their male counterparts. If anything, the tables are reversed: male candidates are penalized for inexperience far more than female candidates. More generally, this chapter shows that in the current era there is no evidence that public attitudes cause women candidates to begin their campaigns at an inherent disadvantage simply because they are women.

Existing Research on Descriptive Gender Stereotypes for Candidates

What does the existing literature tell us about the baseline assumptions that people make about male and female candidates? Some studies have found that female candidates are assumed by the public to be less agentic than male candidates—that is, less tough, less assertive, and less leadership oriented.[12] In turn, it has commonly been thought that female candidates will be evaluated relatively lower than men on particular issues that are associated with agentic traits. In this regard, military and defense issues—and more recently, the ability to handle terrorism—have often been seen as being a weak area for women candidates, and many studies have supported that view.[13] In an associated manner, women politicians are sometimes seen as being weaker on crime.[14]

---

[12] See, e.g., Alexander and Andersen 1993; Lawless 2004. For a review of this topic, see McGraw 2003; Huddy and Terkildsen 1993a.

[13] See, e.g., Alexander and Andersen 1993; Dolan 2010; Lawless 2004; Rosenwasser and Dean 1989; Sanbonmatsu 2002; Sapiro 1981–82.

[14] See, e.g., Sanbonmatsu 2002; Sanbonmatsu and Dolan 2009.

At the same time, many studies have also found that women benefit from positive stereotypes. Female candidates have been found to have a significant advantage over male candidates on communal traits such as "caring," "compassionate," and "honest." Across a wide range of studies using a variety of different methodologies, female candidates—both real and fictional—have been disproportionately assumed by the public to have these positive traits.[15] In an associated manner, women have been found to have an advantage with the public in terms of perceived ability to effectively handle a range of domestic issues, including health care, Social Security, education, the environment, and civil rights.[16]

One might conclude that, at least during the time period of the above studies in question, female candidates are hurt by some stereotypes and helped by others, so the net effect of those gender stereotypes should be neutral. That would assume, however, that negative evaluations on agency-related traits are equal in significance to positive evaluations on communal traits. However, as discussed in chapter 2, there are mixed findings with respect to whether agentic traits are more important to perceptions of leadership than are communal traits. In general, the gender stereotypes literature has tended to do a better job of identifying the existence of particular descriptive stereotypes than in comparing the power of different stereotypes in order to assess whether women tend to get hurt disproportionately by them overall; as such, it is hard to characterize the findings in the literature on that point. But the general tenor of much of the gender stereotypes literature to date at least suggests that descriptive gender stereotypes are likely to be disproportionately problematic for women candidates.[17]

As discussed in chapter 3, these findings derive from a variety of different kinds of methodologies and samples. I established why the Goldberg-paradigm study is the best approach for studying the kinds of questions that are at the core of the book and that the use of a sample not limited to convenience samples of eighteen- to twenty-two-year-old college students is optimal for the examination of this topic. Kim Kahn's examination of candidate gender stereotypes meets both of these criteria.[18] While not perfect on the geographic representation front (Kahn used samples of local adults), her use of two separate locations (Ann Arbor and Phoenix) minimizes some of the geographic concerns raised by Fox and Smith

---

[15] See, e.g., Alexander and Andersen 1993; Dolan 2010; Fridkin and Kenney 2009; Kahn 1994, 1996; Lawless 2004; Leeper 1991; McDermott 1998.

[16] Alexander and Andersen 1993; Dolan 2010; Fridkin and Kenney 2009; Rosenwasser and Dean 1989; Sanbonmatsu and Dolan 2009; Sanbonmatsu 2002.

[17] For just one example of this conclusion, see Dolan, Deckman, and Swers 2011, 143.

[18] Kahn (1994 and 1996) uses a Goldberg paradigm–style experiment in which candidate gender was varied for fictional candidates.

(1998). Additionally, while many of the previously mentioned studies in this literature examined stereotypes about particular traits or issue strengths in isolation, Kahn measured a wide array of descriptive stereotypes. As such, her study is the most comparable to mine (at least the portion in this chapter that focuses on descriptive stereotypes) and is worthy of a more lengthy discussion.

In contrast to most of the literature to date, Kahn found that, controlling for media coverage, women candidates *only benefit* from stereotypes that the public holds rather than being hurt by them. The net finding of the Kahn study is thus that stereotypes give women an advantage relative to male candidates on Election Day.[19] While Kahn's study represents a compelling portrait of how candidates were regarded by the public from 1988 to 1991 when the data were collected for her study, we need to wonder whether the same stereotypes are still in place more than twenty years later given that women have assumed more prominent leadership roles and now constitute a much larger share of candidates and politicians in office.[20] The fact is that, despite considerable work on the topic of descriptive gender stereotypes for candidates, only a small subset of the studies has been conducted on candidate gender stereotypes with data collected in the past decade (and nearly all of these studies are focused on either real candidates or generic "would a male or female candidate be better?" kinds of questions).[21] Our knowledge about the degree to which the public uses candidate gender stereotypes in the assumptions they make about candidates needs to be continually refreshed, and now is a good time for that reexamination.

Descriptive Candidate Stereotypes and Experience

Although many analysts have made assumptions about a possible relationship between candidate gender and experience, it has not received much scrutiny. We need to know if female candidates will be disproportionately penalized for inexperience (or, conversely, helped by it) as compared to men. Kim Kahn comes the closest to addressing this question,

[19] A key caveat is that Kahn also finds that media coverage disproportionately harms female candidates, especially female Senate candidates; the possible role of the media will be discussed in chapter 8.

[20] Fridkin and Kenney found in 2009 that similar views of real women politicians exist, but as argued earlier, we cannot rule out that women politician may be actually acting differently than men.

[21] See, e.g., Dolan 2008a, 2008b, 2010; Fridkin and Kenney 2009; Lawless 2004; Sanbonmatsu and Dolan 2009. Sanbonmatsu (2002) uses both generic and fictional candidate approaches in her study but does not measure stereotypes using the latter methodology. See also Hansen and Otero 2006; Falk and Kenski 2006; Kenski and Falk 2004.

with a brief mention that she finds that gender stereotypes are exacerbated for Senate candidates who are challengers rather than incumbents.[22] Because her analysis alters the type of media coverage given to male and female incumbents and challengers, the independent contribution of candidate experience is not clear. What her findings do suggest is that a detailed examination of gender stereotypes and candidate experience may be fruitful.

The conventional wisdom has long been that inexperience hurts female candidates disproportionately more than otherwise similar male candidates. In the 1960s and 1970s, it was considered to be a matter of course that women had to be more experienced than male candidates to win. In Geraldine Ferraro's 1985 autobiography, she illustrated this dynamic by recounting a gag gift she once received: "Women were not supposed to be able to play in such a high-stakes arena, let alone succeed. A board game my staff gave me for Christmas one year summed up the double standard in politics. One square read: 'You're twice as qualified as your opponent. You've worked twice as hard. The two of you are now dead even. Move to his square.' And move I did, regardless of the double effort it took. How else were women ever going to make a difference?"[23]

Many argue that women still face a double standard with respect to experience and its corollary, perceived competence. Republican consultant John Deardourff claims that "men are perceived to be competent until proven otherwise, whereas women have to prove they are competent."[24] Democratic pollster and political consultant Celinda Lake argues that "women not only have to be twice as good, they have to prove it twice as often."[25] If, in fact, women candidates are perceived from the start to be less competent than men candidates, experience in office should be disproportionately beneficial for them, because it will allow women to imply a degree of competence that might not otherwise be granted to them by the public. Ruth Mandel, a Rutgers University professor and director of the Eagleton Institute of Politics, claims that "female candidates have often faced the double bind that if they are 'outsiders,' breaking ground for newcomers to electoral politics, their 'outsiderness' looms as a hurdle to political acceptability and viability."[26] Former Environmental Protection Agency chief and governor of New Jersey Christine Todd Whitman argued in 2008 that "the challenges women candidates face remain very different from those of their male counterparts. . . . Why is it still true that a male candidate who has never served in public office

[22] Kahn 1992, 507.
[23] Ferraro 1985, 57.
[24] Witt, Paget, and Matthews 1995, 116.
[25] *St. Petersburg Times*, June 29, 1989.
[26] Mandel 2007, 298.

but may have a business background is considered qualified for public office, yet a woman with the same experience is not?"[27]

Moreover, some analysts contend that even when candidates have substantial political experience people will nevertheless still assume that female candidates are inexperienced. According to Witt, Paget, and Matthews, "comparable credentials, money, endorsements, and hard work, however, do not mean that any political step will be easy. Women with years of office-holding experience have been surprised to find themselves described as 'overnight sensations,' or 'coming from nowhere,' when they announced their candidacies for higher office.[28] "I'm a twenty-two-year overnight sensation," Barbara Mikulski exclaimed in this regard after she first won her U.S. Senate seat 1986, after twenty-two years of political work—ten of them in the U.S. House of Representatives.[29]

These beliefs exist among potential candidates as well. In their 2010 book, Jennifer Lawless and Richard Fox interviewed people in the professions that tend to produce the most politicians and found that nearly one-quarter of the women they talked to (i.e., eligible candidates) "referenced the fact that women need greater qualifications than their male counterparts to succeed."[30] Lawless and Fox cite Karen Doyle, a Washington history professor, as claiming that, "Women don't think they're not as qualified as men to succeed. It's just that we perceive, even subconsciously, that we have to be twice as qualified to be successful."[31]

Most of the assertions just expressed are premised on the assumption that more political experience is always beneficial to candidates; however, that assumption should be critically questioned. A good deal of research has demonstrated that "candidate quality"—typically measured solely as having held elected office—confers substantial benefits to candidates. However, it is not entirely clear whether having prior experience helps because the public views experienced candidates more favorably or whether it is largely because prior political experience confers staffing advantages, fundraising advantages, more strategic race-entry decisions, and the like. Moreover, many recent elections have provided a telling reminder that anti-incumbent sentiment can also potentially be an important driver of voter attitudes. Jayson Ertter, a South Carolina voter, en-

---

[27] Christine Whitman, "The Plight of Women Seeking Elective Office," *The Record* (Hackensack, NJ) March 3, 2008, L7.; see, also, Christine Todd Whitman, "Boys on the Bias," *New York Times*, June 8, 2008, where she wrote, "To this day, a businessman with no elected experience is considered qualified for high public office; a woman with the same background is called unprepared."

[28] Witt, Paget, and Matthews 1995, 121.

[29] Witt, Paget, and Matthews 1995, 121.

[30] Lawless and Fox 2010, 126.

[31] Lawless and Fox 2010, 124.

capsulates this view by noting, "People don't like what's going on in Washington. So they don't want somebody who's been there for decades or 20, 25 years, they want somebody who is new."[32] Certainly many of the Tea Party House members elected in the 2010 elections probably owed at least some of their popularity to their status as "Washington outsiders." In an article entitled, "Running as Outsiders, with a Catch: They're In," the *New York Times* reported that the 2012 elections featured many long-time House and Senate incumbents running campaign ads that implied that they are new to politics in an effort to claim outsider status, even as established insiders.[33]

But are women equally positioned to campaign as "outsiders" as men? Celinda Lake maintains that there is a double standard regarding this dynamic, arguing that being a political outsider can be beneficial, but only for male candidates: "Voters are more intrigued by male candidates who are outsiders. . . . They are wary of women who are outsiders."[34] In contrast, others see upsides for women on the outsider front. Susan Carroll, Rutgers professor and senior scholar at the Center for American Women and Politics at Rutgers University, argues that "women are seen as outsiders to the political system. . . . Whenever voters are eager for change, women candidates fare well. . . . If you want a candidate who embodies change, you look for someone who doesn't look like the traditional office holder."[35] In fact, many of the gains experienced by women candidates in 1992, the noted "Year of the Woman," may have been caused by a strong desire for "outsider" candidates at that point in time rather than to a desire for more women in office per se. In this regard, Harriett Woods, president of the National Women's Political Caucus, argued in 1992 that "women are seen as the outsiders—even when they're inside" and went on to predict, probably correctly, that it would help women get elected in 1992.[36]

There may be another factor in play as well. To the extent that subtyping occurs, experienced women politicians may fall into something along the lines of a "longtime woman politician" subtype, and it is plausible that associations with "longtime politician" may largely swamp the associations associated with "woman" within the subtype. After all, as discussed in chapter 2, scholars have found that broad stereotypes are easily

[32] "Frustration with Washington Makes 'Experience' a Liability," *CNN,* January 2008.

[33] Jennifer Steinhauer, "Running as Outsiders, With a Catch: They're In," *New York Times*, September 23, 2012.

[34] "Women Running for Offices Face Many Obstacles," *USA Today*, March 19, 2001.

[35] "From Seneca Falls to . . . Sarah Palin?" *Newsweek*, September 22, 2008, byline: Julia Baird.

[36] Richard L. Berke, "The 1992 Campaign: Women; With Outsiders In, Female Candidates Come Forward," *New York Times*, April 30, 1992.

overridden by other information because broad stereotypes are expected to be relatively inaccurate.[37] "Woman" is one of the broadest possible categories, but "longtime politician" is relatively specific and precise; as such, one might reasonably expect job-related stereotypes to be more dominant within the "longtime woman politician" subtype than traditional gender expectations. As such, experienced women politicians may not pay many costs or reap many benefits associated with their femininity—and they will certainly lose any benefits associated with their "Washington outsiderness." Inexperienced women, however, may very well have their own subtype ("outsider woman candidate"). Stereotypes associated with "candidates" may be broader and more varied than stereotypes associated with longtime politicians—after all, there is a certain commonality among House members or senators and far more variability among candidates who have not yet won office—and thus, gender may play a stronger role within the subtype because "candidate" is relatively less informative about what to expect out of an individual than "longtime politician."

The preceding discussion raises a series of empirical questions: Does having a great deal of political experience or a lack of past political experience affect male and female candidates differently? Are inexperienced women perceived as being more likely than men to be agents of positive change? Are women automatically perceived to be less experienced than men, even when experience itself is not highlighted and the number of years in office has been held constant? And does experience alter distinctions between insiders and outsiders equally for both men and women? All of these questions are evaluated in the analysis below.

The Analysis

Details about the overall design of the study including sampling details, questionnaire structure, n-sizes for each cell, the types of questions that are asked, and so on are available in chapter 3 (with specific question wording available in appendix 2). However, there are a few details that are specific to this subset of the study—the experience experiment—that need to be clarified here.

The text from the treatment newspaper articles is included in appendix 1. Beyond candidate gender, the critical dimension—political experience—is either no time spent in elected office or ten years in elected office.[38] Why such extremes? Obviously, it would be optimal to carefully

---

[37] See, e.g., Irman 2006.

[38] To see the effects of any of the treatments in this study when gender is held constant

stagger political experience to test for a nonlinear relationship between candidate gender and experience on stereotypes. As is invariably the case with experiments, the ideal needed to be scaled back in order to accommodate reality: further dividing the cells to accommodate more types of treatments would have been limiting analytically because it would artificially increase the likelihood of null results. As such, I utilized the extremes.

I also had to select a nonpolitical profession for the candidates. It could not be as simple as not stating a profession: it would be unlikely that a Senate candidate could be competitive without any political experience and without any work experience. Furthermore, letting people make their own assumptions about the work background of the candidate could produce a gender differential in its own right: for example, women could be assumed to have no professional experience or experience in more feminine professions like teaching or nursing, while men might be assumed to be business leaders. A candidate's work background is typically widely available—in fact, it is often a prominent part of an inexperienced campaign's narrative (CEO-turned-politician, doctor-turned-politician, etc.)—so leaving it unstated would allow people to fill in the blanks in a manner that would probably not map onto most elections.[39] In part prompted by Christine Todd Whitman's question highlighted above ("Why is it still true that a male candidate who has never served in public office but may have a business background is considered qualified for public office, yet a woman with the same experience is not?"), I decided to hold the candidate's nonpolitical career constant by stating that he or she had a business career owning and operating a chain of eight dry cleaning stores for the past ten years. This choice is a reasonable one given that Barbara Burrell found that "business owner" is, by far, the most common career path for female nonincumbent general election candidates for the U.S. House.[40]

(more, when half of the responses are based on perceptions of the male candidate and half on perceptions of the female candidate), see Appendix 3 (for the behavior treatments) and Appendix 4 (for the experience treatments). The results are not especially useful for analyses in which there is a significant interaction between candidate gender and candidate behavior or qualifications; in those cases (including experience), one can only meaningfully interpret the separate results for male and female candidates. However, for the many behavior-based experiments in this study in which there are no interactions with candidate gender, the results can give readers a useful sense of the relative consequence of each of those different candidate behaviors on public opinion.

[39] That being said, examining the degree to which people make different assumptions about men and women with no career information provided could potentially be a fruitful area for future research.

[40] Burrell 1996, 67. Her study shows that 21 percent of female candidates in 1992 were business owners and another 8% were "businesswomen." The next closest category is "lawyer," at 11 percent.

A decision had to be made about whether the experienced politician should have a business background as well (thus causing respondents to compare "political" to "business") or whether the experienced politician should also share the same business career (making it possible to have a clean comparison between "experienced politician" versus "new candidate," holding the career constant). I opted for the latter approach, so that the effects of political experience above and beyond business experience would be as clearly identifiable as possible. It is reasonable to wonder how quickly candidates might gain sufficient experience to cause people to evaluate them as "politicians" and not as women or men running for office. Moreover, it is an open question about whether classifying a woman as a businesswoman might interfere with gender stereotypes, along the lines of Irmen's 2006 research that was discussed in a previous chapter. To indirectly address these questions, I can analyze the control group for my main set of experiments (i.e., I can examine the male and female candidate control groups against which the different candidate behavior treatments will be contrasted in later chapters). In the control group for the behavior-based experiments, the candidates are starting their second term in the U.S. House and are announcing an upcoming bid for an open Senate seat. No business background is mentioned for the candidate. Compared to the experience experiments, the set up is slightly different (it is still Kevin and Karen Bailey, and the candidate is still running for Senate, but some other—albeit relatively inconsequential and nongendered—details in the article are different), and I consequently cannot directly compare this control group to the experience conditions. That being said, it is still possible to conclude whether people use gender stereotypes when assessing politicians with some experience and no business background.

Analysis #1: Descriptive Stereotypes for Inexperienced Candidates

Karen Bailey is new to the political scene. She is a successful businesswoman, but she has never held political office before. According to headlines, "Karen Bailey Feels Ready to Be a Senator Despite Lack of Political Experience." In the eyes of analysts discussed in the article, she lacks a background in politics but does have "interesting ideas" and is inclined to find bipartisan solutions to the country's problems. She has started fundraising for an open Senate seat. In other words, she is like countless outsider candidates who are trying to break onto the political scene with their first electoral win.

Does an inexperienced candidate like Karen face harmful stereotypes solely because of her gender? We can assess this by presenting some respondents with the "Karen Bailey" version of a newspaper article and others with the "Kevin Bailey" version (in which gender is the only difference between the articles). The results for the male and female candidate can be compared in the context of a one-way ANOVA in which we are simply comparing the results for Karen to those of Kevin across a range of different measures.

Starting first with the key measures—the outcome measures—allows us to see most directly if politically inexperienced women candidates are likely to be hurt relative to identical male candidates because of gender. The summary of the results shown in table 4.1 indicates that politically inexperienced women are not at a disadvantage relative to their inexperienced male counterparts (see also the first set of columns in appendix 5 for the full results of this analysis). Likely effectiveness in the Senate seems to come close to suggesting that inexperienced women may possibly have a modest advantage over inexperienced men (about .2 of a point on a 7-point scale), but with a p-value at .11 very little can be drawn from that result.

The absence of clear differences on the outcome measures is an important result. Even if gender stereotypes on individual attributes or traits exist, they do not appear to be contributing to an overall disadvantage for inexperienced female candidates. But there is clearly more that can be explored by examining the individual traits and issues about which people might conceivably be forming gendered opinions. And strong differences on those underlying traits and issue competencies could conceivably affect outcomes. At the least, a gender difference on those measures would suggest that a gendered dynamic is at play in campaigns for inexperienced candidates.

On the component measures, the inexperienced female candidate fares very well as compared to her male counterpart. She performs similarly on her ability to handle domestic issues like Social Security and Medicare and on her ability to handle an international crisis. She is not seen as being more competent or more experienced than her male counterpart either. But on nearly every other measure, she outperforms her male counterpart.

Overall, these results are comparable to those found by Kahn in her analysis conducted in the late 1980s: there are positive stereotypes but no negative ones for women candidates. These results paint an optimistic picture for new female candidates in which they are in a position to leverage stereotypes about feminine strengths on honesty, compassion, intelligence, and the like without paying costs associated with negative stereotypes on male traits. In fact, strong leadership has typically been thought of as an agentic trait on which men have a natural advantage, and inexperienced women actually perform higher on that measure. Perhaps leadership is being conceived of in less masculine terms than has been the case in the past.

Significantly, the largest gender difference is on "will improve things in Washington." This lends credibility to the argument made by some that women are "natural outsiders." In an era like today when outsiders are

TABLE 4.1. Summary of the Effects of Candidate Gender for
Inexperienced Candidates

For LOW EXPERIENCE candidates, being a woman...		
has no significant effect	*on*	**favorability**
has no significant effect (p=.11)	*on*	likely **Senate effectiveness**
has no significant effect	*on*	likely **presidential effectiveness**
For LOW EXPERIENCE candidates, being a woman also...		
has no significant effect	*on*	ability to handle **domestic issues**
HELPS modestly	*on*	ability to handle the **economy**
has no significant effect	*on*	ability to handle an **international crisis**
HELPS significantly	*on*	**"honest"**
HELPS significantly	*on*	**"knowledgeable"**
HELPS significantly	*on*	**"intelligent"**
HELPS significantly	*on*	**"strong leader"**
HELPS significantly	*on*	**"gets things done"**
HELPS significantly	*on*	**"cares about people like you"**
HELPS significantly	*on*	**"compassionate"**
HELPS significantly	*on*	**"important person"**
HELPS modestly	*on*	**"would enjoy talking to"**
HELPS significantly	*on*	**"will improve things in Washington"**
has no significant effect	*on*	**"competent"** (vs. "incompetent")
has no significant effect	*on*	**"experienced"** (vs. "inexperienced")

Note: Helps "significantly" = p equal to or <.05; helps "modestly" = p between .06 and .10; for full results, see appendix. The above results are based on a one-way ANOVA model for each individual dependent variable, in which only low-experience candidates are analyzed and differences between male and female candidates are assessed.

often prized, women are in a strong position to use that perception to their advantage. Certainly we have seen hosts of candidates, male and female, try to claim that mantle by emphasizing their lack of political experience. Sarah Palin, perhaps, is the epitome of this approach: a candidate selected, in large part, to balance McCain's Washington insider status with an outsider. While Sarah Palin was not entirely inexperienced (she had held office as governor of Alaska for over a year before she was nominated for the Republican vice presidential slot, and was mayor of tiny Wasilla, Alaska, for several years before that), in the scheme of presidential politics, she was politically inexperienced. The McCain team saw this as an advantage, and may also have had an awareness that her gender would help to magnify her image as an outsider.

While Palin eventually faltered vis-à-vis public opinion (the results I present in chapter 7 on the effects of knowledge gaffes help to explain why; as I show, knowledge gaffes are a significant problem for candidates, male or female), my findings suggest that in a political environment in which being an outsider is an asset, an inexperienced female candidate was probably a better choice than a similarly inexperienced male candidate. While the outcome measures do not suggest a dramatic advantage for inexperienced women in terms of their electoral prospects, they are imbued by voters with a range of positive characteristics from the start that they can potentially use to their advantage throughout a campaign.

Analysis #2: Descriptive Stereotypes of Experienced Politicians

Clearly women are not penalized more for being inexperienced than men—in fact, the relationship appears to work in the opposite direction—but what about experienced women? When Karen Bailey has significant political experience (i.e., she remains successful businesswoman but is now a woman who has been in the U.S. House for six years and a state assembly seat for four years before that), how does she compare to her male counterpart? A candidate like this is likely to be regarded as a "politician" rather than merely a "candidate" in the minds of voters—a distinction that can carry both advantages and disadvantages among the public.

Table 4.2 shows that the trait-based advantages that inexperienced Karen Bailey had over inexperienced Kevin Bailey disappear for experienced candidates (see the second set of columns in appendix 5 for detailed results). This is the case across the entire range of measures studied in this experiment. For better or for worse, male and female politicians with a great deal of experience are evaluated in nongendered terms; people simply do not appear to use gender stereotypes when evaluating them.

It is important to note that this is not merely a case of the respondents knowing more about the experienced candidates; other than information

TABLE 4.2. Summary of the Effects of Candidate Gender for
Experienced Candidates

For HIGH EXPERIENCE politicians, being a woman...		
has no significant effect	*on*	**favorability**
has no significant effect	*on*	likely **Senate effectiveness**
has no significant effect	*on*	likely **presidential effectiveness**
For HIGH EXPERIENCE politicians, being a woman also...		
has no significant effect	*on*	ability to handle **domestic issues**
has no significant effect	*on*	ability to handle the **economy**
has no significant effect	*on*	ability to handle an **international crisis**
has no significant effect	*on*	**"honest"**
has no significant effect	*on*	**"knowledgeable"**
has no significant effect	*on*	**"intelligent"**
has no significant effect	*on*	**"strong leader"**
has no significant effect	*on*	**"gets things done"**
has no significant effect	*on*	**"cares about people like you"**
has no significant effect	*on*	**"compassionate"**
has no significant effect	*on*	**"important person"**
has no significant effect	*on*	**"would enjoy talking to"**
has no significant effect	*on*	**"will improve things in Washington"**
has no significant effect	*on*	**"competent"** (vs. "incompetent")
has no significant effect	*on*	**"experienced"** (vs. "inexperienced")

Note: Helps "significantly" = p equal to or < .05; helps "modestly" = p between .06 and .10; for full results, see appendix. The above results are based on a one-way ANOVA model for each individual dependent variable, in which only high-experience candidates are analyzed and differences between male and female candidates are assessed.

about political experience, this experiment holds the amount of information provided about the candidates constant, so we can specifically isolate the effect of having held office on public attitudes. Of course, it is also true that in a real campaign situation, people will typically have more background information about experienced candidates than inexperienced candidates. Yet, as discussed in chapter 2, more information should generally reduce, rather than increase, the use of stereotypes. Of course, if the candidate information provided by the media is highly gendered, then experienced candidates could still conceivably be affected by gender stereotypes. But the public itself does not appear to be inclined to use gender stereotypes when evaluating politically experienced candidates. They appear to be evaluated more as leaders than as ladies.

Analysis #3: The Mediating Role of Experience

We have established that both inexperienced and experienced female candidates do not suffer from a priori stereotypes that will place them at a disadvantage as they begin their campaigns. In fact, inexperienced female candidates were found to enjoy some advantages relative to their inexperienced male counterparts. But that does not directly address the question of whether political experience has a different effect on men and women. Tables 4.1 and 4.2 provide a general sense of what is likely to be found, but they leave out some of the story. In particular, some differences in either one of the analyses may have been too modest to be picked up as significant; yet when combined into a single analysis, relatively slight movement in two different directions (e.g., inexperienced women are very slightly higher than inexperienced men on one attribute, while experienced men are very slightly higher than experienced women on the same attribute) might result in a significantly different effect of experience for men versus women.

When the data are analyzed this way—that is, in the context of a two-way ANOVA, in which the two factors are candidate gender and candidate experience, and the focus is on the interaction between them—the outcome measures show no significant difference for male and female candidates (see table 4.3 for a summary of the results and see the third set of columns in appendix 5 for detailed results). In other words, experience does not have a significantly different effect on overall views of the male and female candidates.

On the individual traits and issues, men seem to benefit from experience more than women. At first glance, that appears to be an odd finding: women who have been in office for ten years do worse on many measures than women who have never held office before (not on the overall outcome measures; on those, there is simply no difference for experienced vs. inexperienced women). Experience helps male candidates but seems to

TABLE 4.3. Summary of the Effects of Candidate Gender by
Candidate Experience

Does experience affect men and women candidates differently on the overall outcome measures?		
no significant difference	*on*	**favorability**
no significant difference	*on*	likely **Senate effectiveness**
no significant difference	*on*	likely **presidential effectiveness**
Does experience affect men and women candidates differently in other respects?		
no significant difference	*on*	ability to handle **domestic issues**
no significant difference	*on*	ability to handle the **economy**
MEN are **HELPED** significantly **MORE** by experience	*on*	ability to handle an **international crisis**
no significant difference	*on*	**"honest"**
MEN are **HELPED** significantly **MORE** by experience	*on*	**"knowledgeable"**
no significant difference	*on*	**"intelligent"**
WOMEN are **HURT** modestly more by experience	*on*	**"strong leader"**
no significant difference (p =.11)	*on*	**"gets things done"**
no significant difference	*on*	**"cares about people like you"**
no significant difference	*on*	**"compassionate"**
MEN are **HELPED** significantly **MORE** by experience	*on*	**"important person"**
no significant difference	*on*	**"would enjoy talking to"**
MEN are **HELPED** modestly **MORE** by experience	*on*	**"will improve things in Washington"**
no significant difference	*on*	**"competent"** (vs. "incompetent")
no significant difference	*on*	**"experienced"** (vs. "inexperienced")

Note: Helps "significantly" = p equal to or <.05; helps "modestly" = p between .06 and
.10. For full results, see appendix. The above results are based on a two-way ANOVA
model, in which the interaction between candidate gender and experience is assessed.

hurt women in some ways. Yet that interpretation would probably be misleading. Inexperienced women start far higher than inexperienced men on most of the measures, and this is where I would argue that we are seeing the effects of the "outsider bump" that seems to be given only to inexperienced women. That bump goes away as women continue in office, as longtime male and female office holders start to be regarded in the same longtime politician light (e.g., less honest, less caring, more knowledgeable, etc., than outsider women candidates). Inexperienced men never started with that outsider bump, so they only go up in the esteem of the public. Thus, we see male candidates benefiting disproportionately from experience in office, but I would argue that it is because the outsider bump that inexperienced women initially receive is lost over time as they continue on in their political careers, rather than owing to some special kind of distaste for experienced women candidates.[41]

Analysis #4: Descriptive Stereotypes for Newer Incumbents

The analysis above includes candidates for which past business experience has been held constant for all candidates. Additionally, the treatments for experience were held at extremes—no political experience at all versus a great deal of political experience. But what about candidates without business experience who are at more of an in-between stage in their political careers?

Looking at the control group I use in the chapters that follow allows for an analysis of this kind of in-between candidate: someone who has been in politics for a little while (in this case, starting a second term in the House and announcing a bid for an open Senate seat). As noted previously, it would be inappropriate to directly compare these results to those from the previous experience experiments that were just discussed: enough details in the article were changed such that a direct comparison would be problematic (the means should certainly not be compared between the experiments because they are based on different underlying news articles, with different quotes, different candidate backgrounds, etc.). But it is reasonable to analyze whether gender stereotypes are actively applied to moderately experienced candidates. Moreover, it is useful to delineate these results because it establishes the baseline descriptive stereotypes that are in play for the control group prior to introducing different candidate behaviors in future chapters.

In fact, table 4.4 shows that the stereotype profile for the moderately qualified Karen/Kevin Bailey is very similar to that of the experienced

[41] If it were that people did not like experienced women candidates (e.g., because they found powerful women to be unappealing), I would expect to see some kind of negative rating for them relative to either inexperienced women or to experienced men on the outcome measures, perhaps especially on "favorability," but that is not the case.

TABLE 4.4. Summary of the Effects of Candidate Gender for Newer Incumbents (i.e. Control Group Candidates)

Among newer incumbents, being a female (vs. a male) candidate…		
has no significant effect	*on*	**favorability**
has no significant effect	*on*	likely **Senate effectiveness**
has no significant effect	*on*	likely **presidential effectiveness**
Among newer incumbents, being a female (vs. a male) candidate also…		
has no significant effect	*on*	ability to handle **domestic issues**
has no significant effect	*on*	ability to handle the **economy**
has no significant effect	*on*	ability to handle an **international crisis**
has no significant effect	*on*	**"honest"**
has no significant effect	*on*	**"knowledgeable"**
HELPS significantly	*on*	**"intelligent"**
has no significant effect	*on*	**"strong leader"**
has no significant effect	*on*	**"gets things done"**
has no significant effect	*on*	**"cares about people like you"**
has no significant effect	*on*	**"compassionate"**
has no significant effect	*on*	**"important person"**
has no significant effect	*on*	**"would enjoy talking to"**
has no significant effect	*on*	**"Will improve things in Washington"**
has no significant effect	*on*	**"Unemotional"** (vs. "Emotional")
has no significant effect	*on*	**"Calm"** (vs. "Angry")
has no significant effect	*on*	**"Assertive"** (vs. "Unassertive")
has no significant effect	*on*	**"Caring"** (vs. "Uncaring")
has no significant effect	*on*	**"Strong"** (vs. "Weak")
has no significant effect	*on*	**"acts Appropriately"** (vs. "acts Inappropriately")
has no significant effect	*on*	**"competent"** (vs. "incompetent")
has no significant effect	*on*	**"experienced"** (vs. "inexperienced")

Note: The above results are based on one-way ANOVA models, in which the differences between male and female candidates are assessed for each of the individual dependent variables. The control group treatment describes incumbents who have completed one term in the U.S. House and are starting a second term.

candidate: people do not appear to apply gender stereotypes to a moderately experienced candidate (see appendix 6 for the full set of results). There is one area of difference—Karen Bailey is assumed to be significantly more intelligent than Kevin Bailey (a difference of .3)—but other than that, there are simply no statistically or substantively significant gender differences.

Discussion

The bottom line from these experiments is that women candidates do not start out at a disadvantage vis-à-vis men candidates with reference to public perceptions. At least in the current era, the notion that women candidates suffer from harmful descriptive stereotypes is incorrect; in fact, this study finds that to the extent that gender stereotypes do exist, they only benefit female candidates. That being said, female candidates only do better than men on specific individual traits: those areas of assumed superiority do not translate directly to higher candidate affect or assessments of the woman's likely effectiveness in the Senate or the presidency later on in the future. Regardless of experience level, women remain roughly at parity with the male candidate on those critical outcome measures.

Digging beneath the surface, my results suggest that the beneficial stereotypes that do exist for women are confined to brand-new candidates—in other words, women who are political outsiders. Once women became insiders—and my results loosely suggest that could potentially occur after a single term in office—they are judged similarly to men in the same position. Perhaps experienced women officeholders start to be coded by the public as something like "longtime politicians" and are judged accordingly, or perhaps they are subtyped as "longtime women politicians," in a manner consistent with the parallel processing model. Either way, experienced women politicians face stereotypes that are essentially identical to those of longtime male politicians, whereas the same is not true for inexperienced candidates, for whom gender plays a more powerful role. If subtyping is occurring, the subtype for "longtime women politician" leans heavily in the "leader" direction and not in the "lady" direction, with no traditional stereotypes for women applied to women who fall within that subtype.

It may well be that any benefits for female candidates who are new to the political scene receive an "outsider bump" only in eras during which "throw the bums out" is an effective political rallying cry. The time at which this study was conducted—April 2009—would seem to clearly be part of such an era. Republicans had recently been ushered out of the White House largely on the mantel of "change," and the economic crisis continued to unfold. The value of being an "outsider" also appeared to be high in the 2010 and 2012 elections.

Would women new to politics disproportionately benefit at all from their "outsiderness" relative to novice men in an era characterized more by a desire for stability and constancy rather than by a desire for change? That is an open question. In a stability-oriented period—perhaps one in which security concerns are especially prominent, especially if trust in government increases—the value of being an outsider in terms of perceptions of specific competencies might be diminished; if so, the gap between novice politicians and experienced politicians would widen, such that inexperience could be a handicap even for women. While novice women may cease to benefit at all from their inexperience in a stability-oriented era, nothing about the data suggest the gap would be likely to reverse and that novice men would enjoy an advantage relative to notice women in a stability-oriented era (as might have been expected to happen if inexperienced men outperformed inexperienced women on, for example, strength-oriented measures). The fact that experienced candidates may possibly be perceived in more favorable terms than inexperienced candidates in such an era could nevertheless disadvantage women for the simple reason that relatively fewer of them are incumbents and have served in office.

To conclude, the results from this chapter are empowering news for present and future women candidates as well as for those who would like to see more women in office. Many potential women candidates believe that they need better qualifications than men to have a chance at winning a campaign. This study shows that those perceptions are quite clearly wrong. Rather than being hampered by unfavorable descriptive stereotypes as a new legislative candidate, women appear to start out with somewhat of an advantage relative to similarly inexperienced male candidates, at least with reference to perceptions of specific candidate qualities. And once women are in office, they are not assumed to be any less capable or any different overall when compared to their male counterparts. Unlike in previous eras in which even the most seasoned female politicians reported experiencing incidents of gender stereotyping and bias, this appears to be a new and better era, indeed, for female politicians.

CHAPTER 5

Tears and Anger on the Campaign Trail

"Do not cry. No matter what. If you've got to bite your
tongue off or close your eyes so tight that nobody can see
what's in them, do it. Because a man can cry and somehow it
doesn't bother anybody. If a woman cries, it's an immediate,
destructive thing that goes out and that everybody seems to
remember, no matter how bonafide the situation is."

— DIANNE FEINSTEIN[1]

A woman had not mounted a bid for a major party's presidential nomination since Representative Shirley Chisolm ran in 1972, but Representative Patricia Schroeder felt like 1987 might be the right time to try again.[2] To that end, she ran a serious exploratory campaign to consider pursuing the Democratic nomination. In an exhaustive—and exhausting—attempt to assess her chances for the nomination, she visited twenty-nine states during the year. Vowing to run only if she could drum up enough money for a serious bid ("no dough, no go" was her motto), Schroeder ended her campaign in the fall of 1987 when she fell far short of the financial goals she had set.

Despite her failure to launch a winning bid for the nomination, her attempt was viewed as a success in many ways.[3] She ran a serious race, and she earned the respect of many potential voters and political insiders in the process. Many thought that she helped the public to consider the idea of a woman president in a way that allowed later women to more successfully run for higher office. While she fell short of her financial goals, she did raise a great deal of money in the process. Even though she did not formally attempt to win the nomination, her role in the race would have been viewed largely as a success for women in politics, except for one important caveat: she cried.

---

[1] Diane Feinstein as quoted in Carol Pogash, "Mayor Dianne Feinstein's Twelve Rules for Getting Ahead," *Working Woman Magazine*, January 1986.

[2] This chapter draws on Brooks 2011.

[3] Warren Weaver, "Assessing the Lessons of Schroeder's Brief Run," *New York Times*, October 4, 1987.

Schroeder's infamous tears occurred as she was announcing her with-drawal from the primary race. As her crowd of passionate supporters in Denver chanted, "Run, Pat, run," and groaned when she announced that she would not run, Schroeder said, "I learned a lot about America and I learned a lot about Pat Schroeder [this summer]. That's why I will not be a candidate for president. I could not figure out how to run." Tears were flowing at that point, and she wiped her face with a handkerchief. She went on to say, "there must be a way, but I haven't figured it out yet. I could not bear to turn every human contact into a photo opportunity," at which point her husband urged her to take a minute to recompose herself before continuing.[4]

The criticism poured in immediately, both from the media and from the public. The incident was described as a "spectacular flood of tears" by the *London Times*. A *Washington Post* reporter said, "We are not talking misty eyes here. We're talking weeping."[5] Schroeder recounts that, at the time "[people were] saying things like, 'never again can a woman run for president in my lifetime because she shed tears.' You don't see anybody saying never again can a man be governor of New Hampshire because [John] Sununu [Jr.] cried so hard he couldn't even finish his speech when he was saying goodbye. Or never again could a man run for president because I think every single one of them has shed tears in public now."[6] Decades later, Schroeder reports, "I got a devastating e-mail about it [in 2007] from a woman writer just a couple of days ago. I want to say, 'Wait a minute, we are talking 20 years ago.' It's like I ruined their lives, 20 years ago, with three seconds of catching my breath."[7]

For years, Pat Schroeder kept a file of incidents of candidates crying, but she eventually discontinued it because "it has become almost manda-tory for male candidates to cry occasionally, as a way to humanize them-selves. But if a woman cries, it's 'Oh my god, do we really want her finger on the button?'"[8] In a 2008 interview, Schroeder continued to express

[4] John Dillin, "Presidential Race; Schroeder Stays Out for '88," National section, *Chris-tian Science Monitor*, September 29, 1987, 1, See also L. Swayn, "Schroeder Out of 1988 Race," *QNP Telegraph*, September 29, 1987.

[5] Michael Binyon, "Washington View: Soap Opera Image Could Cost Democrats the White House," October 5, 1987; Judy Man, "Tears, Idle Tears," *Washington Post*, October 2, 1987, B3.

[6] Melissa Healy, "Patricia Schroeder: Fighting for 24 Years to Expand Women's Role in Government," *Los Angeles Times*, December 1, 1996.

[7] Nancy Benac, "Shedding Tears on the Campaign Trail," *USA Today*, December 19, 2007.

[8] Libby Copeland "Debating the Tissues: What Makes a Good Cry," *Washington Post*, January 13, 2006, C01, http://www.washingtonpost.com/wp-dyn/content/article/2006/01/12/AR2006011202161_2.html.

frustration with the double standards that she sees on crying: "Dozens of male politicians cry. But when a man cries, he's applauded for having feelings. When a woman cries, she is attacked as being weak."[9]

Congresswoman Schroeder makes a good case that she suffered from a double standard for crying. And there very well may have been one at the time that she cried, held either by the media, the public, or both. Yet, even back then, Edmund Muskie would probably have disagreed with the characterization that male candidates are not hurt by tears. After accusations that he had referred to Canadians with a derogatory term and that his wife had acted in an "unladylike" and "drunken" manner, Muskie had an emotional moment in February 1972 while campaigning in New Hampshire for the Democratic presidential nomination. Characterized as "tears" by many and as "snowflakes on his cheeks" by a few, his emotional display occurred during the course of making a statement to reporters about a recent news story that had contained negative assertions about his wife.[10] The crying incident greatly undermined his candidacy: Muskie later told author Theodore White that the incident "changed people's minds about me, of what kind of guy I was. They were looking for a strong, steady man, and there I was, weak."[11] The term "Muskie Moment" is now regularly applied to harmful tearful displays by both men and women.

Regardless of whether a gendered double standard does in fact exist, many women politicians report that they feel enormous and disproportionate pressure to avoid crying in public, as the quote from Diane Feinstein at the outset of this chapter indicates. While still mayor of San Francisco in 1986, Feinstein followed up her "rule" that women should never ever cry in public by admitting, "very frankly, there are plenty of times that I cry. And what I'll do is I'll go into the shower, I'll turn on the water, and I'll just let it come out. And I'll turn it off the minute I turn off the water. But no one will see me cry."[12] Madeleine Kunin begins her memoir by recounting an admonition she made to herself before her announcement that she would not be seeking a fourth term as Vermont's governor:

> Don't cry, I told myself fiercely, stay in control. . . . Controlled emotion is essential on the political stage, and this is what I strived for. . . . In

---

[9] Katha Pollitt, "Hillary Shows Feeling, Is Slammed," *The Nation*, January 8, 2008.

[10] "Muskie Dies at 81; Served as Senator, Secretary of State," *Los Angeles Times*, March 27, 1996. See, also, David Broder, "The Story That Still Nags at Me—Edward S. Muskie," *Washington Monthly*, February 1987.

[11] "Muskie Dies at 81; Served as Senator, Secretary of State," *Los Angeles Times*, March 27, 1996.

[12] Diane Feinstein as quoted in Carol Pogash, "Mayor Dianne Feinstein's Twelve Rules for Getting Ahead," *Working Woman Magazine*, January 1986.

theory, women and men should be allowed to cry in public but rarely have they been permitted to reveal such human frailty. Strong men, such as Ronald Reagan and George Bush, whose tough credentials are not debated, have more leeway. A tear in the corner of the eye at a poignant moment is a welcome sign of compassion in them, but a woman crying prompts mixed reactions, the depths of which are difficult to comprehend.[13]

When Hillary Clinton was asked during the 2008 New Hampshire primaries about the double standards that a woman running for president faces, she discussed the matter of crying. She noted: "It's that difficult position that a woman candidate is in, because if you get too emotional, that undercuts you. A man can cry. We know that. Lots of our leaders have cried. But, you know, a woman, that's a different kind of dynamic."[14] She made that statement just a day before she had her own emotional moment, and just two days before she pulled off a surprise win in that primary.

The Clinton incident notwithstanding, what is the logic that lies behind the prevalent assumption that female candidates will be penalized more for crying than male candidates? In the eyes of many journalists and pundits, the answer is obvious: crying during campaigns is "especially problematic for women"[15] because "it's different for girls . . . [crying] would show womanly weakness."[16] "Women who aspire to leadership best not admit to 'doing tears' no matter what the circumstances," and "men more than women get away with showing sensitivity."[17] After all, "when a woman cries it reinforces stereotypes and tells us that her toughness was just a front and she has revealed herself to be weak underneath."[18]

---

[13] Kunin 1994, 3–4.

[14] "Women Respond to Hillary's Emotion," *New York Daily News*, January 10, 2008; Fox News Network, January 9, 2008, *Fox Special Report with Brit Hume*. This clip is available at the *Access Hollywood* site at http://watch.accesshollywood.com/video/access-exclusive:-hillary-clinton-talks-life-politics-part-ii-/1309544480001. She makes this specific statement at the 3 minute, 22 second mark; however, the entire interview (including other segments of it posted on the site) is likely to be interesting to readers of this book both as an example of her effort to soften her image at that point in the campaign and because she addresses issues related to gender at various points in it.

[15] Amy Chozick, "Do Tears Signify Political Suicide?" *Wall Street Journal*, January 8, 2008.

[16] Kate Muir, "We Can Do with Less British Stiff Upper Lippiness, but the Currency of Crying Is Being Degraded by Overuse," *Times Magazine* (London), October 27, 2007, 9.

[17] Suzanne Fields, "The Politics of Tears; a Male President Can Cry, but Could Hillary?" *Washington Times*, September 10, 2007.

[18] Journalist Conor Feehan, characterizing the views of professor Tom Lutz, in "Cry Me a River," *The Independent* (Ireland), November 20, 2007.

Despite avid speculation that women politicians are penalized more than their male equivalents for crying, empirical support for this proposition is absent. It is not simply that scholars have not studied this question the right way. No one has studied it at all. The entire intellectual space on this question has been occupied by people who lack methodology beyond anecdotal speculation for analyzing the question.

Crying is not the only area in which a different standard for women is thought to exist, but is rather one part of a larger issue: emotional displays. According to Republican pollster Linda DiVall, "the number one negative for women [candidates] is emotional instability."[19] Besides crying, anger is the other principal emotional behavior that is seen as being particularly troubling for women candidates. As Libby Copeland recounts, "A strong man is admired. A strong woman is—well, with due deference to a line Barbara Bush once used about Ferraro—it 'rhymes with rich.' Female candidates traverse a narrow path, avoiding behaviors that might give rise to stereotypes. Be firm, but not angry. Be compassionate, but not weepy. Too much emotion: dangerous."[20]

Widespread attention was drawn to the issue of anger regarding Hillary Clinton's presidential campaign even before it officially began when Ken Mehlman, the chairman of the Republican National Committee, argued in a 2006 interview that, "I don't think the American people, if you look historically, elect angry candidates . . . Hillary Clinton seems to have a lot of anger."[21] Maureen Dowd argues that the frequent Republican attack against Clinton for being too angry was due to her gender, noting that portraying her "as an Angry Woman, a she-monster . . . handcuffs Hillary: If she doesn't speak out strongly against President Bush, she's timid and girlie. If she does, she's a witch and a shrew. . . . It's the riddle of the Sphinx that has been floating around since the selection of Geraldine Ferraro. Betty Friedan worried then that a woman seen as a threat to men would not get to the White House. But how can a woman who's not a threat to men get there?"[22] Joking about this line of attack from Republicans on Clinton, David Letterman noted: "Did you hear what the Republicans have said about Hillary Clinton? They say she's too angry to be president. Hillary Clinton, Senator Hillary Clinton, too angry to be president. When she heard this, Hillary said, 'Oh yeah? I'll rip your throats out, you bastards.'"

[19] Clift and Brazaitis 2000, 120.

[20] Libby Copeland, "The Rules for Female Candidates," *Washington Post*, November 7, 2007, C01.

[21] Adam Nagourney, "Calling Clinton 'Angry,' G.O.P. Chairman Goes on the Attack," *New York Times*, February 6, 2006.

[22] Maureen Dowd, "Who's Hormonal? Hillary or Dick?" *New York Times*, February 8, 2006.

Of course, many male politicians have also labored under the reputation of being "too angry." For example, even before the infamous "Dean Scream," Howard Dean was frequently criticized for having a pugnacious temperament. And many of John McCain's colleagues in the military and the Senate argued that his frequent angry outbursts made him unfit for the presidency: for example, after watching one infamous committee exchange in which McCain repeatedly called Pete Domenici an "a—hole," one Republican senator who watched the proceedings noted to a reporter, "I didn't want this guy anywhere near a trigger."[23]

Roadmap

At present, we have no scientific basis for evaluating whether displays of emotion are a special danger for women on the campaign trail. Although some scholars have speculated that gendered standards apply to emotionality, the question has not been analyzed empirically.[24]

In this chapter, I analyze how the public responds to displays of crying and anger to understand whether female candidates are, in fact, held to higher standards than male candidates; in the next chapter, I analyze public reactions to toughness (without anger) and lack of empathy. Anger is distinct from toughness (which does not involve the affective state of anger), and it is also distinct from lack of empathy (which represents a lack of emotion, rather than an explosion of it). By centering my analysis in this chapter on crying and anger, I am thus specifically focused on the question of whether candidate gender influences how the public responds to emotional displays. Examining these two behaviors is especially useful not simply because the avoidance of these kinds of emotional displays is so frequently held up as a "rule" that female candidates should follow, but also because these two behaviors are both assumed to be associated with especially strong descriptive stereotypes.

This chapter does not simply investigate empirically how the public responds to these two emotional displays but also helps us to better conceptualize the larger theoretical questions at stake. In this regard, the first part of this chapter delineates a series of hypotheses regarding how displays of crying and anger are likely to influence the evaluation of female and male candidates. In deriving these hypotheses, I focus on the two

[23] Evan Thomas, "Senator Hothead," *Newsweek*, February 21, 2000. See also Mark Benjamin, "It's 3 a.m. Who do you want answering the phone? Not John McCain say some military leaders: 'I think his knee-jerk response factor is a little scary,'" *Salon*, March 6, 2006.

[24] See, e.g., Shields and MacDowell 1987; Glaser and Salovey 1998.

theories in psychology most relevant for understanding this issue: the first focuses on descriptive stereotypes and posits that negative stereotype-consistent behavior will be punished more than stereotype-inconsistent behavior; the second focuses on prescriptive stereotypes (i.e., the "should" and "should nots") and posits that stereotype-inconsistent behavior will be punished more than stereotype-consistent behavior. As I show, when applied to candidates' emotionality and gender, these two theories predict diametrically opposed results that only partially overlap with the double standards theory.

Although the hypotheses that emerge from these psychological theories differ, both posit that female and male candidates will be evaluated in different ways if they display strong emotions. An alternative possibility is that leaders may be relatively immune to the gender stereotypes about emotionality that apply to ordinary people; more precisely, the prediction associated with my leaders-not-ladies theory is that emotional displays by women and by men are not evaluated differently by the public. As I show, studies from the business literature that focus on the significance of status provide a basis for understanding why this is likely to be the case.

The last part of the chapter then evaluates these hypotheses empirically. The main conclusion of this chapter is that male and female candidates are similarly penalized by the public for both anger and tears, an overall finding that supports the leaders-not-ladies theory and runs contrary to the double standards theory.

Hypotheses Regarding Crying

Descriptive gender stereotypes about emotionality, crying, and weakness abound. Lombardo et al. (1983) found that 80 percent of people believe that women cry more frequently than men, and they confirmed this result with 1996 data.[25] For crying, these descriptive stereotypes are rooted, at least for the average man and woman, in some degree of truth.[26] For example, Lombardo et al. (2001) found that 65 percent of men reported that they "almost never cry," whereas 63 percent of female respondents reported that they cry "occasionally" and 18 percent reported that they cry "frequently."

Prentice and Carranza asked undergraduates, "How typical do you think each one of the following characteristics is in adult American males?" for one hundred different traits, and respondents were also asked

[25] Lombardo, Cretser, and Roesch 2001.
[26] See, e.g., Bindra 1972; Lombardo et al. 1983; Lombardo, Cretser, and Roesch 2001.

about the same traits for adult American females.[27] While they did not measure "crying" or "tearfulness" directly (most likely because these are behaviors rather than traits), their data show that women are assumed to be more "emotional" than men: respondents rated women 3.6 points higher on 1–9 scale, where 1 is "very atypical" and "9" is "very typical." Women are also seen as more "melodramatic" (3.4 points higher) and "weak" (1.5 points higher). These are very sizable differences when compared to many other widely held descriptive gender stereotypes (e.g., the typical woman is rated 2.5 points higher than the typical man on "interest in children").

Such ratings are consistent with the descriptive stereotype perspective and, in particular, the work of attribution theorists who argue that stereotypes cause people to attribute particular behaviors to either internal/dispositional factors or to external/situational factors. As discussed in chapter 2, attribution theorists argue that behavior inconsistent with a stereotype will be more likely to be attributed to situational (i.e., temporary) factors, whereas behavior consistent with that stereotype is attributed to the individual's disposition (i.e., permanent traits).[28] Crying by female candidates will be attributed to disposition (e.g., "She has a tendency to get emotional") because it confirms a stereotype, rather than to external factors (e.g., "It must have been a really tough situation"). Because tearful displays are more likely to be attributed to women's disposition, female candidates who cry should be seen as being weaker and more emotional than their male counterparts. And, as stressed previously, if a behavior is attributed to a candidate's personality, it should logically have a stronger effect on evaluations of candidates by the public because it will be seen as more relevant to future governance as compared to behavior that simply arose out of idiosyncratic events.

In psychological research, attributions are generally the dependent variable rather than the overall outcomes that political scientists often focus on. But it seems reasonable to extend the theory from attributions to outcomes: if crying reveals a personality deficit in female candidates (while men are presumed to face a challenging context), women will be penalized more than men on outcome-based measures like favorability because their behavior will be deemed evidence of personal weakness.

Outside of the political realm, studies have shown that women will tend to get punished more for many negative workplace behaviors and

<hr />

[27] Prentice and Carranza 2002. While they only focused on the results for a subset of traits within the published article, the authors very generously shared the full dataset with me for a full analysis of all of the traits they measured.

[28] See, e.g., Barrett and Bliss-Moreau 2009; Jackson, Sullivan, and Hodge 1993; Heilman 1983; Nieva and Gutek 1980.

less rewarded for many positive behaviors than men, largely due to attributions that people make for the behaviors on the basis of gender stereotypes (e.g., "What is skill for the male is luck for the female" is a telling part of the title for one article on the topic).[29] With reference to emotionality in particular, Kelly and Hutson-Corneux (2000) found that women's strong reactions to sadness-inducing scenarios were considered less appropriate than men's analogous strong reactions. If these findings do extend to the political realm, then we would expect to find that women candidates are disproportionately harmed by crying.

This is the same basic thinking that undergirds the double standards theory with respect to crying. From that perspective, female candidates are frequently assumed to be weaker and more emotional than male candidates; therefore, when they cry, the behavior confirms those prior assumptions, and they will be penalized far more than male candidates. However, prior assumptions aside, the double standards theory also holds that female candidates will simply be held to a higher standard of behavior than male candidates. That is, even in the absence of harmful descriptive stereotypes for female candidates, the double standards theory would still predict that female candidates will get penalized more than male candidates for crying. Either way—that is, regardless of whether female candidates are assumed to be weaker and more emotional than male candidates from the start or not—the same hypothesis emerges with respect to crying:

$H1_{crying}$: Crying will damage public opinion about female candidates more than male candidates.

There is, however, a different perspective within psychology that predicts the opposite relationship between gender, crying, and public opinion. As discussed in chapter 2, Prentice and Carranza argue that normative "shoulds" (or "prescriptive stereotypes") and "should nots" are more powerful than "are" and "are not" descriptive stereotypes. In other words, people not only assume that women are more emotional and weaker than men; they also think that men *should not* become emotional or show weakness. According to that approach, violations of strong prescriptions and proscriptions (i.e., the "should nots") will involve substantial social sanctions.

Prentice and Carranza use a measure that asked respondents to indicate "How desirable is it in American society for [a woman, a man] to possess each of the following characteristics?" They find that "weak" is, in fact, the single strongest proscriptive stereotype for men they mea-

---

[29] Deaux and Emswiller 1974; see also Ilgen and Youtz, 1986; Yarkin, Town, and Wallston, 1982.

sured, with a difference of 2.4 points on a 9-point scale as compared to women. It is also far less desirable for men to be "emotional" than women (1.5-point difference) and "melodramatic" (1.4-point difference). The prescriptive stereotype perspective would therefore predict that male candidates will be penalized more for crying than female candidates because men are expected not to cry or be weak. This prediction is represented by:

$H2_{crying}$: Crying will damage public opinion about male candidates more than female candidates.

As delineated in chapter 2, there is another compelling theoretical possibility, however: political leaders may be largely immune to the stereotypes about emotions that apply to ordinary men and women because they are ultimately evaluated by the public far more as leaders or candidates than as "gentlemen" and "ladies."

Studies from the business literature provide a basis for understanding why we would expect to find that emotional displays by male and female political leaders will be evaluated similarly. Averill (1997) and LaFrance and Hecht (1999, 2000) find that high-status individuals are penalized less for expressing their emotional states (anger in these studies) than individuals of ordinary status. With respect to both anger and sadness, Hess, Adams, and Kleck (2005) find that gender differences are mediated by perceived dominance: low-dominance men can show anger but not sadness, whereas low-dominance women can show sadness but not anger; however, the gender differences disappear for men and women described as "dominant and forceful." The prevailing explanation for these differences is that low-status or low-dominance individuals must conform to behavioral prescriptions to curry favor with higher-ups, whereas leaders are subject to different prescriptions (i.e., those for leaders, rather than for men and women per se). Emotionality may be proscribed for leaders in some situations, but this research suggests that gender differences are minimized relative to the proscriptions faced by ordinary people.

To date, all of the studies on this topic are derived from the business sphere; the findings from this realm may not carry over to the political realm. Moreover, some of the findings in this literature are inconsistent; in particular, Lewis 2000 finds that female business leaders are penalized more for both anger and sadness than male business leaders. For that reason, the proposition that leaders face fewer gendered sanctions regarding displays of emotion needs further empirical analysis in general and needs to be tested in the political sphere specifically. Because political candidates are "dominant" relative to the average person, if the overall finding from the business sphere carries over to politics, a double standard will not apply to crying by political candidates. In fact, at the reasonably high-status and socially-distant level of political leadership I examine in my analysis (U.S. congressional races), we would expect this general finding that individuals of high status face fewer gendered sanctions to apply especially strongly to the political realm; the reason why is that the status difference between members of Congress and ordinary people is arguably greater than the status difference between the public and most business leaders.

In combination with the theoretical discussion of the leaders-not-ladies theory in chapter 2, these findings lead to the following prediction:

$H3_{crying}$: Crying will damage public opinion about male and female
    candidates similarly.

In addition to the overall findings from the business literature and the underlying theoretical reasons outlined in chapter 2 in favor of $H3_{crying}$, the hypothesis also seems compelling in light of the findings from chapter 4. While descriptive stereotypes very likely still hold for ordinary women, we saw from the results in table 4.4 in chapter 4 that female candidates are not perceived to be descriptively more emotional than male candidates.[30] This undermines the prevalent idea that female candidates will be disproportionately penalized for crying because it will confirm prior expectations that they are weak or overemotional. At the same time, female candidates might nevertheless still face a different standard for their behavior—after all, women could simply be held to a higher standard, or the act of crying could be so gendered that it could make stereotypes associated with "women" more dominant than stereotypes associated with "leader" when evaluating a woman candidate who has cried. A careful empirical analysis of public responses to crying by female candidates is thus required to properly evaluate the theories under consideration.

Hypotheses Regarding Anger

As with crying, there are some strong theoretical reasons to expect that displays of anger by a politician will have a differential effect on voters if the candidate is a woman. Crying is not the only emotional behavior subject to strong descriptive gender stereotypes: people also think men

[30] Recall that these results showed that the control group (i.e., nonemotional) male and female candidates do not differ substantively or significantly on assumed emotionality (a mean of 3.9 for male candidates and 4.0 for female candidates on "unemotional"). Female candidates are not assumed to be more calm (vs. angry) than male candidates, a priori (a mean of 4.4 for male candidates and 4.4 for female candidates). And female candidates are not assumed to be weaker, a priori, than male candidates (a mean of 4.4 for male candidates and 4.4 for female candidates on "strong" and a mean of 4.4 for male candidates and 4.5 for female candidates on "provides strong leadership").

are more likely to display anger than women (see, e.g., Eagly, Wood, and Diekman 2000; Fabes and Martin 1991; Grossman and Wood 1993; Plant et al. 2000).[31] Prentice and Carranza (2002) did not measure perceptions of anger, but they did measure the related traits of "aggressiveness" (on which men scored 2.7 points higher on a 9-point scale with 9 indicating that the trait is "very typical") and "forcefulness" (2.3 points higher than women).[32] Of the one hundred traits measured by Prentice and Carranza, "aggressiveness" is the trait that has the highest male-female difference on which men score higher than women. "Forceful" is in the next cluster of traits with the second largest gender differences.

Many in the public sphere have posited that aggression is forbidden for female candidates. As Vennochi notes, "Many women have walked in Clinton's shoes, trying to ignore the insults as they strive to strike the acceptable balance between mushiness and aggressiveness. As a presidential candidate, Clinton has to sound strong, not shrill. She has to look in command, not manly. And no matter what she does, there always will be men and women who look at her and see a witch."[33] Some observers link anger and toughness ("Be firm, but not angry. . . . Too much emotion: dangerous"), viewing anger as an emotional version of toughness that is dangerous for female candidates to display.[34] The following hypothesis expresses this general prediction regarding candidate displays of anger:

$H1_{anger}$: Anger will damage public opinion about female candidates more than male candidates.

The preceding prediction is the one that emerges from double standards theory and is identical to the one that the theory makes regarding the effects of crying on female candidates. Yet, whereas the descriptive stereotype perspective predicts the same result as double standards theory for crying, and the prescriptive stereotype perspective predicts the opposite result, the theories switch places with respect to anger. In this case, the prescriptive stereotype perspective aligns with double standards theory. Prentice and Carranza find that people hold strong proscriptions against women being "forceful" (it is 2.2 points less desirable in women

---

[31] For anger, the basis for the common stereotype is also rooted in behavioral differences. A multitude of studies have documented that men are more physically aggressive than women in conflict-oriented situations, especially when the situations are not prosocial in nature (see, e.g., Eagly and Steffen 1986; Knight et al. 2002; Archer 2004). Men also tend to be more verbally aggressive in face-to-face disagreement and argumentation (see, e.g., Archer 2004).

[32] The next most closely related trait—"assertiveness"—also has a substantial gender difference, with men 2.1 points higher on typicality and 2.3 points higher on desirability.

[33] Joan Vennochi, "Trumping the Witch Factor," *Boston Globe*, November 18, 2008.

[34] Libby Copeland, "The Rules for Female Candidates," *Washington Post*, November 7, 2007, C01.

than men) and "aggressive," which of all traits measured shows the largest male-female difference (2.6 points more desirable in men than women). Both traits function as prescriptions (defined as exceeding 5.0 on the 1–9 scale) for "men" and for "people," while falling comfortably within the "proscriptive" (should not) threshold for "women." With such strong proscriptions for women in play, the prescriptive stereotype perspective predicts that displays of anger by women will be seen as less appropriate than such displays by men, and that women accordingly will be penalized for them more than men.

In the only study that focuses at all on gender, emotionality, and political candidates, Hitchon, Chang, and Harris (1997) find that female candidates are penalized more than male candidates for running negative advertisements. The parallel between the tone of television advertisements and the spontaneous emotions I examine is fairly tenuous, but Hitchon, Chang, and Harris try to make the case that negative ad tone is a form of emotionality. Their findings suggest that the double standards theory and prescriptive stereotype perspective may be on target because women candidates are disproportionately punished for engaging in negative emotions through ads. Outside of the political realm, Brescoll and Uhlmann (2008) find that female job candidates who express anger are penalized far more than men across several dimensions, including assumed status, competence, and salary.

In contrast, the descriptive stereotype perspective and the findings of attribution theorists would suggest the opposite outcome: male candidates will be punished more for getting angry. Because anger is consistent with the descriptive stereotype that men get angry, displays of anger will likely be attributed to the personality of male candidates. At the same time, because women are not descriptively stereotyped as being likely to express anger, angry outbursts by female politicians will be more likely to be attributed to the difficulty of the situation. Again, while the attribution literature does not focus on the kinds of dependent variables that are relevant to politics, in the political realm, it is reasonable to expect that it will be more harmful when a candidate's negative behavior is attributed to her personality than when it is attributed to a difficult situation. The following hypothesis expresses this prediction:

$H2_{anger}$: Anger will damage public opinion about male candidates more than female candidates.

Although not focused on political candidates, a prior study that is compatible with this hypothesis is Kelly and Hutson-Corneux (2000); they found that men's strong reactions to anger-inducing scenarios are considered less appropriate, and sanctioned more, than such reactions by women. They also found that women's strong reactions to sadness-inducing scenarios are considered less appropriate than such reactions by men.

As mentioned above, several studies indicate that businesswomen are not held to the same emotional double standards as ordinary women because they are at different status levels.[35] Significantly, most of this research is specifically focused on anger. Again, these studies find that ordinary women are expected to restrain their negative emotions and be prosocial because of their typically lower status in social and work environments; however, once men's and women's roles are elevated and equalized, such as at the level of male and female business leaders, such prescriptions have been found to disappear. As noted above, the general finding of this literature (lack of gendered evaluations for leaders) should be especially likely to apply to political leaders because the difference in status between members of Congress and ordinary people is arguably even larger than the difference between most business leaders and their subordinates. Extended to the political realm, this corresponds to the prediction associated with the leaders-not-ladies theory outlined in chapter 2: political leaders will be largely immune from gender stereotypes and the behavior of female candidates will not be subject to different standards.

H3$_{anger}$: Anger will damage public opinion about male and female candidates similarly.

The Examined Emotional Behaviors

Crying and anger are important behaviors to study not only because they are both behaviors that have been known to be displayed by candidates on the campaign trail but also because they are fascinating mirrors to one another for which descriptive stereotype perspectives and prescriptive stereotype perspectives would predict precisely opposite results. Moreover, these behaviors provide a useful means for evaluating the double standards theory and the leaders-not-ladies theory. Double standards theory would, of course, predict the same relationship in each case: women will be penalized more for both behaviors. In contrast, the leaders-not-ladies theory predicts that female leaders will not be subject to different standards by the public for these behaviors than men are. Let me now briefly describe the key features of the analysis that is used to evaluate these theories.

[35] Averill 1997; LaFrance and Hecht 1999, 2000; Hess, Adams, and Kleck 2005; see Lewis 2000, however, for a gender difference.

Chapter 3 described the overall methodology for the full set of studies; as a result, I concentrate here on the components of my analysis of emotional displays that are unique from those of the other experiments. As with the other experiments, the treatment articles varied from the control group article with the addition of one or two paragraphs that describe two incidents of the behavior in question (crying or anger), a different headline, different subheadline, and a different pull quote (see appendix 1).

There is, of course, no such thing as a "typical" example of anger or crying, and choices thus had to be made on both of those fronts. In the case of crying, a key decision was whether to examine sympathetic crying or nonsympathetic crying. I selected the latter. Examples of sympathetic crying range from tears at a funeral to eyes watering during moving stories told by constituents, especially where illness or deaths are involved. Bill Clinton regularly welled up during funerals, and the Bush brothers are frequent sympathetic criers as well, along with numerous other male candidates.[36] House Speaker John Boehner is a regular sympathetic crier as well; for example, he once choked up while speaking on the House floor about Democrats abandoning U.S. troops in Iraq and is known for crying every year during fundraisers he ran with Ted Kennedy for poor Catholic schools.[37] Because we might expect that sympathy-related tears could potentially have primarily positive effects, it is not as central to the question at the core of this book—that is, whether women candidates face disproportionate perils on the campaign trail due to double standards.

Given my focus on likely penalties for female candidates, it is preferable to examine a kind of crying that could potentially reflect emotional instability or weakness. Perhaps the most famous example along these lines is Edmund Muskie getting teary in 1972 when a news outlet called his wife "emotionally unstable." This is the type of crying episode that is most likely to confirm prior assumptions that a candidate was overly emotional or not strong enough for the tough game of politics. That is, it is the kind of behavior that is likely to play into the weakness-related descriptive stereotypes that many assume female candidates are subject to, and thus is an area in which we would expect to find disproportionate penalties for female candidates if they exist.

In this experiment, the headline of the treatment article reads, "Congresswoman/man Karen/Kevin Bailey Has a Teary Week" with a subheadline of "Cries over Campaign Rigors, Legislative Challenges" and a

[36] Jill Lawrence, "Woman's Plight Pushes Kerry to Tears," *USA Today*, September 4, 2003.

[37] Holly Baily, "John Boehner, Verklempt Speaker-in-Waiting," *Yahoo News: The Upshot*, November 3, 2010; Michael Grunwald and Jay Newton-Small, "Tanned, Tested, Ready: New Speaker John Boehner," *Time*, November 5, 2010.

pull quote that says, "'I really can't talk about this right now,' with tears in her eyes." As with all of the experimental treatments, two different examples of the same basic behavior were provided in order to deepen the treatment. In one incident, the member is described as crying during a speech he or she was giving while discussing the rigors of campaigning in his or her last election. The second incident involves crying while being questioned by reporters who were pressing him or her to comment on the failure of a recent bill that was important to him or her.

The anger scenario was based on a composite of multiple anger incidents in which various politicians have been reported to engage. Among contemporary politicians, John McCain is arguably the one with the most prominent reputation for angry outbursts. During the height of the Keating Five scandal, McCain cursed at and insulted reporters, often hanging up on them.[38] When it seemed that Senator Richard Shelby was going to sink the nomination of John Tower for defense secretary, John McCain screamed at him from a distance of about one inch, a general scenario (McCain yelling at people within inches of their faces, often jabbing a finger at them at the same time) that has been reported by numerous other legislators and congressional aides.[39] McCain also famously yelled at Senator John Cornyn during a bipartisan meeting, shouting, "[Expletive] you! I know more about this than anyone else in the room."[40]

While McCain seems to engage in these kinds of angry outbursts more often than the average legislator, he is of course not the only prominent U.S. politician to show a fiery temper in this way. George Stephanopoulos described Bill Clinton's angry outbursts as "purple rages."[41] Harry Truman was known for angry displays, and he once threatened a reviewer who had criticized the musical abilities of his daughter with physical harm.[42] Lyndon Johnson was known for what James Thurber describes as "calculated displays" of temper.[43] Dwight Eisenhower and Richard Nixon were both known for blowups as well. As one of many more recent examples, in September 2010, a New York Republican gubernatorial candidate Carl Paladino yelled, "I'll take you out, buddy" as part of an angry five-minute exchange with a reporter (the reporter replied, "You'll

---

[38] Larry Margasak, "McCain: I Learned from the Keating Five Case," *USA Today*, March 23, 2008.

[39] Michael Leahy, "McCain: A Question of Temperament," *Washington Post*, April 20, 2008.

[40] Paul Kane, "McCain, Cornyn Engage in Heated Exchange," Capitol Briefing, May 18, 2007.

[41] Michael Leahy, "McCain: A Question of Temperament," *Washington Post*, April 20, 2008.

[42] Michael Leahy, "McCain: A Question of Temperament," *Washington Post*, April 20, 2008.

[43] James Thurber, as quoted by Michael Leahy in "McCain: A Question of Temperament," *Washington Post*, April 20, 2008.

take me out? How are you going to do that?" to which the candidate yelled, "Watch." The reporter shouted, "Are you threatening me?" in response; eventually, aides effectively restrained Paladino and pulled him away from the situation).[44]

The experimental treatment for anger in this situation includes a headline, "Congresswoman (Congressman) Karen (Kevin) Bailey Erupts at Colleague, Reporter," with a subheadline of "Calls Colleague 'Obstinate S.O.B.,'"and a pull quote of "He could have made the same point without pushing me and yelling,' says reporter." The article describes one incident in which the congresswoman or congressman shouts an expletive to a committee chair who was trying to block Bailey's bill from coming to the House floor and a different situation in which reporters cornered the congresswoman or congressman outside of a restaurant to ask for her or his comments on a bill she or he had sponsored. When the reporters persisted in their questioning and followed the member down the street, he or she shoves one of the reporters out of the way and yells, "I said I was through taking questions tonight, and I meant it."

While different permutations of both of these emotional scenarios certainly could be tested, the conventional double standards theory would not expect women candidates to face disproportionate penalties just in response to some kinds of emotional displays. No one has yet hypothesized that only certain kinds of tears or anger are problematic for women. As such, the selected scenarios are sufficient to evaluate the general question of whether female candidates are held to a higher standard than male candidates regarding emotional displays.

Findings

General Response to Emotional Displays

The first question at hand is whether the experiment worked.[45] It did. Respondents generally reacted strongly to both kinds of emotional displays (for full results and all of the associated means for each behavior as compared to the control group, holding candidate gender constant—more precisely, while averaging the responses for male and female candidates—see appendix 3). Overall, angry candidates receive favorability ratings that are significantly lower than candidates in the control group:

---

[44] "Paladino Gets into Angry Argument with NY Reporter," Associated Press. September 29, 2010.

[45] In the experiment, the anger and crying analyses were conducted separately. The crying analysis includes the crying condition plus the control group (i.e., candidates not described as displaying an emotion). The anger analysis includes the anger condition plus the control group.

a difference of 0.8 on a 7-point scale. Angry candidates are deemed more emotional than the control group by 1.2 points, and they are seen also as more angry (versus calm) by 1.8 points. Candidates who display anger are thought to engage in far less appropriate behavior than control group candidates (a difference of 1.6 points).

The results for crying were more subtle on the overall outcome measures, with crying candidates rating just 0.2 points lower on favorability and Senate effectiveness and 0.4 points lower on likely presidential effectiveness than unemotional (i.e., control group) candidates. But there are more sizable differences underneath the surface: for example, candidates who cry are deemed to be less strong ("strong" gets reduced by 0.8 of a point) than the control group and are also deemed to be more emotional (a difference of 1.9). Tearful candidates are viewed as being less able to handle an international crisis (–0.6) than the control group. Furthermore, crying candidates are seen as engaging in less appropriate behavior than the control group candidates (a difference of 0.7). At the same time, candidates who cry are also thought to be significantly *more* "caring" (0.7) and more "honest" (0.3), relationships that presumably help to compensate for the negatives associated with crying.

CANDIDATE GENDER AND CRYING

$H3_{crying}$—the prediction of no difference for male and female candidates generated by the leaders-not-ladies theory—is confirmed by these results (see table 5.1 for the summary results; see also appendix 7 for the ANOVA results and associated group means). The interaction between gender and crying is not significant—or close to significant—for any of the three overall outcome measures (favorability, likely Senate effectiveness, likely presidential effectiveness). There are no gender differences in situational versus dispositional attributions. Perceived appropriateness of crying also did not vary by gender. Furthermore, there are no gender differences on perceptions of strength versus weakness, providing strong leadership, or emotionality in interaction with tearfulness. In short, these findings show that there is no double standard for men and women when they cry.

"Unemotional" is significant at $p = .07$, although the difference is fairly modest substantively. This finding is generally consistent with previous research, which finds that ordinary women who emote (anger, fear, sadness, or disgust) are perceived to be more emotional than ordinary men who display those emotions.[46] However, further analysis suggests that in the political context, increased emotionality may well be a net positive for candidates rather than a net negative: "unemotional" is nega-

[46] Barrett and Bliss-Moreau 2009.

TABLE 5.1. Summary of Crying Results

Do displays of TEARS affect perceptions of male and female candidates differently on the overall outcome measures?		
no significant difference	*on*	**favorability**
no significant difference	*on*	likely **Senate effectiveness**
no significant difference	*on*	likely **presidential effectiveness**

Do displays of TEARS affect perceptions of male and female candidates differently on other measures?		
no significant difference	*on*	ability to handle **domestic issues**
no significant difference	*on*	ability to handle the **economy**
no significant difference	*on*	ability to handle an **international crisis**
no significant difference	*on*	**"honest"**
no significant difference	*on*	**"knowledgeable"**
no significant difference	*on*	**"intelligent"**
no significant difference	*on*	**"strong leader"**
no significant difference	*on*	**"gets things done"**
no significant difference	*on*	**"cares about people like you"**
no significant difference	*on*	**"compassionate"**
no significant difference	*on*	**"important person"**
no significant difference	*on*	**"would enjoy talking to"**
WOMEN who cry **DECREASE** disproportionately	*on*	**"unemotional"** (vs. "emotional")
no significant difference	*on*	**"calm"** (vs. "angry")
no significant difference	*on*	**"assertive"** (vs. "unassertive")
no significant difference	*on*	**"caring"** (vs. "uncaring")
no significant difference	*on*	**"strong"** (vs. "weak")
no significant difference	*on*	**"acts appropriately"** (vs. "Acts Inappropriately")
no significant difference	*on*	**situational attribution** (vs. behavioral)

Note: Summary results are based on two-way ANOVA models in which the significance of the interaction (candidate gender * behavior) is assessed for each of the individual dependent variables (note that the last measure is based on one-way ANOVA; see the appendix for details). The significance of the associated F-test and the means for each experimental cell can be found in the appendix. Differences with a p-value of .10 or better are noted.

tively correlated with perceptions of likely effectiveness in the U.S. Senate (–0.4) for the control group.[47] Thus, being perceived as more emotional is not necessarily a problem for candidates; if anything, it may have some benefits.

The most important conclusion from this analysis is that there is no evidence that female candidates are penalized for crying more than men. Most candidates would be wise not to cry because they will suffer a slight drop in favorability for doing so, with moderate penalties for likely effectiveness in the Senate and likely presidential effectiveness, but women do not seem to be affected any more or less by it than men. I would also go so far as to argue that this particular pattern of results suggests that some candidates—male or female—might potentially find that they improve their relationship with the public after a crying episode, specifically candidates who already have a lock on strength-related attributes but who are having a hard time connecting with the public at a more human, authentic level. I will return to that idea in the conclusion of this chapter, with a discussion of Hillary Clinton's emotional incident.

CANDIDATE GENDER, RESPONDENT GENDER, AND CRYING

If we look beneath the surface, it appears that people penalize candidates of their own gender more for crying.[48] For example, on favorability, women penalize female candidates by about .5 of a point while they do not penalize male candidates at all; conversely, men penalize male candidates for crying by about .3 of a point, while they do not penalize female candidates at all. This dynamic of penalizing the candidate of one's own gender while not penalizing (or penalizing less) the candidate of the other gender is seen across all three outcome measures. Distancing theory may help to explain this dynamic: scholars posit that "collective threat" reactions can be induced when members of a stereotyped group observe ingroup members engaging in negative behaviors.[49] Former Vermont governor Madeline Kunin informally articulates this view when she hypothesizes that "women often cringe with embarrassment at the sight of other wom-

---

[47] Note, too, that the correlation between "unemotional" and the outcome measures is roughly similar for male and female candidates, so it is not simply that it is positive for men and negative for women.

[48] See Brooks 2011 for the detailed results and further discussion of this issue.

[49] Cohen and Garcia 2005. "Distancing" is a common reaction to collective threat; that is, group members—especially members of groups that commonly face negative stereotypes—will disassociate themselves from a group member who displays negative behavior that conforms to a stereotype; this is often termed the "black sheep" effect (see, e.g., Cohen and Garcia 2005; Marques and Paez 1994; and Steele and Aronson 1995).

en's tears, fearing that they—that all women—will be held responsible for such behavior. Seeking an idol, a woman whose life is under control, they may have little tolerance for disappointment."[50] Given the heavy proscriptions that exist against crying for men, a similar dynamic may be at work for them as well: a male leader crying serves as some kind of embarrassment to them.

That being said, this dynamic—the idea of women penalizing women candidates and men penalizing men candidates—does not appear to carry over to any of the other behaviors in this entire study: it appears to be reserved to crying, exclusively, and therefore will not be discussed elsewhere in the book. To the extent that distancing is in play, it may be that both men and women feel that their own gendered identities are threatened by leaders' crying more than for other behaviors because crying is arguably an especially gendered act.

In any case, those effects for male and female respondents on crying ultimately cancel each other out, and so those dynamics do not produce a net bias that favors male (or female) candidates when they tear up. The bottom line is that this study shows that any such effects do not produce a harmful effect for women in the public overall, which is what ultimately matters for the electoral prospects of women.

Anger

This anaylsis clearly shows that all candidates would be wise to avoid angry outbursts. Scores dropped substantially on all of the outcome measures (–8 on favorability, –.6 on Senate effectiveness, –.8 on likely presidential effectiveness) for anger displays relative to the control group, as well as on all of the component trait measures except for "strong" and "assertive." Anger is particularly devastating to perceptions of compassion: scores are 1.2 lower among angry candidates than control group candidates.

Most of the results are neutral with respect to candidate gender. The results show that there is not a double standard on the outcome measures, with no significant interactive effect of a candidate's gender and angry behavior on favorability, likely Senate effectiveness, or likely presidential effectiveness. Thus, these results are consistent with $H3_{anger}$, the prediction derived from the leaders-not-ladies theory that male and female candidates will not be held to different standards by the public (see table 5.2 for the summary results; see also appendix 8 for the full set of ANOVA results and associate group means).

There is also no gender interaction for the measure of "angry" (vs. "calm"): female candidates who act in an angry manner are not signifi-

[50] Kunin 1994, 4–5.

TABLE 5.2. Summary of Anger Results

Do displays of ANGER affect perceptions of male and female candidates differently on the overall outcome measures?		
no significant difference	on	**favorability**
no significant difference	on	likely **Senate effectiveness**
no significant difference	on	likely **presidential effectiveness**

Do displays of ANGER affect perceptions of male and female candidates differently on other measures?		
no significant difference	on	ability to handle **domestic issues**
no significant difference	on	ability to handle the **economy**
no significant difference	on	ability to handle an **international crisis**
no significant difference	on	**"honest"**
no significant difference	on	**"knowledgeable"**
no significant difference	on	**"intelligent"**
no significant difference	on	**"strong leader"**
no significant difference	on	**"gets things done"**
no significant difference	on	**"cares about people like you"**
no significant difference	on	**"compassionate"**
no significant difference	on	**"important person"**
no significant difference	on	**"would enjoy talking to"**
WOMEN who get angry **DECREASE** disproportionately	on	**"Unemotional"** (vs. "Emotional")
no significant difference	on	**"Calm"** (vs. "Angry")
WOMEN who get angry **INCREASE** disproportionately	on	**"Assertive"** (vs. "Unassertive")
no significant difference	on	**"Caring"** (vs. "Uncaring")
no significant difference	on	**"Strong"** (vs. "Weak")
WOMEN who get angry **DECREASE** disproportionately	on	**"Acts Appropriately"** (vs. "Acts Inappropriately")
no significant difference	on	**situational attribution** (vs. behavioral)

Note: Summary results are based on two-way ANOVA models in which the significance of the interaction (candidate gender * behavior) is assessed for each of the individual dependent variables (note that the last measure is based on one-way ANOVA; see the appendix for details). The significance of the associated F-test and the means for each experimental cell can be found in the appendix. Differences with a p-value of .10 or better are noted.

cantly more likely than male candidates who act in an angry manner to be seen as being angry or less calm. Attribution for the behavior to personality(i.e., dispositional) factors rather than to situational factors is also not significantly different for female and male candidates.

A gender difference that does emerge is that female candidates who get angry are seen as being disproportionately more emotional (i.e., less unemotional) than male candidates who get angry; yet, as with crying, perceptions of greater emotionality will not necessarily hurt a candidate. In that regard, the results show that female candidates who act in an angry manner are also seen as being disproportionately more assertive than their male counterparts; assertiveness, in turn, is positively correlated with the outcome measures in the control group for both male and female candidates. In short, if you are assumed to be more assertive, you are assumed to be a better politician. As such, the fact that perceptions of assertiveness rise relatively higher for angry female candidates than angry male candidates may actually serve to help rather than hurt women at some level.

Regarding the anger results, the main area of potential concern for female candidates is the effect of anger on perceptions that the candidate is acting appropriately. Female candidates who get angry are seen as behaving less appropriately than male candidates who do so. Although that should potentially sound a note of caution for female candidates, the fact that it does not result in a penalty on the outcome measures indicates that its substantive consequences are modest, at most.

Reconsidering Hillary Clinton's Emotional Moment in New Hampshire

At first glance, the results regarding crying might appear at odds with Hillary Clinton's emotional moment during the New Hampshire presidential primary.[51] While I do not find a gender interaction in my study, I do find that candidates overall are hurt by crying, especially on assessments of likely effectiveness as president. And yet many have posited that Clinton was actually helped in the New Hampshire primary by her emotional display, perhaps more so because she is a woman; some even speculated that she won because of her tears.[52] It is impossible to prove or

[51] It should be noted that it is a stretch to describe Clinton's behavior as "crying": it is most accurately described as a "voice breaking" moment, rather than as a "tearful" moment. Overall, it was a very restrained display of emotion, despite numerous headlines about her crying to the contrary.

[52] See, e.g., Katz, Celeste, and Bishop, "Survey Tracks Clinton's Tears, Too," *New York*

disprove that assertion on the basis of available polling data; however, we can look at my results to see if we can discern any basis for how Clinton might have been helped rather than hurt by her emotional display.

The scene of the incident was a New Hampshire coffee shop, the day before the New Hampshire primary. In her book, *Big Girls Don't Cry: The Election That Changed Everything for American Women,* Rebecca Traister paints a thorough picture of the incident.[53]

> During a question-and-answer session with undecided voters in Portsmouth on the day before the New Hampshire primary, sixty-four-year-old Marianne Pernold Young asked Clinton, "As a woman, I know it's hard to get out of the house and get ready. My question is very personal. How do you do it? How do you keep upbeat and so wonderful? And who does your hair?"
>
> Clinton paused before replying, acknowledging the final query by noting, "Luckily on special days I do have help. . . . If you look on some of the websites and listen to some of the commentators they always find me on the day that I didn't have help." Then she paused again, returning to the more serious question. "It's not easy," she said. "And I couldn't do it if I just didn't passionately believe it was the right thing to do." She hesitated again, stammered briefly, and said in a voice that sounded unusually reflective, "You know, I have so many opportunities from this country." Then came the sound of her voice breaking. "I just don't want to see us fall backwards. You know, this is very personal for me. It's not just political. It's not just public. I see what's happening, and we have to reverse it. And some people think elections are a game. They think it's like 'who's up,' or 'who's down.' It's about our country, it's about our kids' futures, it's really about all of us together." . . . The spell broke, and Clinton returned to politicking as usual, noting that some of us (she) were ready to lead and others (Obama) weren't.

According to Karen Breslau, a journalist from *Newsweek,* "the 16 undecided voters—14 of them women—nodded sympathetically, some with their own eyes watering," as Clinton spoke.[54]

Daily News, January 13, 2008, 5; Frank Newport, "Post N.H.—Explaining the Unexpected," *Gallup Poll Online,* January 8, 2008, http://www.gallup.com/poll/103663/PostNH -Explaining-Unexpected.aspx.

[53] Traister 2010, 93.

[54] Karen Breslau, "Hillary Tears Up: A Muskie Moment, or a Helpful Glimpse of 'the Real Hillary'?" *Newsweek,* January 7, 2008.

When reporters asked Pernold about her reaction to Clinton's answer to her question, she reported that only one thing ran through her mind while Clinton was speaking: "I thought 'holy s—. She's showing she's a human being."[55] Interestingly, it was not enough to win Pernold's own vote; she later reported that she voted for Barack Obama in the primary, noting "I was moved by her response to me. We saw 10 seconds of Hillary, the caring woman. But then when she turned away from me, I noticed that she stiffened up and took on that political posture again. And the woman that I noticed for 10 seconds was gone."[56] But the incident may have worked differently with many other New Hampshire voters who did not as directly and personally interact with Clinton as Pernold did that day.

Many different factors can potentially explain why Clinton's emotional moment could produce positive reactions among some voters. Drawing specifically on my empirical results, we can identify one dynamic that was likely important in this instance: the centrality of "strength" to her bid for office. My results show that crying hurts candidates especially on strength-related traits—traits that Clinton had already locked up long before the primaries even started and constituted a guiding theme on which she campaigned during the race (see the next chapter for more on that dynamic). Because a core strength of Clinton was, in fact, her strength, she was in a position to act this way without being concerned that she would ever be viewed as not strong enough by voters. Remember also that my results indicate that crying—even the primarily nonsympathetic kind of crying that I measured—helps a great deal on the very attributes that appeared to be the biggest weaknesses for Clinton, especially compassion, honesty, and "emotional."

Unlike many other journalists who took days to move from believing that Clinton's tears would signal the end of her primary run to believing that it would help her win over voters, Karen Breslau of *Newsweek* predicted on the day that the incident occurred that it would only serve to help Clinton because it would soften an overly hard image:

> Photographers argue to this day whether the moisture on Ed Muskie's cheek during a passionate interview on the eve of the 1972 Democratic primary came from tears or snowflakes. But whichever it was, the moment sealed his fate as a man too emotional to be president.

[55] Tim Harper, "Hillary Clinton Allows Raw Emotion to Show," *Thestar.com*, January 8, 2008.

[56] Kate Snow and Jennifer Parker, "Woman Who Made Clinton Cry Voted for Obama," *ABC News*, January 9, 2008, http://abcnews.go.com/Politics/Vote2008/story?id=4109322 &page=1.

Hillary's teary moment may very well work in the opposite direction: helping a candidate who is seen as aloof and too tightly scripted appear more vulnerable, more human and more appealing. And those qualities could be big assets as the campaign careens out of New Hampshire, especially as a contrast to the angry scenes of Clinton rebutting Obama and John Edwards in Saturday night's debate. Hours before New Hampshire voters go to the polls, Clinton has finally showed "the real Hillary," the one advisers always insisted was there, the one the campaign tried to sell in a clunky road show in Iowa, where longtime friends were rolled out to tell endearing stories.[57]

In short, it may be that because of Clinton's prior reputation for strength that she could only benefit from crying (at least in moderation), while a candidate, like Muskie, who was thought to be somewhat suspect on strength, would be hurt by similar behavior.[58] My study suggests that candidate gender does not affect those priors; after all, I do not find that people assume that female candidates are weaker or more emotional than their otherwise-comparable male counterparts. But to the extent that a candidate's persona is very familiar to the public, reactions to candidate emotionality (or any behavior) might conceivably be affected by priors about that candidate in a nongendered way. That being said, most candidates will obviously not be nearly as well-known as Hillary Clinton.

Discussion

The analysis in this chapter shows that, all else being equal, candidates—whether they are male or female—should do their best not to display anger or to cry. Anger drives down the overall outcome measures and component attributes across the board. Crying, in contrast, drives up perceptions of empathy and honesty measures while modestly reducing scores on other attributes, which nets out to a disadvantage—albeit a relatively modest one—on the overall outcome measures. But there is simply no evidence that female candidates will face disproportionate penalties on Election Day if they cry or get angry. There is thus no empirical support for the double standards theory: while gender stereotypes about

[57] Karen Breslau, "Hillary Tears Up: A Muskie Moment, or a Helpful Glimpse of 'the Real Hillary'?" *Newsweek*, January 7, 2008.

[58] For an fascinating account of the kinds of concerns that many journalists had about the emotional instability of Muskie and how the crying incident tapped into those concerns, see David Broder, "The Story That Still Nags at Me—Edward S. Muskie," *Washington Monthly*, February 1987.

emotionality do exist for ordinary men and women, political leaders seem relatively immune to them.

The lack of applicability of double standards theory to emotional behaviors is further explained by the fact that there is no evidence that female candidates are at a disadvantage a priori relative to male candidates on the relevant measures of strength, strong leadership, emotionality, or anger. In other words, crying does not reinforce a prior descriptive stereotype that female candidates are weak or especially emotional, and anger does not reinforce a prior stereotype that male candidates are more likely to get angry. While such descriptive gender stereotypes about candidates may very well have existed in previous eras (and there is, unfortunately, no way to travel back in history to collect fully comparable data), this study indicates that they are not present for otherwise comparable candidates now. Even if those kinds of gendered descriptive stereotypes do not exist, it is still theoretically possible that emotional behaviors could activate otherwise-latent gender stereotypes for candidates. More specifically, crying could conceivably make stereotypes associated with "woman" more dominant than "leader" when people subtype female politicians; however, I see no indication of that type of dynamic.[59]

There was a notable gender difference in play for emotionality: female respondents penalized female candidates more for crying than male candidates, and male respondents penalized male candidates for crying more than female candidates, but the net effect was a neutral one for tearful male and female candidates with respect to the public overall. Interestingly, those are the only such differences across all behaviors in this entire study on the outcome measures; crying appears to be unique in that respect.

Additionally, there were a few other isolated differences that emerged depending on candidate gender. Angry behavior by female candidates is perceived to be disproportionately less "appropriate" than angry behavior by male candidates; female candidates who get angry are more likely to be seen as "assertive" than their male counterparts; and female candidates who get angry or cry are more likely to be considered "emotional" than their male counterparts. Although these differences are interesting, the key underlying point is that they do not produce disproportionate overall penalties for female candidates on the kinds of outcome measures that are ultimately most pivotal to a candidate's electoral success. The more specific results reported here help to explain why this is the case.

[59] Because men and women respondents view crying male and female candidates differently, it cannot be ruled out entirely that latent stereotype activation could be playing a role; that being said, the mechanism by which a crying women would generate a different type of subtype and associated stereotyping for male versus female respondents is not clear. Distancing more clearly predicts that type of difference.

Crying increases perceptions that a candidate is caring and honest—traits that are helpful to the electoral prospects of candidates. Assertiveness is not necessarily a negative either: higher assertiveness is also positively correlated with the outcome measures. Finally, emotionality is also positively associated with the outcome measures. The only potential result of concern for female candidates is the disproportionate "appropriate behavior" penalty that is accorded to them for acting in an angry manner. However, the higher scores that angry women candidates receive on the positive traits of emotionality and assertiveness may potentially work to cancel out the negative effects of being perceived to be engaging in slightly less appropriate behavior.

My overall finding that anger and crying produce no difference in the critical outcome measures for male and female candidates raises a question: how could so many analysts be wrong about the consequences of emotional displays for female candidates? It is certainly possible that the conventional wisdom has always has been incorrect and that women have never been more heavily penalized for emotional displays. If recent election cycles have proved anything, it is that the conventional wisdom about campaigns and elections on a range of topics is often faulty. An alternative possibility—one that I explore in the concluding chapter of the book—is that it may have been true at one time, but not anymore.

CHAPTER 6

Unbinding the Double Bind

"There's always a tension in bringing people together to find common ground and standing your ground. I've tried to do both. When I have stood my ground I have engendered opposition. In part because I'm a woman doing it."

—HILLARY CLINTON, JANUARY 2007[1]

"Half the time when she [Hillary Clinton] shows how tough she is, people say she's too tough. . . . [She has to deal with the] psychological double-bind women sometimes get caught in."

—BILL CLINTON, JANUARY 23, 2008[2]

There has long been a common perception that women face a double bind in politics: they must prove that they are strong enough to lead (because people will assume that will not be the case without evidence to that effect), but they will be viewed as unfeminine when they demonstrate strength and will therefore be disliked. To succeed on one front is necessarily to fail on the other; as such, women politicians face an extremely difficult task in winning over voters. Yet, of course, we know that many women do manage to win over the public, and there are many examples where female politicians have been unabashedly tough and have seemingly paid few penalties for that "unfeminine" approach. From Bella Abzug to Golda Meir to Margaret Thatcher to Diane Feinstein to Nancy Pelosi, tough women have been running and winning in politics for a very long time. So how are we to reconcile the widespread belief in the conventional wisdom on this point with the fact that many women have managed to successfully navigate these supposedly unnavigable contradictions?

To this end, I start by describing the nature of the conventional wisdom on this topic; along the way, I pay special attention to the common perception that Hillary Clinton's presidential bid might have been derailed by these dynamics. I then address the existing research about politi-

---

[1] Ben Smith, "Clinton Balances Femininity, Toughness," *Politico*, January 29, 2007.
[2] Choire Sicha, "Bill Addresses Hillary's 'Double-Bind,'" *New York Observer*, January 23, 2008.

cians that is most relevant to the question at hand. From a theoretical and analytical standpoint, I first address the issue of toughness. After I establish that women candidates do not face a double bind on that front, I then describe the relationship between toughness and empathy (or lack thereof). I then empirically examine how lack of empathy might, and does, affect public views; again, I do not find that women candidates face special challenges on that front.

The bottom line from my analysis is that I do not find any evidence that women face a gendered double bind. In fact, to the extent that any of the results are related to candidate gender, it is that women *benefit* from toughness more than their male counterparts on a couple of key measures. I conclude the chapter with a discussion of why we should not be surprised by the disparity between these findings and those in the business and organization literatures.

The Nature of the Conventional Wisdom
Regarding the Double Bind

According to Mandy Greenwald, a Democratic consultant, "[Madeline] Albright is one of the few top female politicians who has succeeded in projecting 'an image of strength without being called a bitch.' Think about other prominent female politicians, women like Dianne Feinstein, Christie Whitman, Geraldine Ferraro. Sooner or later that word tends to follow them around."[3] Marie Wilson, former president of the White House Project, wonders "How do women actually convey toughness? How do they convey they will be a strong leader? And how do they do it in a way without losing their femininity? We expect women to display their masculine side all the time and their feminine side at the same time. It's a tough balancing act. Very few women can do it."[4] Some argue that this is an ancient phenomenon: "A woman who displays toughness and ambition often sacrifices being liked. This is not a new discovery. It goes back 3,000 years to the first female pharaoh, Hatshepsut. Women in business, academia, science—you name it—are caught in a double bind. If they are not tough enough, they are not up to the job. . . . If a woman is too tough, she does not fit our stereotype of female behavior. . . . A frequent response to a strong woman leader in any sphere is, 'I just don't like her.'"[5]

[3] Mandy Greenwald as quote by Michael Dobbs in "Albright Reshapes Role of Nation's Top Diplomat," *Washington Post*, 15 June 1997, A01.

[4] Rob Christensen, "Woman's Place: On the Ballot," *News and Observer* (Raleigh, NC), April 15, 2007.

[5] Madeleine Kunin, "Clinton an Ideal nominee for Difficult Times," *Times Argus*, February 17, 2008.

Kathleen Hall Jamieson, a political communications scholar, stresses, "It's gender bias, plain and simple. They [female candidates] are supposed to be warm and accessible, because that's what's perceived to be gender-appropriate. But they also need to be tough and competent. The minute they appear that way, their warmth and accessibility are called into question."[6] In this view, female candidates face an impossible decision; according to journalist George Rede: "A woman has to choose between running as the candidate with the proper competence—and thus, being manly—or as the candidate who is properly feminine—and thus, being unqualified."[7] According to linguistics professor Deborah Tannen, this dynamic is caused by gendered prescriptions: "Our image of a politician, a leader, a manager, anyone in authority, is still at odds with our expectations of a woman. To the extent that a woman is feminine, she's seen as weak. To the extent that she puts it aside and is forceful, aggressive and decisive, she's not seen as a good woman."[8]

Indeed, some argue that the double bind is not simply an obstacle for female candidates, but that it is the single *greatest* obstacle for female candidates. Pollster Celinda Lake claims that the greatest challenge for women candidates is demonstrating toughness in a way that does not alienate voters.[9] To emphasize that point, Lake quotes a woman candidate whom she had interviewed as saying, "If you're too strong, you're labeled a bad word. If you're not strong enough, you get run over."[10]

Many tie the existence of the double bind specifically to national security, an area that may be particularly relevant in the post-9/11 era.[11] For example, Dee Dee Meyers, former press secretary for President Bill Clinton, notes that "when women in positions of authority conform to traditional stereotypes, they are perceived as 'too soft' to be effective (especially on issues of national security). And when they defy those norms, they are considered 'too tough,' too masculine, downright bitchy."[12] Others argue that the double bind is especially difficult for women to manage as presidential candidates: "Female candidates for all elective offices face the conundrum of having to appear strong and confident without looking

[6] Jamieson, as quoted in Jocelyn Noveck, "Clinton's Task: Being Likable AND Tough," *USA Today*, January 10, 2008.

[7] George Rede and Melody Rose, "Women's 'Double Bind': Competence, Femininity Collide in Candidates' Paths," *The Oregonian*, 6 September 2008.

[8] Tannen as quoted in Ellen Goodman, "Rules of the Game Stacked against Women Candidates," *Daily Herald*, December 11, 2007.

[9] "Women Running for Offices Face Many Obstacles," *USA Today*, March 19, 2001.

[10] "Women Running for Offices Face Many Obstacles," *USA Today*, March 19, 2001.

[11] See, e.g., Lawless 2004 for her own work on the matter, and for a review of other research on the topic.

[12] Myers 2008.

unfeminine, according to specialists on women and politics. But the dilemma is more pronounced at the presidential election level, they say, because voters are more likely to be guided by their gut reactions to candidates rather than comparisons of the contenders' records."[13]

Many believe that Hillary Clinton's 2008 presidential primary bid was derailed by these supposed contradictions. Her primary adviser, political consultant Mark Penn, did not seem to believe that the double bind would be a problem for Clinton; he stressed that to win the race, she needed to focus primarily on locking up her credentials on toughness and power. Specifically, he believed that many Democrats had been derailed by appearing to be weak; to win the presidency, Clinton needed to project a Margaret Thatcher–like toughness, even if it was to the exclusion of warmth. He characterized his firm beliefs on this point in a 2006 memo to Clinton by noting, "A word about being human. Bill Gates once asked me 'could you make me more human?' I said 'being human is overrated.' Now don't get me wrong, connecting with people and understanding their problems with passion is a critical part of leadership. But the idea that if only you were warmer and nicer so many more people would like you and you would be in the White House is wrong. True, more people would like you. Fewer would vote for you."[14]

Early in her campaign, Clinton followed Penn's advice and worked hard to consolidate and promote an image of toughness and power, via tough statements of her own[15] and those made by her proxies.[16] The strategy worked in terms of establishing that she was the toughest candidate in the Democratic primary field: in a fall 2007 Pew survey, 67 per-

[13] Susan Milligan, "Clinton's Struggle Vexes Feminists: To Some, Her Skills Losing Out to Style," *Boston Globe*, February 19, 2008, A1.

[14] Mark Penn's "Launch Strategy Thoughts" memo from December 21, 2006, http://www.theatlantic.com/politics/archive/2008/11/penns-launch-strategy-ideas-december-21-2006/37953.

[15] At an Ohio campaign event, for example, Clinton told her supporters, "I'm here today because I want to let you know, I'm a fighter, a doer and a champion, and I will fight for you" (Carroll and Dittmar 2010, 59). In another prominent example, Clinton stressed that "we need a president who can take whatever comes your way" and simultaneously attacked Barack Obama for whining (Julie Boseman and Jeff Zeleny, "Clinton Impugns Obama's Toughness," *New York Times*, April 19, 2008).

[16] In his official endorsement of Hillary Clinton, Governor Mike Easley of North Carolina described Clinton as someone "who makes Rocky Balboa look like a pansy." A day later, an Indiana union leader introduced Clinton to a crowd of supporters by describing her as someone who has "testicular fortitude" ("Gov. Easley Makes It Official," *National Journal Hotline*, April 29, 2008). Clinton responded by saying "[that comment] means a lot to me. I do think I have fortitude. Women can have it as well as men" ("Union Leader: Endorsed HRC, Said Nation Needs a Pres with 'Testicular Fortitude,'"*National Journal Hotline*, April 30, 2008.

cent of Democrats said that Hillary Clinton was the candidate they thought of when they heard the word "tough."[17] Chris Matthews likened her to Luca Brasi (the toughest, most feared enforcer from the Godfather movies).[18] However, various polls showed that Clinton was weak on caring and compassion measures—for example, one Pew poll showed that she was regarded as the "least friendly" of the major Democratic candidates.[19]

Many journalists concluded that Clinton was running up against the double bind. According to a *USA Today* journalist, "Poised to become our first female nominee for president, Clinton has spent most of the campaign trying to dispel the idea that she's *too* feminine—too gentle, too thoughtful, too caring—to lead the nation. But when she adopts a tough persona, especially on foreign policy and defense issues, some voters complain that she's behaving like a man."[20] Similarly, a journalist in the *Washington Post* observed: "Clinton's strength is also a source of uneasiness. Throughout her career, she has stirred an irrational hatred that is not primarily of her own making. To much of the public, when she is tough, she seems unwomanly and therefore inhuman; when she is soft, she seems unfit to be commander in chief. It's the old double bind that women have always faced in acquiring power, but wishing it weren't so won't make the dilemma vanish."[21]

To redress this perceived problem and to try to save her increasingly troubled campaign, Clinton initiated a drive in late December 2007 "to warm up an image some voters perceive as cold" through an online and in-person campaign to "showcase her personal side with testimonials from friends, associates and constituents she has helped."[22] Yet, when Clinton tried to simultaneously display both toughness and empathy, she was then criticized for inconsistency in her message. Was she the tough candidate or the feminine candidate? "Whatever the outcome, history will have to take note of many miscues in Clinton's campaign. Her demeanor has changed as often as her clothing style and is certainly con-

---

[17] Kornblut 2009, 27.

[18] "More Violent Imagery from Chris Matthews," *Media Matters*, January 5, 2008, http://mediamatters.org/research/200801050005.

[19] Jill Lawrence, "Strong Organization Characterizes Clinton," *USA Today*, January 1, 2008.

[20] Jonathan Zimmerman, "Why Gender Still Matters in American Politics," *USA Today*, November 14, 2007, 11A.

[21] Paul Starr, "Watch It, Democrats. You Could Still Slip Up," Outlook section, *Washington Post*, January 20, 2008, B01.

[22] Jill Lawrence, "New Clinton Campaign Out to Show Her Likeability," *USA Today*, December 16, 2007, 4A.

tributing to public disillusionment with her. It's easy to think that's true when she goes from acting like a nails-tough achiever to, well, a girl."[23]

Many weighed in to defend Clinton's situation as being caused less by strategic miscalculations and more by the impossible conundrum presented by the double bind. One journalist used a type of analogy that is very common regarding the discussion of female candidates—a "tightrope" analogy—to describe the challenges faced by Clinton on the toughness front: "The fact is that Hillary has had to walk a tightrope between masculinity and femininity, toughness and sensitivity."[24] In an article entitled "Clinton's Task: Being Likable AND Tough," Mary Trigg of the Institute of Women's Leadership at Rutgers University noted: "Research demonstrates that there's a very narrow bandwidth of acceptable behavior for women in positions of power, because they have to be feminine, but also exhibit the kind of attributes we look for in a leader. . . . A female leader can't be too assertive and strident, because you get into the 'B' word. It's a hard and lonely trail to walk."[25] Similarly, Deborah Tannen made the following argument about Clinton in 2007: "We're a very macho culture, and I think every woman in public office has to find her path to negotiate that. To the extent she's a woman and has to prove she's tough, standing her ground is the best thing to do. And to the extent she's a woman and people don't tolerate toughness in women, she's going to be faulted for that."[26]

Was Hillary Clinton derailed by the double bind? Or was she instead undermined because she followed mistaken guidance from Mark Penn that the public does not care about the human side of presidential candidates? Perhaps that fact that Clinton seemed inauthentic, overly managed, or too malleable to many voters rested at the root of her problem with the public, as much or more than the actual strategy she pursued. Unfortunately, we cannot disentangle all of the numerous different influences on public opinion to answer these questions with any level of confidence for a particular campaign. But it is clear that many believe that women candidates, including Hillary Clinton, have been greatly hampered by impossible expectations that they demonstrate strength without being strong.

[23] Karen Burshtein, "Dressed to Imprez," Weekend Post, *National Post* (Canada), March 1, 2008, WP5.

[24] Lisa Stevens, "Hillary-Baiting Shows Extra Barriers Ambitious Women Face," *Western Mail*, June 6, 2008, 23.

[25] Mary Trigg as quoted by Jocelyn Noveck in "Clinton's Task: Being Likable AND Tough," *USA Today*, January 10, 2008.

[26] Patrick Healy. "Politics Means Sometimes Having to Say You're Sorry," *New York Times*, March 4, 2007.

Related Empirical Research about Politicians

We currently lack an empirical basis for determining whether female candidates actually do face a toughness double bind. However, that is *not* to say that political scientists have failed to explore issues related to candidate gender and toughness. In particular, many scholars have studied whether the public holds descriptive stereotypes that female leaders are less tough or less capable of handling "tough issues" like crime or the military. As discussed at many points already in this book, most studies have found that people are more likely to project "feminine" traits (e.g., compassion, caring, honesty) onto female candidates and that people are more likely to project "masculine" traits (e.g., strength, resolve, toughness) onto male candidates. These trait stereotypes have been linked in some studies to perceived issue competencies; in this perspective, men tend to be perceived to be superior on foreign policy and defense issues and women tend to be perceived as being better on domestic issues. At the same time, other studies have failed to find that male candidates or politicians benefit from strength-related or other stereotypes. In particular, Kahn finds that fictional male and female candidates were not perceived to be significantly different on traits like the ability to handle leadership or military issues.[27] Fridkin and Kenney (2009) confirm that same general pattern in their analysis of senators running for office in 2006: no beneficial stereotypes for male candidates on any attributes, including leadership-related traits. In short, there is evidence—albeit quite dated evidence in many of those cases, sometimes using methodology that is not quite up to this particular task—that people may have some stereotypes about male and female politicians, but the evidence is more mixed for agentic traits.

There has been no attempt to date to quantify whether acting tough can change any of these priors and differentially affect preference for candidates. Thus, although an understanding of baseline stereotypes about candidates is relevant as a starting point, it does not directly address whether the double bind exists because it cannot tell us if women are disproportionately penalized for acting tough if they choose to do so.

A few studies have come closer to the question at hand by examining public perceptions of tough female versus tough male politicians, but none of those studies discusses the double bind and none of the study designs fully permits an assessment of it. In the early 1980s, Virginia Sapiro and Mark Stephen Leeper analyzed how people react to tough male and female candidates, but their studies both lacked a control group for candidates who were not tough; as a result, they cannot determine

---

[27] Kahn 1992, 506; 1994, 183; 1996.

whether their results reflect the effects of reactions to tough candidate behavior or simply the effects of standard descriptive gender stereotypes that may be applied to candidates.[28] Leonie Huddy and Nayda Terkildsen examined how people react to male and female candidates who are described in masculine versus feminine terms and found that the trait descriptions largely overrode the effects of gender stereotypes.[29] However, they focused only on changing perceptions of a particular trait or issue competencies rather than on the kinds of overall candidate assessments that would allow us to determine whether tough female candidates are likely to face disproportionate penalties on Election Day.

In her book, *Beyond the Double Bind: Women and Leadership*, Kathleen Hall Jamieson uses case studies to claim that women have traditionally faced a double bind between femininity and competence. She also suggests that some women leaders were starting to overcome that bind by 1995, when the book was written. Her book does not analyze public opinion on the matter, however.

In the end, it remains unclear whether female candidates face a double bind for acting tough that may harm their electoral prospects. It is a remarkable lacuna in our field, especially given the intensity of public attention focused on the issue.

Hypotheses Regarding a Double Bind for Toughness

In the case of toughness, double standards theory predicts that female candidates will face a double bind. Yet, as with the other behaviors, there are also good reasons to believe that female candidates will not face a double bind for toughness. The basis for these competing hypotheses is established below.

With reference to toughness-related attributes, people hold strong descriptive stereotypes about men and women. Examining both descriptive and prescriptive stereotypes for ordinary men and women across one hundred widely ranging traits, Prentice and Carranza find that, as compared to women, men are assumed to be far more aggressive, more force-

---

[28] Sapiro 1981–82 and Leeper 1991.

[29] Huddy and Terkildsen 1993a, 1993b. The "typically feminine" trait treatment described the candidate as "intelligent, compassionate, trustworthy and family-oriented opponent with proven leadership skills and strong people skills," whereas the "typically masculine" trait treatment described the candidate as "intelligent, tough, articulate and ambitious and as having strong leadership and administrative skills" (1993b, 127). They find that "it was relatively easy to reverse trait stereotypes of both male and female candidates by describing them in counterstereotypic terms. For most respondents, information about the candidate's traits—not gender—shaped inferences about their gender-linked personality traits" (1993b, 128).

ful, less yielding, more assertive, more competitive, and more decisive (out of the one hundred measured traits, those six characteristics were all in the top fifteen largest gender differences).[30] Men are also thought to have more business sense, be less weak, be less naïve, more controlling, more ambitious, and have more leadership ability than women.

With reference to prescriptions about toughness-related behaviors, the gender differences are even more notable than the descriptive stereotypes. In terms of the ranking of the magnitude of gender differences on the desirability of each trait for men and women, all twelve of the toughness-related traits rank within the top sixteen out of one hundred; moreover, "aggressive," "weak," and "assertive," capture the first, second, and third spots, respectively. In other words, there tend to be much stronger gender prescriptions for toughness-related traits than for other kinds of traits.

Thus, at least for ordinary men and women, the psychology literature shows that fairly strong descriptive stereotypes are in place for many toughness-related traits and extremely strong gendered prescriptions exist for toughness-related behavior. But is the same true for leaders? As compared to female leaders, ordinary women would not necessarily be expected to face a double bind because they may not need to demonstrate toughness in order to be seen as good people. To the extent that toughness by women is penalized, it is likely that ordinary women will simply try to avoid that behavior. But for female leaders, such conformance to expectations may not be possible, because toughness may be required for success in leadership roles.

While political scientists have not empirically examined the double bind regarding political leaders, business scholars have addressed the question by examining how people react to the tough behavior of male and female business leaders. The business scholarship focuses on "agentic" traits by leaders, such as ambition, self-reliance, competition, aggression, force, and decisiveness. As mentioned in chapter 3, research has shown that idealized leadership is generally conceptualized in agentic "Think Leader, Think Male" terms, while female business leaders are assumed to be more "communal."[31]

Drawing upon role congruity theory, Eagly and Karau (2002) argue that male business leaders are in a favorable position because male stereotypes overlap with the prescriptions of good leadership: they act in an agentic manner, and they get rewarded for it. In contrast, the difficulty faced by female business leaders is that negative consequences known as "backlash effects" can result from women's attempts to counter gender stereotypes in the workplace by acting in an agentic manner. The litera-

---

[30] Prentice and Carranza 2002. Thanks are due to Prentice and Carranza for generously sharing their data with me.
[31] Catalyst Report 2007.

ture shows that women in the business realm who establish themselves as agentic tend to face sanctions in terms of favorability or likeability.[32] This can have tangible consequences for agentic women, such as a lower likelihood of getting hired, promoted, fairly compensated, or favorably evaluated on the job.[33] Women who act in an agentic manner while also displaying communal characteristics like warmth and niceness can minimize backlash.[34] However, Rudman and Glick argue that those findings apply only to competence-related agentic behavior, while backlash from dominance-related agentic behavior may be impossible for women to avoid because dominance by women inherently lowers perceptions that they are nice.[35] In their review of the literature to date on the topic, Rudman and Phelan ultimately conclude that "ambitious women may have to choose between being liked but not respected (by displaying communal qualities) or being respected but not liked (by displaying agentic qualities), a dilemma not faced by men."[36]

There are indications that these dynamics exist within higher education as well. Using both evaluations of actual professors and an experimental design involving actors acting as instructors in a management course, Sinclair and Kunda found that undergraduates who received negative feedback from instructors derogate the competence of a female instructor but not a male instructor.[37] In turn, the final evaluation scores of female instructors were found to be far more dependent upon the amount of positive feedback they gave to students than was the case for male instructors. But, interestingly, when respondents merely observed a third person receiving praise or criticism, the effects of instructor gender disappeared.

Thus, on the basis of both ample anecdotal evidence about women in politics and the compelling body of research demonstrating that women face a double bind when working within nonpolitical professions, we might expect that female candidates will be penalized more than male candidates for acting tough. Specifically, the double standards theory would predict:

H1$_{tough}$: Acting in a tough manner will disproportionately hurt the female candidate.

[32] See, e.g., Rudman and Glick 2001.

[33] See, e.g., Rudman 1998 on hiring; Babcock and Laschever 2003 on salary negotiations; Heilman et al. 2004 on promotion; Eagly et al. 1992 and Eagly, Karau, and Makhijani 1995 on leadership evaluations.

[34] See, e.g., Carli, 2001; Johnson et al. 2008.

[35] Rudman and Glick 2001, 758.

[36] Rudman and Phelan 2008, 65.

[37] Sinclair and Kunda 2000.

I have discussed a fair amount of evidence that demonstrates that women face a double bind in the business world: women have to prove that they are tough enough to lead a business but then are disproportionately penalized when they do so. However, while the world of politics has some similarities to the business sphere—leading groups, a premium placed on agentic traits, and so on—there are also many important differences between leadership in the political and nonpolitical professional spheres. Chapter 2 discusses several reasons why we might generally expect such differences.

Moreover, chapter 4 showed no descriptive stereotypes about female candidates and strength-related measures. All indications from my study are that women politicians are on equal footing with male politicians (or even better footing, in the case of low-experience female candidates) in strength-related domains from the start with the public overall. This does not eliminate the possibility that women candidates will be subject to prescriptive stereotypes about feminine behavior—it is at least conceivable that tough behavior could activate some latent gendered expectations—but it does make it less likely, given that female candidates do not start out at a disadvantage on the relevant measures.

Finally, for all of the reasons described in chapter 2, the leaders-not-ladies theory makes the case that women candidates, at least in the current era, will be judged by the public according to the same standards and prescription they apply to male candidates. Ultimately, the leaders-not-ladies theory would predict:

$H2_{tough}$: Female candidates who act in a tough manner will not be disproportionately penalized by the public.

STUDY DESIGN FOR TOUGHNESS EXPERIMENT

The overall experimental design I employ was described in chapter 3. As such, I address here only the issues that are specific to the toughness experiment. As with the crying and anger experiments, the treatment articles varied from the control group article with the addition of two paragraphs that described two incidents of tough behavior, a different headline, different subheadline, and a different pull quote (the full text of each of the newspaper treatments is included in appendix 1 and the n-sizes for each cell are listed in table 3.2 in chapter 3).

A choice existed as to what kind of tough behavior to use for the treatment. In their studies of perceptions of male and female business leaders, Rudman and Glick (2001) specifically identified dominance—not competence—as being the agentic trait that puts businesswomen in the double bind (because dominance inherently lowers perceptions of niceness for women). As such, behaviors related to dominance were selected. The headline for the toughness treatment was "Congresswoman Karen Bailey Threatens to Hold up Bills: 'I Will Be Heard,' Bailey Says," while the pull quote was "I won't let anyone stand in my way." The treatment situations involved refusing to yield the floor and continuing to give a speech when leaders asked the politician to stop. Bailey's response to the situation was "I don't take 'no' for an answer, and I won't let anyone stand in my way. I will be heard." The article also reports that an email was anonymously leaked in which Bailey threatened to "hold up the House leaders' favored bills in committee unless they agreed to hold hearings to consider the provisions [he or she] was demanding."

The hypotheses derived from the theories are generalizable and thus should apply to a wide variety of toughness-related scenarios, including the one I selected. This scenario also is a fair representation of the kinds of rough-and-tumble legislative situations that policy makers may often have to navigate. It is behavior that is neither entirely admirable nor entirely appalling, which is a realistic representation of the kind of toughness often displayed in politics. In short, this scenario is useful for evaluating whether the double bind exists.

Beyond the standard outcome measures that are of key interest for this topic, there are a few traits and issues that are especially interesting for the study of this topic (see appendix 2 for exact question wording). I included several complementary measures of strength in the survey. One is the standard "provides strong leadership" measure that is included in many surveys of candidate traits, including the National Election Studies, and has been found to correlate highly with outcome measures. Because "provides strong leadership" is as much a measure of good leadership as it is of "strength" per se, I also measured "strong" (vs. "weak") as a separate measure. Additionally, because strength-related traits are likely to have issue-based implications, I included a measure of "ability to handle an international crisis."

In order to test whether toughness takes a disproportionate toll on communal measures for women, it is the caring and compassion measures that are particularly relevant. First, I included a measure for "really cares about people like you," which captures a combination of empathy and personal identification with the candidate commonly utilized by the National Election Studies. I also included "compassionate" and "caring" (vs. "uncaring") as measures because they remove the personal identification element to focus more precisely on perceived warmth and empathy-related communal values.

Additionally, I used two measures to capture assessments of the appropriateness of the behavior and attributions for that behavior. I asked about whether the candidate's behavior was "appropriate" or "inappropriate." For the treatment group only, I also asked whether the candidate's behavior could best be explained by "the nature of the situation" ("7") or with "the personal characteristics of the candidate" ("1"), because behavior that it associated with the personal characteristics of the candidate is likely to have a larger effect on overall candidate assessments. Finally, I measured the degree to which candidates were thought to be "assertive" (vs. "unassertive") as a manipulation check for the toughness treatment but also as a check to see if tough women are perceived to be more assertive than tough men.

Analysis of Toughness Results

The first question is whether the experimental design worked—that is, did respondents react to the toughness treatment? The answer is yes (for full results and all of the associated means for each behavior as compared to the control group, holding candidate gender constant—more precisely, while averaging the responses for male and female candidates—see appendix 3). Setting candidate gender aside (i.e., assessing the overall means on the basis of half of respondents randomly viewing a male candidate and half viewing a female candidate), acting tough significantly increased the degree to which a candidate is viewed as being assertive (a 1-point difference on a 7-point scale). Tough-acting candidates were also viewed as being "stronger" (.5 difference) as compared to the control group.

Overall, tough behavior is seen as being significantly less "appropriate" than the ordinary behavior of the control group candidates (a difference of .3). There was a significant difference between the control group candidates and the treatment candidates for "compassionate" (the measure that most directly taps into the feminine trait of empathy): tough behavior takes a significant toll on perceptions of candidate compassion, with a .3 difference between the tough and control group candidates. Given the push-pull effects operating under the surface (with toughness increasing perceptions of candidate strength but decreasing perceptions of compassion), it is perhaps not surprising that there is no overall effect of tough behavior on the three outcome measures (favorability, likely effectiveness in the Senate, or likely presidential effectiveness ten years in the future).

Although these results are interesting, the critical question at stake is whether there is an interaction between the "tough" condition and candidate gender. I find no interactions between candidate gender and toughness that indicate damage to female candidates (relative to male candidates) for acting in a tough manner, which is consistent with the expectations of the leaders-not-ladies theory (see table 6.1 for a summary of the results, and see appendix 9 for the ANOVA results and associated means). Indeed, whereas the double standards theory predicts that women would be penalized more than men for toughness, on several measures the opposite is actually the case. Although there is no interaction between candidate gender and toughness regarding likely effectiveness in the Senate, on likely presidential effectiveness—an especially key measure because of the assumed linkage between perceived strength and executive leadership—women who acted in a tough manner were actually viewed as having more potential for the presidency than women who did not act in a tough manner, whereas the opposite was true for men. In short, women improved their prospects of being viewed favorably for the presidency by acting tough, while men hurt their prospects with the same behavior. On favorability itself—a key measure, given that violations of prescriptions have so often been thought to result in being "disliked"— there is a suggestive effect ($p = .08$) that men, but not women, are viewed less favorably if they act tough (women remain unchanged on favorability regardless of their behavior).

Strength appears to be responsible for some of these differences in the outcome measures. "Strong" (vs. "weak") was the only individual trait to approach significance for the gender interaction ($p = .07$). Male candidates increase on perceived strength when they act tough (+.3), but female candidates increase to an even greater degree (+.7).[38] There is not a significant interaction effect for ability to handle an international crisis.

The conventional wisdom regarding the double bind was predicated, in part, on the idea that toughness would specifically cause scores for feminine traits such as compassion to fall and that they would fall farther for women. This was also the dynamic predicted and found by Rudman and Glick with reference to business leaders.[39] However, in my analysis of political candidates, I find no evidence of a backlash effect occurring at all. Perceptions of compassion are compromised somewhat by toughness for all candidates but not disproportionately more for women. And women were obviously not penalized more than men on the overall outcome measures either, which helps to rule out the alternative possibility

[38] There is not a significant gender interaction for leadership strength, although the means are directionally consistent with those of the "strong" versus "weak" measures.

[39] Rudman and Glick 2001, 753.

TABLE 6.1. Summary of Toughness Results

Do displays of **TOUGHNESS** affect perceptions of male and female candidates differently on the overall outcome measures?		
Tough **MEN** are disproportionately **LOWER**	*on*	**favorability**
no significant difference	*on*	likely **Senate effectiveness**
Tough **WOMEN** are disproportionately **HIGHER**	*on*	likely **presidential effectiveness**

Do displays of **TOUGHNESS** affect perceptions of male and female candidates differently on other measures?		
no significant difference	*on*	ability to handle **domestic issues**
no significant difference	*on*	ability to handle the **economy**
no significant difference	*on*	ability to handle an **international crisis**
no significant difference	*on*	**"honest"**
no significant difference	*on*	**"knowledgeable"**
no significant difference	*on*	**"intelligent"**
no significant difference	*on*	**"strong leader"**
no significant difference	*on*	**"gets things done"**
no significant difference	*on*	**"cares about people like you"**
no significant difference	*on*	**"compassionate"**
no significant difference	*on*	**"important person"**
no significant difference	*on*	**"would enjoy talking to"**
no significant difference	*on*	**"unemotional"** (vs. "emotional")
no significant difference	*on*	**"calm"** (vs. "angry")
no significant difference	*on*	**"assertive"** (vs. "unassertive")
no significant difference	*on*	**"caring"** (vs. "uncaring")
Tough **WOMEN** are disproportionately **HIGHER**	*on*	**"strong"** (vs. "weak")
no significant difference	*on*	**"acts appropriately"** (vs. "Acts Inappropriately")
Tough **WOMEN** are disproportionately **HIGHER**	*on*	**situational attribution** (vs. behavioral)

Note: Summary results are based on two-way ANOVA models in which the significance of the interaction (candidate gender * behavior) is assessed for each of the individual dependent variables (note that the last measure is based on one-way ANOVA; see the appendix for details). The significance of the associated F-test and the means for each experimental cell can be found in the appendix. Differences with a p-value of .10 or better are noted.

that compassion (as a key measure of empathy) is simply more important for female candidates than for male candidates.

A final interesting result concerns the attributions that people make for the causes of tough behavior. People are more likely to attribute the behavior to situational factors for women and dispositional factors for men (a difference of .4). In other words, when men act tough, it is assumed to be due to their personal characteristics, whereas when women act tough, it is assumed to be in response to a difficult situation. While the implications of situational attributions for wholly negative behaviors are fairly clear—a candidate should be better off if a negative behavior is attributed to the situation rather than to his or her personality—the implications for a trait that is neither wholly positive nor wholly negative are less clear. It may be that being tough mainly when a situation demands it is beneficial for a candidate—and that women benefit from the assumption that they were being tough in response to a difficult situation; this could potentially help to partially explain the positive results for women on the favorability and likely presidential effectiveness measures.

The Relationship between Toughness and Empathy

Toughness is generally assumed to negatively affect the perceptions of women either directly or indirectly through empathy-related measures like caring and compassion. However, the double bind could potentially operate in a couple of different ways. It might be that a tough female candidate will be perceived to be less empathetic than a similarly tough male candidate—in other words, toughness may take a disproportionate toll on favorability for female candidates at least partly by making them seem more uncaring than comparably tough male candidates. Conversely, it may be that a tough man and a tough woman will be perceived to be similarly uncaring; however, empathy may simply be more important to assessments of favorability for women candidates than men candidates.

In addition to examining how the public reacts to tough candidates, an examination of how the public reacts to uncaring candidates can thus help us to further evaluate whether the double bind exists. After all, if people are penalizing women for either seeming less caring or not being as caring as women are expected to be when they act tough, we should see similar dynamics when women candidates simply act in an uncaring manner. And even if we do not see a similar relationship for nonempathetic behavior as we see for tough behavior, this will still help us to identify the mechanisms through which toughness might actually affect female candidates.

HYPOTHESES REGARDING LACK OF EMPATHY

As stressed previously, the conventional wisdom is that toughness negatively affects the perceptions of female candidates either directly or indirectly through empathy-related measures. In this view, an underlying trade-off exists between agentic and communal traits: to signal toughness is to deemphasize empathy-related traits. This could potentially be harmful to female candidates in one of two ways: toughness could lower perceptions of empathy more for women than men, or, alternatively, it could lower perceptions of empathy similarly for women and men in an environment in which empathetic traits are more critical to overall evaluations of women. The previous analysis demonstrated that neither was accurate.

However, it may be that the kind of agentic, legislatively oriented toughness that was measured was not the kind of behavior that leads some female candidates to be seen as an "ice queen," or the equivalent. Maybe people expect candidates—male and female—to be legislatively tough, but when candidates seem interpersonally cold, then that produces gender differences in terms of how people evaluate candidates. Toughness might be fine for politicians, but coldness may produce the kind of assessments that could put female candidates at a disadvantage as compared to their male counterparts.

In sum, it is useful to evaluate the two general theories under consideration specifically with respect to empathy. As applied to empathy, the prediction from double standards theory is that female candidates will be penalized disproportionately for displaying a lack of empathy. In this view, women are expected to be especially caring and empathetic, so if they fail to display those traits, they will be disproportionately penalized for it:

$H1_{empathy}$: Acting in a nonempathetic manner will disproportionately hurt the female candidate.

It should be noted that that $H1_{empathy}$ could be validated in two different ways. As with toughness, it is possible that we could find that empathy-related scores will be lower for nonempathetic female candidates than nonempathetic male candidates; such differences should, in turn, produce disproportionately lower scores on the outcome measures for female candidates who act in a nonempathetic manner. That pattern of results would suggest that a lack of empathy disproportionately affects female candidates by making them seem less caring and compassionate than identical male candidates. Alternatively, the outcome measures could be lower for nonempathetic female candidates than nonempathetic male candidates without differential scores on empathy-related items. That pattern of results would suggest that empathy is simply more important for female candidates than for male candidates.

As with other behaviors, the leaders-not-ladies theory would expect that female candidates will not face disproportionate penalties for acting in a nonempathetic manner. Candidates are likely to face major penalties for acting in a nonempathetic manner, but to the extent that female candidates are regarded as leaders and not as women, they are likely to be held to the same standards as male candidates:

$H2_{empathy}$: Female candidates who act in a nonempathetic manner will not be disproportionately punished by the public.

Study Design for Lack of Empathy Experiment

The underlying design for this experiment is identical to the toughness study and the other experiments in the rest of this book (see table 3.1 in chapter 3, for n-sizes). For the treatment groups, the news article for the lack of empathy treatment has a headline reading, "Congresswoman(man) Karen(Kevin) Bailey Is Curt with Constituents in Recent Encounters," a subheadline, "Cuts Off Parent of a Disabled Child: Is There a Question Here?" and a pull quote, " 'I just wanted to know that she cared,' says disappointed elderly man." The first incident described in the article involves Bailey's response to a constituent who recounted the challenges facing parents of developmentally disabled children. Bailey is described as checking his or her watch during the constituent's story and interrupting to say, "I'm sorry to cut you off—and I don't doubt the extent of your hardships—but is there a question here?" and then moving onto the next question. The other situation described in the news article involves moving quickly through the hallways of a nursing home and brushing past an elderly man who was trying to show her a family photo.

As with all of the experiments, different examples of lack of empathy could have been provided to respondents. Yet, as with the other experiments, the hypotheses under consideration are generalizable, and the treatment would be expected to tap into gendered prescriptions regarding empathy if people do, in fact, apply them to their candidate evaluations. In this case, these are examples of interpersonal coldness that should translate to expectations that people might have about the empathy of female candidates.

The key dependent variables of interest—the overall outcome measures, agentic measures (e.g., strength, ability to handle an international crisis) and communal measures (e.g., cares about people like me, compassionate, caring vs. uncaring)—are the same as for the toughness experiment.

Results for Lack of Empathy

The treatment clearly worked in a general sense: as expected, nonempathetic candidates were viewed much less favorably by voters. While the drops were most dramatic on the empathy-related measures, scores dropped on all of the relevant measures. On the empathy related measures, candidate scores fell precipitously, on the order of 2–2.5 points on a 7-point scale. Overall candidate evaluations fell dramatically, too, by approximately 1–1.5 points. Regardless of gender prescriptions, the nonempathetic candidate was clearly failing a prescription for political leaders that they be kind and compassionate.

Regardless of the strength of lack of empathy to feelings about candidates, it did not have a gendered effect on overall candidate evaluations (see table 6.2 for a summary of the results, and appendix 10 for the ANOVA results and associated means). People heavily penalized candidates, male or female, for acting in an uncaring manner, but they did not penalize women more than men on the outcome measures. This finding rules out $H1_{empathy}$, the hypothesis associated with double standards theory.

Lack of empathy did, however, differentially influence perceptions of men and women candidates regarding two subsidiary measures: intelligence and knowledge. Recall from chapter 4 that intelligence is the only measure on which descriptive gender stereotypes existed for the control group candidate (with female candidates being viewed as more intelligent than male candidates). My analysis shows that when a female candidate is nonempathetic, her underlying advantage on intelligence disappears. Moreover, she ends up falling behind the male candidate on the "knowledgeable" measure after displaying a lack of empathy (even though she started just slightly—but not significantly—above the male candidate in the control group on that measure). It may well have been a "she should know better than that" kind of reaction, but that is just conjecture.

Regardless, these subsidiary results do not amount to anything particularly consequential in light of the overall lack of gendered effects on the outcome measures and all of the other measures. In short, candidates should be empathetic—if they are not, they will be swiftly and harshly punished by the public—but female candidates are not penalized more

TABLE 6.2. Summary of Lack of Empathy Results

Does LACK OF EMPATHY affect perceptions of male and female candidates differently on the overall outcome measures?		
no significant difference	*on*	**favorability**
no significant difference	*on*	likely **Senate effectiveness**
no significant difference	*on*	likely **presidential effectiveness**

Does LACK OF EMPATHY affect perceptions of male and female candidates differently on other measures?		
no significant difference	*on*	ability to handle **domestic issues**
no significant difference	*on*	ability to handle the **economy**
no significant difference	*on*	ability to handle an **international crisis**
no significant difference	*on*	**"honest"**
WOMEN who act non-empathetically **DECREASE** disproportionately	*on*	**"knowledgeable"**
WOMEN who act non-empathetically **DECREASE** disproportionately	*on*	**"intelligent"**
no significant difference	*on*	**"strong leader"**
no significant difference	*on*	**"gets things done"**
no significant difference	*on*	**"cares about people like you"**
no significant difference	*on*	**"compassionate"**
no significant difference	*on*	**"important person"**
no significant difference	*on*	**"would enjoy talking to"**
no significant difference	*on*	**"unemotional"** (vs. "emotional")
no significant difference	*on*	**"calm"** (vs. "angry")
no significant difference	*on*	**"assertive"** (vs. "unassertive")
no significant difference	*on*	**"caring"** (vs. "uncaring")
no significant difference	*on*	**"strong"** (vs. "weak")
no significant difference	*on*	**"acts appropriately"** (vs. "Acts Inappropriately")
no significant difference	*on*	**situational attribution** (vs. behavioral)

Note: Summary results are based on two-way ANOVA models in which the significance of the interaction (candidate gender * behavior) is assessed for each of the individual dependent variables (note that the last measure is based on one-way ANOVA; see the appendix for details). The significance of the associated F-test and the means for each experimental cell can be found in the appendix. Differences with a p-value of .10 or better are noted.

for lacking empathy than male candidates on any of the key outcome measures. As with the analysis of toughness, these results run contrary to double standards theory and are consistent with the expectations of the leaders-not-ladies theory.

Discussion

The key conclusion from this analysis is that the conventional wisdom about a double bind for female candidates is wrong. People do not seem to hold an unwinnable combination of mutually exclusive expectations for female candidates that they simultaneously act in a nondominant and leader-like manner. My results show that women can be tough in a highly "unfeminine," dominant, and forceful manner and not get penalized for it by the public. In fact, it appears to benefit them in some key respects: women benefit from toughness more than men with respect to their perceived effectiveness in the presidency and possibly to a modest degree with respect to favorability as well. And the empathy results indicate that although all candidates should be in touch with their empathetic, "feminine" side, that women do not have to be more attuned to it than men.

Why is there a divergence between these findings about candidates from the existing findings regarding nonpolitical leaders and professionals? Many of the potential reasons for this discrepancy were previously outlined in chapter 2. Beyond these general reasons, there may also be a more fundamental difference at the root of this discrepancy that pertains to this specific set of behaviors. Setting aside the matter of gender, different roles require a different balance between toughness and compassion: business executives "should be" agentic nearly all the time in order to lead their companies, while professors "should be" tough only when absolutely necessary (at least in the eyes of students). As for ordinary people, the need for agency and compassion are entirely context dependent. In contrast, politicians—male and female—have always faced the need to project power and the ability to stand up to tough situations while also projecting care and compassion nearly all the time. They need to be able to project that they feel your pain *and* that they will be able to stand up to those who would try to cause you pain. Male politicians are expected to display both agentic and communal traits, as are female politicians, and those who cannot do so tend to get selected out of the pool by not winning elections. The public has grown used to politicians, male and female, who can kiss a baby one minute and deliver a hard-hitting speech the next. Tough female candidates and compassionate male candidates are unlikely to surprise anyone in the current era.

Indeed, the more general point to underscore is that to be judged as a leader and not as a lady is not necessarily a wholly positive experience; it simply means that women and men are not judged by different standards. In this regard, Madeline Kunin evocatively recounts that, for her, one representation of being judged as a leader and not a lady is simply being called a different profanity. When Kunin, later the first female governor of Vermont, first started in the state legislature, she recalls that, "Orrin Beattie [the Speaker's right-hand man] reported that he had been asked how he liked having two women on his committee—Judy Rosenstreich, a Republican, and me. 'Oh, they're bastards like everyone else' is what he said. I laughed with the others. A bastard was fine, I knew. As long as I wasn't called a bitch."[40]

To Kunin, it represented progress for women in politics that she could be tough without being saddled with the particular word that has been launched at so many strong women. For her, it was fine that she was being criticized for being demanding in exactly the same way that her male colleagues were being criticized for the same behavior. Women like Bella Abzug, Nancy Pelosi, Diane Feinstein, and so many other women politicians have indeed now set a strong precedent that female leaders can be tough, powerful, and electable. Perhaps partly in response to their success, it appears that female candidates are no longer subject to a toughness double bind imposed by the public that would serve to constrain them on the campaign trail.

[40] Kunin 1994, 119.

CHAPTER 7

Knowledge Gaffes

Fox Reporter Greta Van Susteren: What do you think: are women
treated differently than men in politics on gaffes?
Sarah Palin: Yes, of course.

—FOX NEWS, MARCH 23, 2011

In both business and politics, many have claimed that women leaders face
double standards for their behavior that produce disproportionate penalties for errors and gaffes they commit. Whereas men can be excused a
slip-up (or two or three), women are frequently seen as facing a much
higher threshold for their competence.

In the corporate world, one female Wall Street executive describes the
issue as follows: "We have to know everything before we take action. A
guy can be more brazen. If he gets caught with his pants down, he just
laughs and says, 'No big deal,' whereas a woman looks like an utter fool.
If you ever show any weakness in nuts-and-bolts knowledge, you really
are never forgiven."[1] Psychologists Alice Eagly and Linda Carli argue
that, "because the bar is set higher for women, the old adage that a
woman must be 'twice as good as a man' to get a job holds true, at least
for jobs that are traditionally male-dominated, including most leadership
positions."[2] By extension, any evidence of a slip-up should therefore
make it that much harder for a woman business leader to prove that she
is sufficiently superior to a male counterpart such that she can be seen as
his equal.

These kinds of concerns are not exclusive to the corporate world;
women political leaders report the same dynamics. In 1963, Canadian
politician Charlotte Whitton cited the same ratios when she said, "Whatever women do they must do twice as well as men to be thought half as
good."[3] Madeline Kunin similarly believed that, at least several decades
ago, she was held to a higher standard of knowledge as a woman politi-

---

[1] Swiss 1996, 57.

[2] Eagly and Carli 2007, 115.

[3] As cited in Anna Quindlen, "Still Stuck in Second; The double standard is alive and
well; it's just more nuanced. And to those guys in New Hampshire? Iron your own shirts!"

cian: "As the first woman governor of Vermont, I felt I had a special obligation to master the facts. A man in my position might be able to slide
over what he did not know. As a woman, I continued to feel the need to
prove that I was qualified for the job. If I said the words 'I don't know,'
the aura of power might fade under the hot lights. Not informed? How
can she govern?"[4]

This belief that women are held to a higher overall standard has persisted throughout the years. During her 2000 race for U.S. Senate, Hillary
Clinton observed that women candidates had to be better than their male
counterparts: "You can be who you are but you just have to be very conscious that you're given no benefit of the doubt as a woman."[5] Later, after
Hillary lost her 2008 primary bid, Bob Hepburn wrote a newspaper article entitled, "How Sexism Killed Hillary's Dream," and declared in it,
"The truth is that women *are* treated unfairly in politics. The bar for
performance is set higher for them than for men."[6] Nicolle Wallace, a
journalist, echoes this sentiment and explains, "While many male candidates have recovered from shaky performances on the stump, women
often seem doomed after a major flub."[7] And Sarah Palin, in the quote
that leads this chapter, expresses certainty that women are held to a
higher standard.[8]

The previous chapters have gone a long way toward establishing that
campaign imperfections—even in arenas that might potentially be fairly
explicitly gendered such as emotionality, toughness, and empathy—are
challenges for all candidates, not just women candidates, vis-à-vis the
public. And inexperience proved to be more of a problem for male candidates than for female candidates, so clearly women are not disproportionately penalized for having short resumes. That strongly suggests that
slip-ups might not generate disproportionately negative reactions for female candidates relative to their male counterparts, but there is room still
for a more direct test of this "higher competency" hypothesis. We have
not yet directly considered the classic "oops" scenario, the knowledge
gaffe: the all-too-common blink-of-an-eye situation in which a candidate
seems to express incompetence through factual inaccuracies.

Newsweek, March 17, 2008, 70. Whitton served as mayor of Ottawa, the capital city of
Canada, from 1951 to 1956 and from 1960 to 1964.

[4] Kunin 1994, 63–64.

[5] Clinton as quoted in Clift and Brazaitis 2000, 20.

[6] Bob Hepburn, "How Sexism Killed Hillary's Dream," *Toronto Star*, June 5, 2008.

[7] Nicolle Wallace, "What Michele Bachmann Learned from Sarah Palin—and Hillary
Clinton," *Washington Post*, Outlook section, August 7, 2011.

[8] It should be noted that in Palin's case, her concerns seem to rest as much or more on
how the media reports on women candidates—conservative women candidates, in particular—than on how the public regards women candidates. I will return to a discussion of the
possibility of gendered media effects in the next chapter.

Did the public punish female candidates like Sarah Palin or Michelle Bachman more for their knowledge gaffes than they would have punished a male candidate? Dan Quayle, Rick Perry, Herman Cain, and the many other male candidates who have faced the disdain of voters over their own knowledge gaffes would likely underscore that getting caught in a gaffe can be quite problematic for men too. Yet answering this question requires more than anecdotal evidence: it needs to be tested. This chapter explores the "knowledge gaffe" scenario to further address whether women fall harder when they slip up. I will first examine the nature of gaffes in American politics. I will then briefly discuss the methodology that is specific to this experiment, followed by an analysis and discussion of the findings. Yet again, I find that women candidates are not held to a higher standard than men candidates or even a different standard; along the way, I help to establish why knowledge gaffes tend to be problems for all candidates, gender aside.

Why Focus on Knowledge Gaffes?

This study focuses on the "oops"-type scenario: the knowledge gaffe in which a politician lacks the kind of information that a political candidate would normally be expected to possess. However, there are gaffes other than knowledge gaffes, to be sure. A brief exploration of other types of gaffes and why the findings from my analysis should still generally be applicable to those kinds of situations is in order.

One type of gaffe is the physical gaffe, such as President George H. W. Bush throwing up on the Japanese prime minister or Bob Dole falling off of a stage during a campaign event in 1996. There are also lack-of-judgment gaffes (which are often, but not always, tied to "hot microphone" gaffes), such as Ronald Reagan's pronouncement during the height of the Cold War that, "My fellow Americans, I'm pleased to tell you today that I've signed legislation that will outlaw Russia forever. We begin bombing in five minutes," over a microphone that he had incorrectly assumed was turned off. There are exaggeration gaffes about matters that are later proved decisively to be untrue, such as Hillary Clinton's rendition of her trip to Bosnia, during which she reported "landing under sniper fire" and running for safety with "our heads down," which video footage of her ceremonial and sniper-free arrival in Bosnia quickly disproved. There are also gaffes that seem to indicate arrogance or lack of compassion: the "you are likeable enough, Hillary" comment by Barack Obama, or the epic sighs by Al Gore in a 2000 debate in response to several of George W. Bush's debate statements.

Gaffes of malapropism are probably best thought of as a subcategory of the knowledge gaffe and tend to be fairly common on the political scene. These are gaffes such as when George W. Bush observed that, "Rarely is the question asked: Is our children learning?" or Dan Quayle's comment to the United Negro College Fund that "You take the UNCF model that what a waste it is to lose one's mind or not to have a mind is being very wasteful. How true that is."

Yet, for this study, the specific nature of the gaffe should not matter much; the hypothesis that women will face a greater penalty for missteps should be broadly generalizable. Nearly any gaffe should thus work for our purposes. Surely, if women were held to a higher standard, we should see it with reference to the knowledge gaffe. And given its great prominence in the political sphere in recent election cycles, the knowledge gaffe is a timely and relevant type of behavior to study.

It is also an interesting area to explore, because we know that women candidates with no political experience, as well as women candidates who are relatively new incumbents, are both assumed to be slightly more intelligent than their male counterparts; in fact, it was the only significant gender stereotype held by the public for the control group candidates. It is not a dramatic difference, to be sure, but it is clear from my data that political women do not start out behind their male counterparts in terms of perceptions of intelligence.

Knowledge Gaffes and Gender in American Politics

In the political world of today—one with a 24/7 media where there seems to be a video camera in every pocket recording almost every utterance of politicians—knowledge gaffes seem to be becoming more and more prominent. If this is the case, and if women are especially damaged by them, then this would constitute an ever growing constraint on their electoral prospects.

If awards were given for uttering memorable knowledge gaffes, Sarah Palin would almost certainly be in line for one. In an interview with Charles Gibson, she awkwardly expressed no apparent knowledge about the nature of the "Bush Doctrine." In multiple interviews, she cited Alaska's proximity to Russia as proof of her foreign policy credentials, which was mocked widely. Moreover, when pressed by Katie Couric on how that proximity demonstrates foreign policy expertise, Palin replied, "As Putin rears his head and comes into the air space of the United States of America, where do they go? It's Alaska. It's just right over the border," thus generating further rounds of public ridicule.[9] Moreover, after insisting that John McCain had pressed for more regulation in some situations,

[9] Christine Lagorio, "New Sarah Palin Clip: Keeping an Eye On Putin," September 25, 2008, CBS News.

Palin was unable to cite a single example of it. Perhaps most famously in the same interview, Palin seemed unable to cite to Katie Couric a single news source that she reads regularly.

But it did not end there. At a 2008 campaign stop in Laconia, New Hampshire, Palin referred to the state as being part of the "Great Northwest." She referred to Afghanistan as "our neighboring country" at a fundraising in San Francisco. When discussing the role of the vice president of the United States in response to a "Questions from the Third Grade" segment of a Colorado TV station, Palin rather questionably expanded the role of the vice president to say that "they're in charge of the United States Senate, so if they want to they can really get in there with the senators and make a lot of good policy changes" (this was only a few months after saying on a CNBC interview that, "As for that VP talk all the time, I tell you, I still can't answer that question until somebody answers for me, 'what is it exactly that the VP does every day?'").[10] In Boston, Palin creatively revised history when she claimed that Paul Revere, "warned, uh, the British that they weren't going to be takin' away our arms, uh, by ringing those bells."[11]

Palin is not the first, nor the last, female politician to face the knowledge gaffe scenario. In recent years, Michelle Bachmann is particularly notable in this regard. She appeared to struggle with her command of facts at a number of points in the campaign. She started her campaign for president in 2011 with the statement that her hometown of Waterloo, Iowa, was the birthplace of John Wayne and "that's the kind of spirit that I have, too," without realizing, until it was too late, that the person named John Wayne who was born in Waterloo was actually the serial killer John Wayne Gacy. Among other examples, she noted Americans' fear of "the rise of the Soviet Union," claimed that the Revolutionary War started in the wrong state (she declared in Concord, New Hampshire, that the "shot heard round the world" had been fired there), credited the Founding Fathers of the United States, as a group, with working to end the institution of slavery, and she asserted that if she were president, "we wouldn't have an embassy in Iran" (an odd remark in light of the fact that the United States had not had an embassy in Iran for more than thirty years when she made that point).

Of course, the fact that Palin and Bachmann seemed to be hurt by their knowledge gaffes hardly indicates that this dynamic exists only for female politicians; there are many examples of male politicians who have been similarly damaged in this way. Perhaps most notably, Dan Quayle was regularly pilloried for the gaffes he made during his time in office.

[10] Karen Harper, "Sarah Palin Doesn't Know What the Vice-President Does," October 23, 2008, Examiner.com.

[11] Andrew Malcolm, "Sarah Palin Claims Paul Revere Warned the British," *Los Angeles Times*, June 3, 2011.

For example, in a press conference on September 15, 1988, he said, "The Holocaust was an obscene period in our nation's history. I mean in this century's history. But we all lived in this century. I didn't live in this century." In another gaffe, he told a reporter in 1989, "I believe we are on an irreversible trend toward more freedom and democracy, but that could change." And, of course, Quayle famously corrected a student who had correctly spelled potato in a spelling bee by saying, "Add one little bit on the end [the 'e'] . . . You're right phonetically, but what else?" Those were not the only examples of Quayle's statements that earned him scorn from the public and the media, but the "potatoe" incident, in particular, seemed to galvanize public concern about him as a politician. His attempt to run for president in the 1999 primaries was a short one, and he has not held public office since he left the vice presidency.

In the 2011 Republican presidential primary races, voters were treated to a range of knowledge gaffes by unsuccessful male candidates, most notably Rick Perry and Herman Cain. Cain's most memorably awkward knowledge gaffe came in response to the straightforward question "So you agreed with President Obama on Libya or not?" during a videotaped interview with the *Milwaukee Sentinel* editorial board. Cain's tortured, painfully convoluted answer was pilloried in the media with headlines like "Does Herman Cain know anything at all about foreign policy? No, judging by gaffe" (*Milwaukee Progressive Examiner*, November 16, 2011) and "Herman Cain Has a 'Rick Perry Moment' on Libya Policy" (*Chicago Tribune*, November 14, 2011). Perry is perhaps the politician most damaged by a knowledge gaffe, an "oops moment" (in fact, the source of the term itself) that not only seemed to derail his campaign but will likely always be remembered as a landmark in the annals of presidential debate history. With a series of problematic debate performances marring his late entry into the 2011 race—a race in which debates played an unusually frequent and central role—he needed to improve his perceptions with voters quickly in order to redeem his candidacy. Instead, he managed to set it back even further with the inability to name the third of three federal agencies that he had proposed to eliminate as part of his presidential platform. Pressed by the debate moderator to name it, he awkwardly stumbled around for the name and then ultimately had to concede, "I can't—the third one, I can't. Sorry. Oops." Described by Larry Sabato on Twitter as "the most devastating moment of any modern primary debate"—and with more than 4,400,000 Google entries for the combined terms of "Rick Perry," "oops," and "debate" less than two weeks after the event—Rick Perry's "oops" moment is an unforgettable reminder of the potential power of knowledge gaffes in campaigns.[12]

[12] Debbi Wilgoren, "Rick Perry Makes Light of Gaffe, Vows Not to Quit," *Washington Post*, November 10, 2011.

Yet, it is obviously not the case that all gaffe-prone politicians have been unsuccessful electorally. Ronald Reagan was notoriously gaffe prone. Discussing his time as a candidate on the campaign trail, an aide of Reagan's reported, "the only good news for us at this time is that we were making so many blunders that reporters had to pick and choose which ones they would write about."[13] George W. Bush also, of course, faced many of his own "oops" moments. In one prominent example, asked to name the leaders of Taiwan, Chechnya, Pakistan, and India, in November 1999, Bush could name only the leader of Taiwan. His communications director, Karen Hughes, responded to criticism by Democrats of the incident by saying, "the person who is running for president is seeking to be the leader of the free world, not a Jeopardy contestant."[14]

The cases of Reagan and George W. Bush clearly show that it is possible to be highly gaffe prone and yet also be highly successful in terms of garnering political victories, which raises a key question: Could a woman be similarly successful electorally with those kinds of missteps? Although it would be premature to write off their political careers at this juncture, Palin and Bachmann did seem to be harmed by their missteps. Were they disproportionately harmed in this regard because of their gender? The conventional wisdom would suggest that women will, in fact, be disproportionately penalized for their gaffes; yet, to the extent that political women are regarded as leaders rather than ladies, we would not expect to find a gender difference. That proposition will now be tested.

Study Design for the Knowledge Gaffe Experiment

The overall experimental design for this analysis is the same as those featured in the previous several chapters. I will therefore concentrate on the unique features of this part of the study.

As with the behavior-based experiments (but not the experience experiment), the treatment articles differed from the control group articles with an additional section that described the behavior in question (in this case, a knowledge gaffe). And, as with the other experiments, "Karen Bailey" was featured in one treatment and one control group article and "Kevin Bailey" was featured in one treatment and one control group article, and the articles were identical in every other respect.

In the treatment articles, the information provided beyond the control group boiler plate article is a headline that "Congresswoman(man) Karen(Kevin) Bailey Short on Facts," with a subheadline, "Wrong on

[13] Roger Simon, "Dumb, Dumber, Dumbest," *Politico*, November 22, 2011.
[14] Glen Johnson, "Bush Fails Quiz on Foreign Affairs," *Washington Post*, November 4, 1999.

Leaders' Names, Veto Procedure," and a pull quote, " 'I guess I should have known that,' admits Bailey." The first incident described is one in which he or she misstated the names of two foreign leaders and a second incident in which he or she misstated the number of votes required by the House and Senate to override a presidential veto and was corrected by a sixth grader (see appendix 1 for the full text of the news article). This scenario taps into the general kinds of knowledge gaffes that have been seen in politics, and also addresses the specific concern about the need for women politicians to not slip up on facts, as expressed by Madeline Kunin earlier in this chapter. To the extent that women are subject to higher standards of behavior than men by the public in general—and to the extent that women are penalized for "oops" moments in particular—this scenario should elicit that kind of reaction from respondents.

As with all of the previous parts of the study, the outcome measures are of key interest. Those will allow us to assess the overall penalties applied to Karen and Kevin Bailey for their gaffes. But there are other component measures that, while not as critical as the outcome measures, can also provide us with some specific information of interest. In this case, "intelligent" and "knowledgeable" are central to understanding the dynamics at hand. "Competent" (vs. "incompetent") might also cast some light on the matter. Assessments of the candidate's ability to handle different issues (help to make America strong economically; effectively handle an international crisis) could also help us understand the mechanisms through which penalties are assessed.

As in all of the behavior-based studies, I asked whether the candidate's behavior could best be explained by the personal characteristics of the candidate or by the nature of the situation. Differences on those measures could help to make it possible to discern the causes of any differences observed in the other measures. An underlying element of the conventional wisdom is that people are likely to attribute mistakes on the part of women candidates to personal flaws, while male candidates are likely to be let off the hook by an attribution to the "difficult" nature of the situation they were facing at the time.

Results

These results indicate that knowledge gaffes can be quite problematic for candidates, but—consistent with the findings from the rest of the book—they are no more problematic for female candidates than for male candidates.

With respect to the effects of a knowledge gaffe overall (male and female candidates combined), appendix 3 shows that the "oops" moment is significantly more harmful to candidates on the overall outcome measures than crying, anger, and toughness (the latter of which was not harmful at all).[15] The lack of empathy scenario was more harmful to candidates than the knowledge gaffe scenario, but still the gaffe produced a drop of over a full point on each of those three measures (favorability, likely effectiveness in the Senate, likely effectiveness as president about ten years from now). Similar patterns are observed for the issue competencies. The trait of "knowledgeable" (falling from 4.6 in the control group to 2.6 in the treatment group) took a much bigger hit than "intelligent" (falling from 4.8 in the control group to 3.2 in the treatment group). "Competence" was not nearly as affected, falling from 4.4 to 4.0.

Some of the unrelated measures such as "compassionate" and "cares about people like you" take relatively substantial hits as well (.8 in both cases). That suggests that knowledge gaffes have a somewhat "global" effect on all assessments of an individual that are not just specific to the nature of the trait at hand. This is not unique to knowledge gaffes though; for example, angry candidates were seen as being substantially less knowledgeable than the control group candidates and nonempathetic candidates were seen as being less important people than the control group candidates; the same is the case across a number of the behaviors and unrelated traits. Viewing a candidate in a negative light in one respect causes voters to view them in a more negative light in other, unrelated respects.

With respect to the matter of gender, however, I find no evidence that female candidates are held to a higher competency standard than male candidates (see summary results in table 7.1; for full results, see appendix 11). That is the case across all of the overall outcome measures as well as for all of the individual attributes. In short, while all candidates would be wise to avoid these kinds of knowledge slip-ups, women are not penalized more than men for them.

Conclusion

In this analysis, we see yet again that the conventional wisdom regarding how female candidate behavior influences public opinion is off base. Female congressional candidates are not penalized more than male candidates for knowledge gaffes. If female legislative candidates were in a tenuous position regarding competency on the campaign trail vis-à-vis

[15] These results certainly resonate with Rick Perry's 2011 experiences on the campaign trail, where his knowledge gaffes during the debates were thought by many to take him out of contention for the presidency.

TABLE 7.1. Summary of Knowledge Gaffe Results

candidates differently on the outcome measures?

no significant difference	*on*	**favorability**
no significant difference	*on*	likely **Senate effectiveness**
no significant difference	*on*	likely **presidential effectiveness**

Do KNOWLEDGE GAFFES affect perceptions of male and female candidates differently on other measures?

no significant difference	*on*	ability to handle **domestic issues**
no significant difference	*on*	ability to handle the **economy**
no significant difference	*on*	ability to handle an **international crisis**
no significant difference	*on*	**"honest"**
no significant difference	*on*	**"knowledgeable"**
no significant difference	*on*	**"intelligent"**
no significant difference	*on*	**"strong leader"**
no significant difference	*on*	**"gets things done"**
no significant difference	*on*	**"cares about people like you"**
no significant difference	*on*	**"compassionate"**
no significant difference	*on*	**"important person"**
no significant difference	*on*	**"would enjoy talking to"**
no significant difference	*on*	**"competent"** (vs. "incompetent")
no significant difference	*on*	**"experienced"** (vs. "inexperienced")
no significant difference	*on*	**situational attribution** (vs. behavioral)

Note: Summary results are based on two-way ANOVA models in which the significance of the interaction (candidate gender * behavior) is assessed for each of the individual dependent variables (note that the last measure is based on one-way ANOVA; see the appendix for details). The significance of the associated F-test and the means for each experimental cell can be found in the appendix. Differences with a p-value of .10 or better are noted.

the public as is widely suggested, we would expect to see at least some evidence of it here, and we do not.

While the present study allows us to understand that women legislative candidates do not face harmful double standards due to knowledge gaffes while campaigning, future research will need to delve into why and when knowledge gaffes seem to derail some candidates and not others. Clearly, the media play a role in the dynamic, but the viral nature of video on the Internet arguably takes some of the power to focus public attention on gaffes away from the media, and places it more directly in the hands of the public. Now that nearly every American is a potential "citizen reporter" with a pocket-sized video camera on hand, knowledge gaffes are sure to play a visible role in campaigns moving forward. Understanding why such gaffes sometimes derail campaigns, while other times they quickly fade from public interest, will help us to understand their role in political campaigns in this changing era.

CHAPTER 8

Reassessing the Parity Problem

The best hope for improving the lot of all women, and for closing what Wolfers and Stevenson call a "new gender gap"—measured by well-being rather than wages—is to close the leadership gap: to elect a woman president and 50 women senators; to ensure that women are equally represented in the ranks of corporate executives and judicial leaders. Only when women wield power in sufficient numbers will we create a society that genuinely works for all women. That will be a society that works for everyone.... You should be able to have a family if you want one—however and whenever your life circumstances allow—and still have the career you desire. If more women could strike this balance, more women would reach leadership positions. And if more women were in leadership positions, they could make it easier for more women to stay in the workforce.

—ANNE-MARIE SLAUGHTER[1]

After decades of protests by advocates for women's political rights, the Nineteenth Amendment to the United States Constitution became law in August 1920 and guaranteed women the right to vote. Not until fairly recently, however, has there been anything resembling a critical mass of female legislators. The U.S. has never had a woman president or vice president and is still not even near gender parity in the percentage of women holding elective legislative positions; it is likely to be many years, at best, before parity can even be on the horizon. The conventional wisdom suggests that a key reason that gender parity has not been achieved is because the public employs a wide range of gender stereotypes and double standards that hurt women candidates. Yet I do not find that to be the case.

My analysis shows that the public as a whole does not apply harmful descriptive stereotypes to their evaluations of female candidates relative to men: they are not assumed to be more emotional, less tough, or less

[1] "Why Women Still Can't Have It All," *Atlantic Monthly*, July–August 2012.

able to handle many different types of issues; in fact, some women candidates (i.e., "outsiders," with no prior political experience) tend to be viewed in a more positive light on many dimensions relative to their low-experience male counterparts. Moreover, this study shows that female candidates are not penalized by the public for violating gendered prescriptive stereotypes (men should not cry, women should not get angry, women should be empathetic, women should not be tough), which suggests that prescriptive gender stereotypes for politicians do not determine the electoral fates of women. Similarly, the notion that women are simply held to higher competency standards by the public than male candidates is also not confirmed by this study. It is certainly not easy to be a candidate for office, but the findings from this study do not support the idea that it is any harder for women than men to win over the hearts and minds of the American public.

Along the way, a few mostly modest differences for male and female candidates were uncovered, all on fairly peripheral measures. Upon closer scrutiny, however, nearly all those differences were limited to the kinds of measures ("emotional," "assertive," "strong," etc.) that are themselves related to higher, rather than lower, overall assessments of candidates.[2] Thus, even in the few areas where differences are observed in public responses to the behavior of male versus female candidates, the data do not support the idea that women candidates are disproportionately penalized for being women.

Might some individuals, or might some groups, still engage in gender stereotyping, or routinely apply gendered standards in their evaluations of candidates? We know that there will always be individual-level variation in views, and often some group-based differences as well, that reside within any finding that characterizes the views of "the public" as a whole. This book does not focus on delineating any such differences but instead is directed toward systematically evaluating the validity of the conventional wisdom that women candidates are at an electoral disadvantage relative to their male counterparts.[3] Some differences can be located in the data for analyses involving particular dependent variables within particular experiments, but I did not find consistent patterns of differences for major subgroups, such as male versus female respondents or respon-

---

[2] The only two findings where that is not the case are "acts appropriately" in the anger experiment (which drops somewhat more for women than men when they get angry), and "knowledgeable" and "intelligent" in the lack of empathy study (where women in the treatment condition fall disproportionately more than their male counterparts).

[3] In addition, illustrating potential subgroup differences with three-way interactions (candidate gender by behavior/control by grouping variable) for six separate experiments, plus a separate analysis for the control group, for up to twenty-four different dependent variables for each experiment is not viable, since the tables alone would require hundreds of pages.

dents who are Republicans versus Democrats, that track across multiple dependent variables and across multiple experiments in a manner that tells a clear story about particular segments of society that tend to be more or less likely to favor women candidates as a general rule.[4] Even for the most theoretically interesting subgroup finding—which concerns older voters and pertains to possible generational differences—the relationship is confined to specific dynamics involving the presidency and toughness (this is a matter which will be returned to in chapter 9).

Do my findings mean that all women candidates absolutely never, under any circumstances, face a playing field that is different from what male candidates face? Specific exceptions may exist. Perhaps especially attractive or especially unattractive women,[5] more femininely dressed versus more masculinely dressed women,[6] women with young children,[7]

---

[4] On a related point, I also do not see any evidence in my data that female candidates are assumed to be more liberal than men, a finding from the previous literature that had raised concerns that Republican women might have a harder time winning over their base than Democratic women, even absent any direct antiwoman sentiment (see, e.g., Alexander and Andersen 1993; King and Matland 2003; Koch 2000; McDermott 1997; Sanbonmatsu and Dolan 2009).

[5] Women candidates might need to be disproportionately attractive to earn the support of the public; conversely, maybe attractiveness detracts from perceptions of leadership competence. The smattering of work that has been done on the topic has not identified that physical appearance is disproportionately important for women candidates. Sigelman, Sigelman, and Fowler (1987) study only women candidates and find that, while attractiveness had some effect on trait measures, it did not affect voter preference for the candidate. Rebekah Herrick, Jeanette Mendez, Sue Thomas, and Amanda Wilkerson (2012) found that the faces of women members of Congress were perceived to be both less competent and less mature than the faces of their male counterparts, even controlling for actual candidate age. Kathryn Lewis and Margaret Biely (1990) looked at the interaction between candidate gender and appearance by studying both men and women. They found that perceptions of attractiveness were found to increase perceptions of candidate competence for both men and women candidates at roughly equal levels.

[6] Politicians and consultants often believe that the clothing choices of female candidates are fairly high-stakes decisions, yet I am not aware of any academic research that addresses the issue. Outside of academia, a recent study conducted by Democratic pollsters analyzed public reactions to male and female candidates different types of settings and outfits (formal vs. informal) and concluded that women candidates were disproportionately better off when they appeared in formal business dress and settings (dark suits in offices). Moreover, the report concluded that "voters, both male and female, are much more likely to comment on the appearance of the female candidates than the male candidates (The White House Project 2002).

[7] Stalsburg (2010) has done the only empirical work I could find to date on the topic of public attitudes toward candidates with children, and her experimental evidence showed that, in fact, childless women are at a relative disadvantage as compared to women with children. She finds female candidates with young children are at somewhat of a disadvantage relative to male candidates with young children, but male candidates with young children also face what she terms a "fatherhood penalty" as compared to men without children. There is clearly more work to be done on this (in part, this research was conducted on un-

extremely old or extremely young women,[8] or women involved in certain types of scandals[9] might face more gendered reactions by the public. This study reminds us that we should not assume that any gender dynamics are in play or that the effect of any or all of those extremes, or other potential ones, would necessarily be negative rather than positive for the electoral prospects of women. Such dynamics should be certainly studied further. Although valuable to pursue, it is extremely unlikely any such research would challenge the basic premise of this book that, contrary to the conventional wisdom, women legislative candidates do not face a public that is, on balance, hostile to them as a matter of course. Too many different situations were tested in this study with no indication of gender bias or double standards to think that Americans as a whole are unsupportive of women leaders. An environment in which women candidates regularly face an inherently hostile public by dint of their womanhood would simply not allow for the kinds of results that populate this study.

In some ways the lack of evidence in my analyses for the conventional view that female candidates face damaging double standards that harm them on the campaign is surprising: it is remarkable that so many candidates, potential candidates, consultants, pundits, and journalists regularly and emphatically claim that women candidates are disproportionately penalized for various campaign behaviors and characteristics when empirical evidence for that proposition does not exist. Perhaps it was always a misperception or perhaps it is simply that the status of women in society and politics has changed so rapidly that the conventional wisdom has not yet had an opportunity to catch up to a new reality (an issue I discuss in the next chapter). But even if such a lag effect is in play, the continued belief in gendered double standards by many political observers and practitioners is still rather stunning.

---

dergraduates, and undergraduates might have atypical reactions to parenthood), but it is an interesting start to addressing the question.

[8] Perhaps women candidates need to be younger looking (or, conversely, perhaps they need to be older and more mature looking) than their male counterparts to appeal to the public (for some research on related questions, see Herrick, Mendez, Thomas, and Wilkerson 2012); if so, this issue could potentially be magnified in its effect due to the fact that women tend to run for office about three years later in their lives than men (Burrell 1996, 63–66; see also Lawless and Fox 2010, 167).

[9] There have been a couple of interesting findings regarding scandals and candidate gender. Smith, Powers, and Suarez (2005) do not find that female candidates are penalized more for indiscretions, overall, than male candidates; they do, however, find that men and women are somewhat less penalized when they are involved in a scandal that is inconsistent with gender stereotypes (the authors considera sexual relationship with a superior and a "Nannygate" type situation of hiring an illegal alien for household work to be stereotypical female scenarios, while the consider accepting illegal gifts from contributors and sex with a subordinate to be stereotypical male scenarios). With a finding that is consistent with the Smith et al. results, Huddy and Capelos (2002) find that male candidates fare poorly relative to female candidates after disclosure of a financial scandal.

In another way, however, the overall conclusion of this study should be unsurprising. As mentioned earlier, the literature shows that female candidates are not at a relative disadvantage on Election Day. There is unusually broad agreement on this finding: once standard factors like incumbency, the partisan split of the district, and candidate experience are included as controls, numerous findings have shown that women candidates do just as well as their male counterparts.[10] Thus, my study helps to resolve a perplexity that has loomed within both applied politics and political science: if the conventional wisdom about gender stereotypes and double standards is right, how can we not see strong evidence from electoral returns that women are winning at disproportionately lower rates than men? With my general finding that the public does not have more challenging expectations for women candidates, my analysis provides an intuitively satisfying solution to that long-standing puzzle.

But an important question remains: If gender stereotypes can be taken off of the table, why is there a parity problem? This chapter assesses the most unlikely and most likely contributors to the imbalance of women serving in office. By sorting through key findings from the relevant literature at large, and by leveraging my data on some matters to help to shed additional light where possible, this chapter aims to provide clarity regarding where our knowledge as a field currently stands. In so doing, this chapter provides the foundation for the final chapter, where I show that a core contributing factor to the parity problem can perhaps somewhat be ameliorated by recognizing the findings from this book. Specifically, I argue that my findings can potentially help to encourage women to run— and may encourage political power brokers to recruit more women candidates —by correcting a prevalent misperception that women face disproportionate challenges vis-à-vis public opinion. Recognition of my findings will not rectify the parity problem entirely, to be sure, but for a problem that has many components that are likely to be tenacious, it is an important step.

From Whence the Parity Problem?

If gender stereotypes are not the cause of the gender parity problem, then what is? After scrutinizing a series of alternative possible causes for the continued relative lack of women in office, I evaluate these potential con-

[10] See, e.g., Tolleson-Rinehart and Josephson in Tolleson-Rinehart and Josephson 2000, 5; Erika Falk and Kathleen Hall Jamieson in Watson and Gordon 2003, 48; Burrell 1996, 55; Carroll 1994, 48; Lawless and Pearson 2008; Palmer and Simon 2001, 62; Fox 2000, 232; 2010, 194; Pearson 2010, 237; Darcy, Welch, and Clark 1994, 67 and 100; Seltzer, Newman, and Leighton 1997; Smith and Fox 2001.

tributors to the parity problem and try to provide some direction to scholars and students regarding the particular issues that I believe call for further inquiry.

1. Fundraising Disparities and Opponent Campaign Strategies

In considering the parity problem, it seems reasonable to posit that women candidates might face disproportionate fundraising challenges. A look at campaign receipts without controls can yield an apparent disparity between male and female candidates; yet much of that difference stems from the fact that most women running for office are running as challengers, and incumbents tend to have a much easier time of fundraising, regardless of gender.[11] Once appropriate controls are included, most indications are that women do quite well in terms of fundraising: numerous scholars find that women candidates fare as well, or in some cases slightly better, than comparable male candidates.[12] This topic has been studied comprehensively by Barbara Burrell, who argues, "At the beginning of the twenty-first century, the story about women's capacity to raise campaign funds continues to be that their fund-raising prowess equals men's."[13] Burrell intentionally uses the phrase "continues to be" in that statement in part because she does not find that it is a recent change: she had documented in prior studies that women did as well as men on the fundraising front in earlier eras[14] Fundraising differences thus do not seem to help explain why fewer women hold public office than men in the current era.

Another potential question is whether more or better opponents emerge in order to challenge women candidates, thereby making the election of women candidates more difficult. Scholars have found that women candidates tend to face more competitors in congressional primaries than men; yet, even so, they do not fare worse in the electoral arena than men.[15] In fact, Lawless and Pearson find that women win primaries as frequently as their male counterparts; and, since 1990, they even find that Democratic women have done *better* than Democratic men.[16] Thus, the

---

[11] Dolan, Deckman, and Swers 2011, 167.

[12] Adams and Schreiber 2011; Crespin and Deitz 2010; Milyo and Schosberg 2000; Uhlaner and Schlozman 1986; Werner 1997.

[13] Burrell 2005, 39.

[14] With reference to some of her earlier findings, Burrell examined House candidates from 1972 to 1992 and found that "on each of the elements of fund-raising—total amounts raised and spent, PAC contributions, large donations, and the acquisition of early money—women candidates have either competed equally with male candidates or, in recent elections, surpassed them" (Burrell 1996, 128).

[15] Lawless and Pearson 2008.

[16] Lawless and Pearson 2008, 77.

stronger challenger dynamic does not provide a good explanation for why there are not more women in office.[17]

One might also wonder whether male opponents run more aggressive campaigns against female candidates than male candidates, thereby disadvantaging women. In fact, if anything, women may be at a slight advantage on this front. Research findings suggest that male candidates believe attacking women is a bad strategy.[18] To illustrate one reason that male candidates may be reluctant to go negative against female candidates, Richard Fox cites an anonymous male candidate who observes: "I don't think it is proper to attack a woman. I was completely constrained in how I went about campaigning. It was a constant struggle to show the proper politeness towards my opponent. Women cannot handle criticism or high stress so I had to watch what I said closely so that I would not appear to be causing my opponent any grief."[19] Moreover, other research finds that this general strategy may be a wise choice: scholars have found that in a race with a male attacker, negative messages against a male opponent work much more effectively than when the same messages are launched against a female opponent.[20] To the extent that female candidates are viewed more as leaders than as ladies by the public in the current era, my hypothesis is that male candidates do not need to artificially hold back from attacking a woman candidate. It still may not be socially acceptable to "hit a lady," but on the basis of the other findings in my study, I would expect that the public would consider it to be as acceptable for a male candidate to attack a female candidate as to attack a male candidate, at least in the current era. But regardless, aggressive opponent strategies do not seem to provide traction for explaining the parity problem that exists today.

2. Media Bias

Might the media treat female candidates more harshly than male candidates? Anecdotal evidence suggests that women candidates at least sometimes face very hostile, and occasionally outright sexist, treatment. But is the coverage of women candidates systematically less favorable than that

---

[17] Lawless and Pearson (2008, 78) suggest, however, that because women face tougher primary contests, that might help to explain part of why women are more reluctant than men to run for office. In other words, tougher primaries could indirectly contribute to the parity problem by discouraging women from running for office.

[18] Bystrom et al. (2004, 63–65), found that it was especially true among incumbent women (versus incumbent men) and among Democratic women (versus Democratic men).

[19] As quoted in Fox 2000, 248.

[20] Fridkin, Kenney, and Woodall 2009. They did not test the effect of having a female attacker in that study, which would have been very interesting.

of male candidates or focused on different matters that could unfairly hurt women candidates in their quest for office?

It is fairly clear from the research to date that the media tends to give more coverage to women candidates than male candidates regarding personal appearance and family members, a problem commonly referred to as the "hair, husband, and hemline problem."[21] While relatively greater media coverage of those matters for women candidates appears to be fairly well established and has some face validity to it (e.g., one would typically not see headlines like this for a male candidate: "Hillary Reverses Cinderella Story: Glamorous Candidate Transforms into Frumpy Senator," "Hillary Gets Down to Business; Attired in Black Pantsuit, She Takes on Uniform of Power," "Latest Campaign Issue? One Candidate's Neckline"), a causal link between that kind of coverage and its effect on women candidates vis-à-vis the public has not been established.[22] Kim Kahn (1994, 1996) comes closest to demonstrating a causal linkage between the greater coverage of women candidates on personal issues and public views about candidates, but she was examining coverage differences that extended well beyond hair, husbands, and hemlines matters and, moreover, was doing so using data gathered in the late 1980s and early 1990s; this is a topic that could clearly use further study using recent data.

The question of quantity of coverage also often emerges: Do women candidates receive less coverage than their male counterparts? Some studies lend credence to those concerns,[23] while others have found little difference,[24] and still others have demonstrated that female candidates actually receive more coverage than male candidates overall.[25] Given the mix of findings on the issue to date, it is extremely unlikely that overall media coverage overwhelmingly favors of male candidates; if so, there would likely not be so many findings in the other direction.

Perhaps the amount of coverage matters less than the focus or favorability of the coverage in determining the chances of female candidates. After all, obtaining an enormous amount of coverage that happens to be

[21] See, e.g., Kahn 1994, 1996 (although she found variation between Senate vs. gubernatorial races); Falk 2010; Banwart, Bystrom, and Robertson 2003; Niven and Zilber 2001.

[22] For example, it is possible that disproportionate coverage of hair, hemlines, and husbands issues makes a candidate seem frivolous or less substantive; however, it is also possible that it helps the candidate seem more human, relatable, and memorable than the more substantively covered male candidate.

[23] See Kahn and Goldenberg 1991 and Heldman, Carroll, and Olson 2005.

[24] See, e.g., Atkeson and Krebs 2008; Devitt 2002; Fowler and Lawless 2009; Smith 1997.

[25] For studies that have shown disproportionately greater coverage for women, see, e.g., Banwart, Bystrom, and Robertson 2003, Jalalzai 2006; see also Miller, Peake, and Boulton 2010 regarding Hillary Clinton versus Barack Obama, in particular.

focused on whether the woman can really win the race, or coverage that is disproportionately negative, may potentially hurt a woman candidate more than it helps her. Some findings suggest that women receive more "viability coverage"—that is, a greater focus on the horse race and whether they can win it, rather than on the substance of the campaign— than male candidates,[26] while others do not find a significant difference on that front.[27] With respect to the tone of coverage, the findings are equally mixed. Some studies, such as those of Erika Falk (2010) and Miller, Peake, and Boulton (2010) have found that women candidates receive disproportionately critical media coverage, while others such as Fowler and Lawless (2009) have found that the tenor of the coverage largely lacks gender bias. Still others, such as Banwart, Bystrom, and Robertson (2003) and Smith (1997), have found that women candidates enjoy an advantage over male candidates in terms of the tone of coverage. And Kim Kahn (1994, 1996) found a mix of results depending on the level of office.

Why are there so many different findings with reference to candidate gender and media coverage? One compelling explanation rests in a change over time. Writing in 2010, Diana Bystrom argues that a notable improvement in the coverage of women candidates occurred in recent decades: "In the mid-to late 1990s, women political candidates began to receive more equitable media coverage, in terms of both quantity and quality, when compared with male candidates. . . . While some stereotyping does exist, the playing field for female candidates is becoming more level, at least for women running for governor and for the U.S. Senate."[28] A change over time does not explain all of the divergent findings (there are still a handful of studies that show that women received worse coverage than men in recent years), but the findings that show that women are at a pervasive disadvantage to men with reference to media coverage are relatively few and far between in research published after the late 1990s.[29]

[26] Kahn and Goldberg 1991 and Smith 1997; Kahn (1994) finds variability between level of office (female senate candidates receive more horse race coverage than men, while there is not a difference for gubernatorial candidates).

[27] See, e.g., Atkeson and Krebs 2008 and Bystrom, Robertson, and Banwart 2001. Jalalzai (2006) finds that male candidates receive more horse race coverage than female candidates but does not find a statistically significant difference for competitive races, so the finding can be reasonably characterized as "no difference" because competitive races are the most interesting for this particular question.

[28] Diane Bystrom in Carroll and Fox 2010, 244. Bystrom differentiates the coverage of women candidates for the presidency in 2000 and 2008 as being less favorable to women than coverage patterns in gubernatorial and U.S. Senate races.

[29] A question more specific to my study is whether the media might treat the foibles of female candidates differently than the foibles of male candidates. Did the media cover Hillary Clinton's emotional moment in a more harmful manner than they covered John

It is interesting to consider what ongoing changes in the media environment might mean for female candidates. We are moving away from a
traditional model where information is mediated by a relatively small
group of potential sources to a more fragmented model, including cable,
Internet, and satellite radio programming. On the one hand, the nature of
the changing media marketplace makes it more likely that dramatic foibles and slip-ups by high-profile candidates will garner a flurry of coverage, at least briefly.[30] Gender may potentially have less to do with the
pattern of coverage, however, than how well the candidate is known, the
extremity of the behavior in question, and the existence of natural voids
in news availability that happen to leave room for coverage of such matters.[31] On the other hand, the new media model—a model that disproportionately rewards controversy and opinion-based commentary in a race
for rapidly shrinking audience shares—provides many avenues in which
extremely sexist comments can flourish. In an effort to gain "page hits"
on the Internet and viewers or listeners in increasingly fragmented cable
television and radio environments, controversy, drama, strident opinion,
and disparagement are common.[32] From Tucker Carlson's comments
about Hillary Clinton on MSNBC ("There's just something about her
that feels castrating, overbearing, and scary") to Rush Limbaugh's attacks on female candidates on the radio ("Mrs. Clinton's testicle lockbox

---

Boehner's (many) tearful displays? Was a tough Nancy Pelosi treated differently as a congressional leader by the media than a tough Trent Lott or a tough Newt Gingrich? Were the
media harder on Sarah Palin's or Michele Bachmann's gaffes than, say, Rick Perry's or Herman Cain's similar slip-ups? Was the coverage harsher, was it more frequent, or was there
no difference? Unfortunately, this is an area in which definitive evidence will necessarily be
elusive. For every isolated similarity in those cases, there are manifold differences between
the candidates and the situations they faced. Comparing the amount or type of coverage
between different candidates in different situations would be a fool's errand. As such, while
it is entirely possible that the media covers such situations differently, that hypothesis probably can never be tested.

[30] More mundane behaviors and lesser-known candidates are still likely to largely slip
under the media radar screen, as they always generally have.

[31] The foibles of Herman Cain and Rick Perry, for example, were certainly not treated
with kid gloves due to their gender in the new media environment; for the most part, they
seemed to be eviscerated by the media, widely and mercilessly. I expect that a woman candidate with similar liabilities and similarly tantalizing video footage would be likely to receive similarly harsh treatment in the current media environment.

[32] For example, during the 2010 election cycle, the gossip-oriented Web site Gawker.
com received over 200,000 page views in the hours following the publication of an anonymous account of an alleged sexual encounter with (unmarried) Delaware Senate candidate
Christine O'Donnell three years before; entitled, "I Had a One-Night Stand with Christine
O'Donnell," the source described O'Donnell as "aggressive," "intense," and a "cougar," and
photos of the candidate dressed in a revealing Halloween costume accompanied the article
(Nicole Allen, "Gawker Hits O'Donnell While She's Down," *Atlantic.com*, October 28,
2010).

is big enough for the entire Democrat hierarchy") and the other sexist comments made about Clinton, Sarah Palin, and other female candidates in the blogosphere and in other partisan sources throughout the election, it is clear that female candidates sometimes face extremely demeaning comments in this new media environment.[33]

Most cable programs, talk radio shows, and Web sites individually attract relatively few viewers; moreover, many of those viewers may already be inclined to think a particular way about the candidate in question or may be inured to the strong opinions of the hosts. From that perspective, the damage of sexist comments may be relatively contained. At the same time, insults can potentially take on a life of their own, especially if they get picked up and reported by the mainstream media or "go viral" more generally. How damaging is that likely to be for women on the campaign trail?

An interesting new study sheds some light on how women candidates fare when faced with sexist attacks in the media. In a creative Goldberg paradigm–type study sponsored by several groups focused on women in politics and conducted by Democratic political pollsters, online survey participants read about a House race between a fictional male candidate, Dan Jones, and a fictional female candidate, Jane Smith.[34] All respondents read a basic profile about each candidate. Respondents then registered their initial vote preference and, afterward, read two news stories. Negative but nonsexist criticisms against Dan Jones were outlined in the news story about him, while respondents read a news story with negative but nonsexist comments, moderately sexist comments, or highly sexist comments about Jane Smith.[35] One key finding from this study is that sexist attacks lower preference for the female candidate more than negative but nonsexist attacks.[36] Given that highly derogatory, sexist attacks

[33] Tucker Carlson, "Tucker," *MSNBC*, March 20, 2007. Rush Limbaugh's comment is cited in Emma Tom, "Singled Out by Sex for the Sleaziest Campaign Abuse," *The Australian*, September 18, 2008, 13.

[34] The White House Project 2002.

[35] The moderately sexist attack reports that unnamed people have been saying that she acted like an "ice queen," that she was a "mean girl" when anyone tried to get her to explain her vote, and that commentators remarked on her new hairstyle and designer shoes and dress. The highly sexist news story reports that, because she supported an expensive provision in a health care bill, a radio host commented that "she may be the most expensive prostitute in the history of prostitution. She may be easy, but she's not cheap." It cites another radio host who says that "Stupid Girl" describes the candidate pretty well.

[36] There were ultimately four experimental treatments in this study: Condition A, a moderately sexist story against Jane with a moderately negative story against Dan; Condition B, a moderately negative but nonsexist story against Jane with a moderately negative story against Dan; Condition C, a highly sexist news story about Jane with a highly negative news story against Dan; Condition D, a highly negative but nonsexist news story about Jane with a highly negative news story about Dan. As a result, not all potential comparisons can

do exist in the blogosphere and on the airwaves of cable and talk show radio—and given that the mainstream media outlets with much broader audiences sometimes report on those attacks—the findings of the study are a potential source for concern.

The study did not stop there, however: it also examined how candidate responses to such attacks affect the public. When respondents hear comments by Jane Smith calling the attacks sexist and inappropriate, she more than overcomes the losses among the public due to the sexist attacks. The key conclusion from this study—tellingly called the "Name It, Change It" study—is that publicly identifying and criticizing sexist attacks eliminates their effectiveness. There is still more work to be done on this topic to isolate exactly which kinds of responses minimize the effects of sexist attacks, but the implication for female candidates is that openly criticizing sexist attacks should be a critical component of their campaign arsenal.

Given that there are many reasons to believe that sexist comments will crop up in a fragmented media environment, the results from the "Name It, Change It" study provide a measure of optimism that such attacks will not necessarily hurt female candidates. Although the study finds that candidates themselves can be effective messengers for responses, it may also be that the media can serve that role, perhaps even more effectively. Despite the media's culpability in perpetuating the idea that women are at an electoral disadvantage without questioning it (or, perhaps, because of that tendency), many news articles today directly address gendered aspects of campaigns, including the possibility that some media reports might have been sexist in their coverage. Perhaps it is not just women candidates who can reverse their fortunes by explicitly identifying an opponent's attack as being sexist; it may be that the media can also perform that same function.

The bottom line is that my study did not find that the public is naturally predisposed to penalize women candidates; however that does not mean that women candidates might not still face harsher scrutiny by the media, which could then negatively affect public opinion through that mechanism. That being said, aside from some fairly unified evidence regarding differential "hair, husbands, and hemlines" coverage patterns, the findings on the topic of media coverage do not lead to the conclusion that women candidates are at a clear disadvantage in the media, or that any such differences would necessarily translate into lower support by the

---

be made (e.g., it is impossible to directly compare whether highly sexist attacks are worse for the female candidate than moderately sexist attacks, because the degree of negativity launched against the male candidate is also varied between those conditions. The attacks themselves are also fundamentally different—the attacks consider entirely different issues, moreover, in one, the attack is made by unnamed "people" while in the other the attack is made by radio hosts.

public for women candidates, at least in the current era. If women candidates were at a systematic and substantial disadvantage with the media as compared to male candidates in recent decades, we presumably would have seen far stronger, and far more consistent, evidence of it than we have in the recent literature on the topic.

3. A Glass Ceiling?

The parity problem operates at two levels: women are underrepresented as a percentage of legislators, and they have been underrepresented (or unrepresented entirely) among political executives. My study focuses largely on women running at the legislative level. That is a logical area of focus because most women running in races throughout the United States are running for legislative seats or seats in some kind of local multimember body (school boards, city council, etc.), and because candidates for executive office are likely to make that move after spending some time at the legislative level. But, as discussed in chapter 2, many scholars make the argument that winning executive office—whether it be the presidency or perhaps even governorships—can be even more disproportionately difficult for women than winning legislative seats.[37] As such, even if the parity problem could somehow be resolved at the legislative level, women might potentially continue to be unrepresented at the executive level.

There tend to be two dominant hypotheses regarding the causes of the underrepresentation of women in executive political office. The first is that because of the underrepresentation of women at lower levels of office, there are consequently fewer potential women candidates for the highest level of office. That is typically referred to as the "pipeline" problem and is almost certainly at least part of the explanation for why there has not been a woman occupant in the Oval Office to date, and perhaps why there have been only thirty-four women governors in total to date. The second hypothesis tends to revolve around concerns pertaining to gender stereotypes: specifically, that the public has expectations of executives that are different from those of legislators and that these expectations tend to be disproportionately challenging for women candidates. Scholars speculate that those expectations are more masculine (strong defender, tough, decisive, etc.) than their expectations of legislators (able to make decisions collectively, cares about the people in their districts, etc.). If the public perceives women to generally be weaker on those kinds of agentic traits, women will therefore have a tougher time winning at the executive level.[38]

My study provides some good news on that front: specifically, that women legislative candidates are not viewed by the general public as

[37] See, e.g., Schroedel and Godwin 2005; Dolan 1997; Kenski and Falk 2004.
[38] See, e.g., Murray 2010; Paul and Smith 2008; Rossenwasser and Dean 1989; Smith, Paul, and Paul 2007. Similar logic underlies Lawless 2004.

being weaker on the kinds of agentic traits (toughness, leadership ability, ability to handle the international crises, and so on) that had been feared by some scholars to hold women back from executive positions. Moreover, I do not find that women are penalized disproportionately for acting in a tough manner, as presidents and presidential candidates often need to do.[39] It surely would be a problem for women executives if they faced a double bind vis-à-vis the public for acting as a tough executive, yet I see no evidence that women leaders are in that tough spot. In my study, those questions pertained to candidates who were currently running for legislative office. However, my results still represent good news with reference to a possible glass ceiling issue: not only does my analysis provide evidence that gender is not looming large in the eyes of Americans when thinking about legislative candidates in the current day, but it is also important because legislators are a critical part of the pipeline to gubernatorial roles and the presidency.[40]

With respect to public views on presidential candidates specifically, I am able to address this issue to some extent in my study design. I do so with an admittedly imperfect measure, consisting of a rating regarding whether the (legislative) candidate would be an effective U.S. president about ten years from now.[41] In my data, I find little evidence that the public overall is evaluating future presidential candidates differently in terms of gender, aside from the fact that acting tough seems to especially benefit women in terms of perceptions that they would be good presidents. Those are promising, though not conclusive, findings with respect to the glass ceiling issue for the presidency. There is some indication from my data that another factor, generational change, may be in play with reference to the presidency—that is, that older people are less inclined to view women candidates as promising presidential candidates than are younger people. I discuss that matter in the last chapter as actually providing some cause for optimism regarding women and the White House moving forward.

---

[39] See, e.g., Lawless 2004 and Falk and Kenski 2006. Note that results in the next chapter show that there is some evidence that older individuals may be inclined to stereotype women candidates negatively on a few very specific dimensions (discussed later in this chapter) but there is no relationship in the overall population.

[40] Women in executive positions could potentially face a double bind while legislative women do not, but the theoretical mechanism by which such a difference would be observed is not clear. If anything, given that tough behavior is more likely to be prescribed for executive rather than legislative office, a woman in a legislative office acting tough would arguably result in the most negative public reaction, and we do not see that.

[41] The specific question wording is: "How good of a job do you think that the candidate would probably do with the following," with "be an effective U.S. President about 10 years from now" as one of five questions in that series. The 7-point scale was anchored with "a poor job" and "an excellent job."

It is still possible that the act of actively running for the presidency (or perhaps running for a governor in states without prior women executives) could make the public view a candidate in a different, more gendered light owing to "token status." The mere fact of being among the first women to attempt or to achieve something may highlight gender in a manner that may put women candidates in more of a "lady" light than a "leader" perspective, thus encouraging the application of more traditional female stereotypes by the public. I do not see evidence of this dynamic in the public overall, but the reality is that my experiment cannot replicate token status especially well. Thus, to the extent that being a token rather than one of many might increase the use of stereotypes, it is important to be cautious with respect to the degree to which my data can fully bear on the glass ceiling issue.

4. Incumbency Advantage

At first glance, incumbency effects would appear to be an obvious source of the gender imbalance in representation. Expressing a commonly held view in the field, Dolan deems incumbency to be "perhaps the most significant system barrier to increasing the number of women officeholders."[42] The benefits of office are high enough that legislators, especially at the national level, infrequently choose to vacate their offices voluntarily (in 2008, e.g., only 7 percent of sitting U.S. House members chose not to run for reelection). And the benefits of office—from name recognition to franking privileges to staff support to pork to constituency service, and more—help to ensure that incumbents get reelected at very high rates (generally above 90 percent in the U.S. House—often as high as 98 percent, although 2010 was unusually low at 85 percent), and with very comfortable electoral margins to boot, in most cases. Incumbents are extremely hard to displace in the U.S. House; that is also true, albeit to a somewhat lesser degree, in races for the U.S. Senate (reelection rates have ranged from 79–96 percent in Senate elections in recent decades) and state legislative office. If the potential for improving the parity problem rests in women winning open seats, but seats only rarely open up, then significant strides toward parity will necessarily be slow.

The logic of the incumbency advantage being a key source of the parity problem, however, ultimately rests on a sufficient number of women being willing to run for office. After all, if seats open up, but women do not run for them, the parity problem will not change. With interesting data to leverage on this matter, Thad Kousser (2005) finds that states with term limits do not increase the percentage of women elected to of-

[42] Dolan 2004, 52. See also Alexander and Andersen 1993; Darcy, Welch, and Clark 1994; Carroll 1994; Seltzer, Newman, and Leighton 1997.

fice. This suggests that the problem, at least in the short term, resides in something deeper than incumbency. While the lack of open seats would be impeding women from achieving greater parity *if* they were willing to run in sufficient numbers, the much bigger problem is that not enough women are inclined to throw their hats into the ring.

5. Recruitment Bias

A few people have been on a political trajectory since birth, but for many it is not until much later in life they come to the realization that they would be good political leaders and that they would have a reasonable chance at winning an election. This realization tends to be planted, or at least bolstered, by encouragement from others. If men are encouraged more often than comparable women to run for office, then recruitment bias could be a source of the parity problem.

Recent studies have found recruitment bias that ultimately serves to encourage a disproportionate number of men to run for office. In their survey of people who are in professions that tend to function as pipelines to political careers, Jennifer Lawless and Richard Fox found that women are 16 percent less likely to be encouraged to run by a political actor, and they also demonstrated that recruitment attempts by electoral gatekeepers significantly increase the likelihood of a candidate (male or female) running for office.[43] They also found that women are less likely to be recruited with repeat attempts by the same individual, to face recruitment attempts by multiple people, or to be encouraged by friends, family members, and colleagues to run for office.[44]

Taking on the conventional wisdom that strong party leadership enhances the descriptive representation of women, Sanbonmatsu (2006) utilizes a multimethod approach (multiple surveys, in-depth interviews, and time-series, cross-sectional analysis of gender and representation in states across the United States) and finds that greater party involvement in nominations tends to result in a lower proportion of female nominees and state legislators. She also finds that many party leaders believe that women are at an electoral disadvantage with voters. Her results suggest that party leadership can be a source of gender bias rather than a remedy for it, particularly in some less progressive states where party leaders may be more apt to conclude that women candidates are not a good fit for their districts.

The literature is not entirely unified on this issue; Barbara Burrell, in particular, concludes that parties are not "gatekeepers" that prevent

---

[43] Note that in assessing the effects of political recruitment, they wisely controlled for a variety of demographic measures and other measures, including some related to candidate quality, such as political interest, political participation, and political knowledge.

[44] Lawless and Fox 2010, 167.

women from running for office but instead have become positive forces for the recruitment and support of female candidates.[45] But the Sanbonmatsu and the Lawless and Fox findings regarding gender differences in recruitment suggest that some party leaders and elected officials do have lingering concerns about public receptivity to female leaders. This is not hard to believe; after all, the conventional wisdom has been pervasive enough among other political practitioners, so it is likely that at least some party power brokers assume that women candidates, all else being equal, are at a disadvantage vis-à-vis the public. Party leaders, after all, tend to be devoted to the act of winning elections for their party and will typically be loath to waste limited resources or risk seats in order to support candidates whom they perceive to be electorally problematic. By showing that women candidates are not inherently weaker than their male counterparts as far as the national public is concerned, the findings in this book can potentially help to alleviate some misperceptions held by those who have the potential to encourage women to run for office.

6. The "Ambition Gap" (and an Underlying Cause of It, the "Confidence Gap")

Are women less likely to want to hold high office and to want to try to do what it takes to get there? And, if so, why is that the case? Lawless and Fox (2010) explore these questions and find substantial cause for concern. It is not possible to do full justice to their rich and nuanced findings here, but a critical bottom-line finding from their research is that, even within the most promising pool of potential political leaders, women are far less likely than comparable men to have the ambition to seek office.[46]

In particular, Lawless and Fox found that far more eligible men than eligible women candidates (about one-third more) have ever considered running for office.[47] Among those who had considered running for office, only three-quarters as many women as men actually ran for office.[48] These relationships persist even with a wide array of controls and cannot be explained away by demographics or by candidate quality indicators, such as political interest, participation, or political knowledge.[49] Combined with the fact that women tend to be underrepresented in the professions that tend to form the most promising foundations for politi-

[45] Burrell 1996, 99.

[46] Lawless and Fox (2010, 177–78) focused on lawyers, business leaders, professors, college administrators, and political activists for their sample of eligible candidates.

[47] Lawless and Fox 2010, 50–52.

[48] Lawless and Fox 2010, 50–52.

[49] In fact, women in this professionally elite population are more likely to follow the news about politics than their male counterparts (Lawless and Fox 2010, 48).

cal careers, the lower ambition of women to run for office constitutes a major source of the parity problem.[50]

In their work, Lawless and Fox peel back the onion to identify the primary causes of this gendered "ambition gap." The recruitment differences mentioned in the preceding section constituted one of the layers; however, while they find that recruitment is part of the problem, they also find that a substantial portion of the ambition gap exists independently of it.[51] Of particular relevance given the analysis in the present book, Lawless and Fox argue that "some of the most important findings" of their book involve their identification of a critical confidence gap among candidates, which contributes substantially to the ambition gap. In particular, they find that potential women candidates are much less likely than potential male candidates to believe they have the skills to win an election and that they will be able to win over the public.[52] They also find that both men and women doubt that women, overall, face an equal shot at winning elections.[53]

At an individual level, women question their own ability to win an office they seek at a much higher rate than do men: Lawless and Fox found that 37 percent of male respondents view themselves as likely or very likely to win a race for the first office they could seek, versus just 25 percent of female respondents (the authors point out that these results might actually understate the true extent of the difference, because women are also more likely than men to envision lower-level offices, especially local offices, as the first office they might seek).[54] Controlling for a variety of demographic, candidate quality, and recruitment attempts measures, Lawless and Fox find a significant relationship between candidate sex, self-perceived qualifications, and likelihood of considering a candidacy. They find that women's greater propensity to think they are personally unqualified for office, combined with the fact that they are even less likely to run than men who have similarly unconfident perceptions of their own qualifications for office, significantly lowers the likelihood of women considering a candidacy. In short, women seem to hold themselves to higher standards than do men when considering whether to run.

---

[50] See Lawless and Fox 2010, 30–32, for a discussion of the proportions of women in the pipeline professions. See p. 164 regarding the role of the ambition gap.

[51] They cleverly modeled an improbable world in which women are twice as likely as men to be recruited by others to run for office (i.e., 43 percent of men vs. 100 percent of women and found that, even under those implausibly favorable recruitment conditions, fewer potential women candidates (52%) than their male counterparts (57%) would consider running for office (Lawless and Fox 2010, 148).

[52] Lawless and Fox 2010, 112–35.

[53] Lawless and Fox 2010, 115–17.

[54] Lawless and Fox 2010, 117.

It is plausible to hypothesize that women may be less likely to run because they expect that the public, on balance, is holding them to higher standards because of their gender. According to Lawless and Fox, "Some women's self-doubts can be linked to their perceptions of a sexist political environment dominated by a masculinized ethos."[55] The scholars reveal important indications that most eligible women candidates buy into the conventional view that it is harder for them to win than it is for male candidates. A stunning 87 percent of women (and 76 percent of men) in their pool of eligible candidates in 2008 believe that it is not as easy for a woman to be elected to high-level office as a man.[56]

During in-depth interviews, the scholars also found that a quarter of eligible women candidates spontaneously volunteered that they believe that women need better qualifications than men in order to have a chance at electoral success.[57] Multiple women in the Lawless and Fox study were cited as mentioning permutations of the "twice as good rule" ("the unspoken requirement that women be twice as good as men").[58] The authors go on to point out:

> When we asked respondents . . . whether they believe women face significant gender bias in the electoral arena, the levels of perceived sexism were striking. The examples of bias identified in our interviews ranged from claims of overt bias against women at the polls (a phenomenon that aggregate-level studies of vote shares and electoral outcomes do not substantiate) to subtler instances of gender stereotyping. . . . An overwhelming majority of respondents, across professions, do not think that women and men have an equal chance of succeeding when running for high elective office.[59]

They conclude:

> Comments from the respondents, coupled with the data collected from the 2008 survey, indicate that perceptions of a sexist environment convey to women heightened levels of electoral competition and a more challenging campaign trail to traverse. These circumstances lead many women to conclude—perhaps rightfully so—that they have to be more qualified than men to compete successfully against them. Because of the higher standards imposed on women—both internally and exter-

[55] Lawless and Fox 2010, 134–35.
[56] Lawless and Fox 2010, 124.
[57] Lawless and Fox 2010, 126.
[58] Lawless and Fox 2010, 124–26, 167.
[59] Lawless and Fox 2010, 124.

nally—they are more likely than men to conclude that they are not qualified to run for office.[60]

My analysis is unequivocal that this is a misperception on the part of candidates. It may very well affect whether women decide to run for office, and is a misperception that should be corrected.

It is highly problematic that the conventional wisdom has permeated the views of high-powered women to such a remarkable degree. Given the many significant difficulties that necessarily exist for winning a campaign regardless of gender, a pervasive belief that being a woman is an additional substantial hurdle they face very likely contributes to the parity problem, by making a run for office seem less appealing and unlikely to succeed. But compared to the other potential causes of the ambition gap—many of which are deeply rooted in cultural and structural factors that are likely to be quite resistant to change—this particular issue should be relatively easy to fix. The very good news from my study is that we do not somehow have to figure out how to change the views or reactions of the general public in order to give women a fighting chance in politics. That would be a very tall order with, at best, only a long-term hope for a solution. To address this portion of the parity problem, we simply have to correct a common misperception that is disseminated by many political elites. It will not solve the entire problem of representation inequities for women to be sure, but it is certainly an important step to take.

[60] Lawless and Fox 2010, 126; see also Fox and Lawless 2011 for an initial attempt to consider how candidate perceptions of gender bias and personal skills might affect candidates' beliefs about their own qualifications; they do not, however, analyze the key dependent variable of relevance here, which is the decision to run for office. Fox and Lawless argue, "Certainly, women's perceptions of a biased electoral arena and heightened levels of political competition may depress their interest in running for office," but they do not analyze that relationship directly (see pp. 68–69, n. 13).

CHAPTER 9

A Bright Future for Women in Politics

> One of my favorite [congratulatory] messages was written
> on stationary headed with an Eleanor Roosevelt quote:
> "The future belongs to those who believe in the beauty of
> their dreams." What a wonderful sentiment! And what a
> wonderful and exhilarating time to be a woman in
> America, where there are no limits to our futures, no limit
> to the beauty of our dreams.
>
> —NANCY PELOSI, ON HER ELECTION
> AS HOUSE SPEAKER[1]

My results come together to suggest a very promising future for women in politics. The key challenge to resolving representational inequities, then—as many scholars have argued long before me, and scholars long after me are sure to continue to argue—is in encouraging more women to run. Although this dynamic is not going to be changed with any single, simple solution—most of its causes are too deeply rooted within society, culture, and individuals to be so easily rectified—I argue here that a recognition that the public at large is entirely willing to support female leaders may help to give at least some women more confidence to run for office and other people more cause to encourage their ambitions.

This chapter also takes up a question that may be looming in readers' minds: To what degree might the public's receptivity to female leaders represent a change from a darker day for women in politics? As I discuss, there are many indications from the world at large that suggest that the public is significantly more receptive to women in politics now than it once was. I leverage my data to the extent possible on this matter and present some suggestive evidence that the process of generational replacement has had a beneficial effect on women in politics. This provides even greater reasons for optimism regarding the future, particularly with reference to the possibility that a glass ceiling may exist for women who seek the presidency.

[1] Pelosi 2008, 173.

A Bright Day for Women Who Decide to Run for Office

For women who want to make a difference in politics and who are willing to do what it takes to run for office, the very good news from my study is that a pervasive concern held by many potential women candidates can be eliminated. This study found that women candidates do not face a tougher road to winning over the American public than their male counterparts, as many had long feared was the case. Women do not need to be "twice as good" as men to do well in politics. Women do not start on more tenuous ground, and they are not more likely to alienate the public with missteps along the way. This research should give them more confidence that their first slip-up is unlikely to be their last; or, at the very least, that their slip-ups and imperfections would be similarly damaging for their male counterparts. None of the behaviors tested in this study—crying, getting angry, acting tough, displaying a lack of empathy, or engaging in knowledge gaffes—hurt female candidates significantly more than male candidates. The public appears to be receptive to the idea of female political leadership, and that is very good news, indeed.

Thus, women who might want to run for office—and anyone who wants to support a woman candidate in her quest for office—should proceed with the knowledge that being a woman is not a liability on the campaign trail. In fact, female candidates who are new to politics should feel confident that they have an advantage relative to their male counterparts: this study did not find any negative stereotypes about them among the public, while they still benefit from a few isolated positive ones. Specifically, these results suggest that inexperienced female candidates seem to be able to more effectively claim the mantle of "outsider" than their inexperienced male counterparts by benefiting from perceptions of having traits such as greater honesty and compassion that tend to be attached to ordinary women rather than politicians. It is not as if inexperience directly gives women an advantage in winning campaigns relative to similarly inexperienced men; after all, my results show that the benefits conferred to women rest in individual issues and traits rather than in more favorable impressions of women candidates overall. But my results imply that women new to politics may be able to craft effective strategies tailored to their perceived strengths, which could potentially give them a leg up initially, perhaps especially during eras where being an "outsider" is advantageous.

Yet my results show that once a woman is in office, those beneficial stereotypes fade. Aside from seeming slightly more intelligent to voters than men, women politicians who have held office quickly become "politicians" in the eyes of the public. They suffer no negative stereotypes that

are associated with their womanhood, but once they become more established political figures, then they enjoy little particular benefit from being
a woman. From the perspective of feminism, this should be seen as tremendous progress. It appears that women leaders are judged more as
leaders than as ladies by most people on the range of personal traits and
candidate behaviors measured in this study. Yet, from the perspective of
those who would like to see women having an advantage in the electoral
arena, it may be bittersweet that the disproportionate benefits that new
female candidates begin with seem to disappear rather quickly as their
careers progress.

Thus, the explanation for the gender imbalance in representation does
not appear to rest with the public. As the discussion in the previous chapter indicates, the most critical problem seems to be that women do not
run for office in sufficient numbers.

Encouraging Women Who Doubt They Can Win

The research in this book indicates that a key step that should be taken
by those who care about improving the representation of women in politics is an informational one: specifically, an effort to ensure that all
women have accurate information about the nature of the challenges associated with running for office. Women candidates and potential women
candidates, their handlers, their potential supporters, journalists, parties,
and other candidate-supporting organizations need to understand that
being a woman does not belong on the long list of challenges that candidates face when running for office. Most potential women candidates
believe that, if only because of their gender, it will be harder for them to
win a campaign than it will be for a man, yet no evidence was found in
this study to lend credence to those concerns. As such, to encourage more
women to run for office, misinformation about the hurdles faced by
women candidates should be cleared off the decks.

As noted in the previous chapter, recent studies have shown that part
of the reason that women do not run is that they are not recruited to run
by political power brokers as often as men.[2] Given the pervasive nature
of the conventional wisdom regarding greater hurdles for women vis-à-
vis the public, it is reasonable to believe that at least some electoral gatekeepers believe it as well; this may help to explain at least part of the recruitment bias. As such, it is important that political power brokers
understand that a choice to support a promising female candidate is not
an inherently risky move. With the knowledge that the American public

[2] Lawless and Fox 2010; see also Sanbonmatsu 2006.

is far more receptive to female political leadership than many had feared, people in a position to encourage women to run might feel more empowered to do so. Ironically, rather than assuming that the public might not support a female candidate, political power brokers should try to emulate the public and evaluate candidates as leaders more than as ladies.

As a starting point for eliminating the influence of the conventional wisdom about gendered double standards, journalists need to stop perpetuating inaccurate information on this topic. As readers have presumably come to understand through the many quotes and headlines that reside throughout this book, the degree to which the media have embraced the conventional wisdom is truly stunning. It is only rarely questioned and is invariably discussed as being a well-proven fact. At the same time, the media have also increasingly done important work by discussing candidate gender directly and by identifying potentially sexist aspects of some media coverage or campaign dynamics in a manner that can generate useful consideration by media consumers. As with its treatment of so many topics, the media have been doing critical work by generating necessary discussion, but they need to be more careful about presenting definitive conclusions on topics that have not yet been rigorously studied.[3]

Similarly, consultants need to stop repeating the conventional wisdom if candidates are to take it less seriously. Much of what occurs between consultants and candidates takes place behind closed doors. Yet this book presents enough on-the-record quotes from consultants who openly perpetuate inaccurate views about women candidates that it is reasonable to think that at least some misinformation is flowing to candidates through the experts they hire to advise them on how to win campaigns.

Beyond their critical role in candidate recruitment, parties are key conduits for training and supporting many of the men and women who are likely to run for office. It is essential that they use accurate information to that end. Given that local party organizations tend to be the key contact

---

[3] The media's handling of other topics in American politics may be instructive on this matter. For a long time, the media perpetuated the conventional wisdom that negative campaigning harms voter turnout. By the late 1990s and early 2000s, the vast bulk of academic research on the topic did not support that perspective, but still as of 2005 the media's perpetuation of the conventional wisdom persisted, with about two-thirds of the hundreds of stories about the topic inaccurately characterizing the dynamic (Brooks 2006). In recent years, however, the media appears to be handling the topic of negativity and turnout at least somewhat more responsibly. John Geer, a scholar who has studied campaign tone extensively, agrees that progress, albeit slow progress, has been made in reporting about the topic, although he notes that the top-tier media sources seem to have generally updated their reporting on the matter more accurately than lower-tier media sources, which still sometimes tend to rely upon the outdated and overturned views (email exchange with John Geer, July 2012).

points for personal interactions with candidates and national and state party organizations tend to be key sources of candidate funding, it is critical that party leaders throughout the ranks (from the national level on down to local units) understand that the American public is no less receptive to women candidates than to men candidates.

Finally, other organizations that work with candidates need to make sure they do not present an inaccurate account to women about the role that gender plays in campaigns. There are many groups that work specifically with potential women candidates that tend to be key conduits of information for the candidates with whom they work. Among these organizations are groups like the White House Project, the Women's Campaign Forum, the Women's Campaign Fund, the National Women's Political Caucus, Emily's List, the National Federation of Republican Women, WISH List (Women in the Senate and House), She Should Run, the Women's Campaign School at Yale, and the Ready to Run Campaign Training program offered by Rutgers' Center for American Women and Politics at the Eagleton Institute. It is not a given that all of these actors will necessarily work to dispel the conventional wisdom, however, even if they are presented with direct evidence that it is inaccurate. Groups focused on women candidates may potentially be able to generate more publicity, more financial support, and more interest from potential candidates if they overstate the challenges facing women on the campaign trail. Similarly, campaign consultants who want to build reputations for helping women win races might sometimes be tempted to misrepresent the hurdles involved for women when pitching the value of the services they offer. And journalists will have a much harder time wrapping stories around a frame of equal treatment for women candidates than around the much juicer frames of unfair differences; after all, journalists need to generate readership, and the conflict-oriented spin of the latter type of frame fits into typical news values far better than the more responsible approach. To be part of the solution rather than part of the problem, however, any temptation to overplay the challenges facing women candidates relative to their male counterparts needs to be resisted by all of these actors, and by scholars as well.

And once women have made the decision to run for office, I would hypothesize that they might be more likely to run interesting, meaningful, less stressful campaigns if they do not let consultants and others convince them that they need special handling and need to behave (or not behave) in specific ways because of their gender. I hope findings like those in this book may, perhaps, allow more women politicians to focus less on what the public thinks about them as ladies and more on what the public thinks of them as leaders, and the particular strengths they have to offer in this regard. At a minimum, the knowledge that the public does not hold them to higher standards might make the process of campaigning more enjoyable for women and less fraught with concern about unusually harsh consequences resulting from imperfections on the campaign trail.

A Change over Time?

Given that women leaders were still a shocking aberration to the norm of male leadership until not so long ago, how can it be the case that female candidates are in such a seemingly equal position regarding public opinion now? Few people half a century ago probably would have imagined that just a handful of decades later, women candidates could win the public's confidence just as effectively as their male counterparts. Some kind of change has likely been in play. How was that possible?

In her memoir about her time in politics and as the first governor of Vermont, Madeleine Kunin, posits that women political leaders were initially treated differently by people in large part because of their rarity:[4]

> A woman's face in a man's role was still startling, an aberration, and when women play formerly male parts, we go through an unconscious process of translation, like learning a new language. There is an instinctive effort to find familiar words in the language we know. Looking at a woman in a man's role, we focus on the fact that it is a "she" and not a "he." Her neckline, her shoes, the timbre of her voice, her posture, each of her female and male qualities are assessed against standards we know, silently and perhaps unknowingly. The female politician is a new work of art just coming into focus. An element of sexual tension exists: the strong woman playing the part of a strong man is a new variant of the male-female paradigm. Or is it? A female politician conveys an element of disguise, for there is a suspicion that underneath her masculine behavior we would discover a soft and vulnerable woman.
>
> The female politician is unexpected; her presence provokes a brief digression during which the public wanders off into internal musings about how this woman is like a man and yet not like a man. Does ambition fit her, or is it awkward, even unseemly? These distractions become significant when the woman herself cannot be heard or seen for who she really is. Then gender becomes extra baggage, something to be lugged around, adding to the weight of the usual questions and controversies that beleaguer every politician.[5]

---

[4] Kunin began her political career in Vermont state government in 1972 and served as governor of Vermont from 1984–89.

[5] Kunin 1994, 204–5.

In this respect, Kunin believed that her own presence in a gubernatorial role, and that of other women, could help "begin the critical transformation from the traditional male image of political leadership into a female one."[6] The image of political leadership has been changed yet further since her time in office, as women have ascended to a range of different leadership roles for the first time and multiple times thereafter. Beyond elected leaders, women have also risen in greater frequency to nonelected political positions of great authority: of particular note, there had been no female secretary of state prior to 1997, but three out of the past four holders of this position have been women. Enough women have served in leadership positions at most levels of government that politicians no longer surprise voters by simply being women. A new language is thus no longer required; having seen many examples of strong, tough, empathetic female political leaders in their lifetimes, most people probably have available a mental category—a subtype—available for political women. The findings of my study suggest that perhaps this is a subtype which deemphasizes the gender differences assumed to exist for ordinary women and, in contrast, emphasizes the attributes associated with political leaders, especially for women who have held office for any length of time.

Governor Kunin also argues that the increasing presence of women leaders changes the culture of politics for women in more subtle ways. When asked what it was like to work for a female governor, one of her commissioners answered, "No more little jokes about women; not even the deference paid to women in that lovely, gentlemanly way. Nobody does that in state government anymore. You just walk into a room and you realize what the difference is. Nobody dares make even those wonderful, warm statements about a woman being in charge, or a woman's opinion. It is just now taken for granted, and it really is different."[7] The commissioner was speaking mostly about the environment within government, but it is easy to see how that ordinariness of women's leadership would exist in the public sphere as well. Less often would female candidates be treated as tokens or aberrations in public settings.

Women will not be tokens in American politics, at least at the legislative level, again: the genie of female leadership will not go back in the bottle. The fact that a candidate is a woman is not the oddity, problem, or all-defining characteristic that it may once have been. Of course, beyond politics, society itself has changed tremendously in recent decades: one does not need to watch too many episodes of *Mad Men*—or consume too many pop culture remnants, biographies, research papers, or statistics regarding the public's views of women's roles in the 1970s, 1960s,

[6] Kunin 1994, 204.
[7] Kunin 1994, 362.

1950s, or earlier—to recognize that gender equality has improved greatly in relatively short order in society as a whole. It also does not take too much of a leap to believe that there could be some lingering effects of sexism, perhaps especially among older generations. This brings up a looming question that must remain in any reader's mind: do the findings in this book reflect improvements over time in the equality of the public's views toward male and female candidates? Or was the public always more equitable toward women candidates than the conventional wisdom would suggest?

Analyzing the Influence of Generational Change

To directly address the extent to which public views have changed over time, we would need to have the intent of the study hidden from study participants.[8] We would also want to be able to compare public reactions to female and male candidates today versus public views in previous decades (in a perfect world, we would examine the views of the same individuals in a long-term panel study to see how individuals changed over time). But Time's arrow is the bane of every public opinion scholar. Regardless of the fascinating nature of the results we gather today, we cannot go back in the past to collect comparable data. Unless a researcher happened to be interested in the same question—and used replicable methodology to test it—we have to make an educated guess about the degree to which the public or individuals have changed over time. With this study, we now have a baseline about stereotypes and double standards for female candidates that scholars will have the opportunity to return to in the future to assess change moving forward, but that does not help us in looking backward from where we are now. Data of that nature just do not exist on these questions to look back in time from the current day. Although we lack perfect data to draw firm conclusions, there is some information from past scholarship, from the world at large, and indirectly from within my data that suggests that there has been an improvement over time in the political climate for female candidates.

The research about candidate gender stereotypes in the 1970s and 1980s was fairly unified in finding at least some negative stereotypes about female candidates (Kahn's findings being a notable exception). This pattern of results suggests that fairly significant gendered dynamics may have been in play at the time, contrary to what I find is the case today. It is important to note, however, that there was never much solid evidence

---

[8] Otherwise, observed changes over time might merely reflect changing social norms associated with acknowledging preference for male candidates over time.

that such dynamics put female candidates at a marked disadvantage on Election Day, even back then.

Additionally, important changes regarding female candidates have been noted by those who are out in the trenches. Like Madeleine Kunin, many female politicians have noted the immense changes they have observed in the political environment for women candidates in recent decades. According to Senator Barbara Boxer, her womanhood has changed from being a liability on the campaign trail to a strength. Boxer notes that when she first ran for county supervisor in 1971, "You never mentioned being a woman. You never brought it up. You hoped nobody noticed."[9] By 1992, she felt that it was entirely different ballgame. In her 1994 book, *Strangers in the Senate: Politics and the New Revolution of Women in America*, Boxer recounts some of the enormous changes for women politicians she experienced throughout that era:

> In 1972, to be a woman in politics was almost a masochistic experience, a series of setbacks without a lot of rewards. If I was strong in my expression of the issues, I was strident; if I expressed any emotion as I spoke about the environment or the problems of the mentally ill, I was soft; if I spoke about economics I had to be perfect, and then I ran the risk of being "too much like a man." . . .
>
> Any woman who survived a run for public office in those years learned how to take the hits over and over again, and if she was lucky, she learned not to take it personally. On some level she had to know that this was the stuff of pioneers, although it certainly wasn't considered in that way back then. Now, with 20 years' experience, I *know* it was the stuff of pioneers.
>
> In 1992, it was different. Being a woman running for public office in 1992 was a distinct advantage. The polls showed it. "Put a woman against a man in the California Senate race in 1992 and all else being equal, she wins," said my pollster, Mark Mellman . . . in 1992 being a woman was absolutely a help.[10]

Senator Boxer goes on to credit this shift in significant part to different formative experiences across the generations. She argues that when she ran for public office in 1972, most voters had experienced their formative cultural and political years prior to the 1960s, which meant that she was "not the kind of woman [she] should have been" in most voters' eyes.[11] Boxer recounts that in the 1970s her own mother-in-law couldn't understand why she wanted to run for office, recalling that "she was slightly

[9] Barbara Boxer as quoted in Whitney et al. 2001, 102.
[10] Boxer 1994, 73–74.
[11] Boxer 1994, 76.

embarrassed that I wanted to work at all."[12] In contrast, by the time she was running in the 1990s, many of her voters had been socialized after the massive social changes for women of the 1960s and 1970s; as a result, voters had a very different vision of what a woman could do in the public sphere. In 1994, when she wrote her book, women composed only 11 percent of the House and 7 percent of the Senate; one can only imagine how different it was for Senator Boxer to run in 2010 versus 1972.

Looking within my data, there is indeed some suggestive evidence in favor of this notion that generational differences matter, particularly with respect to the highest level of office. While the focus of my book has been on how the public, overall, regards male and female candidates, it is interesting to consider generational issues by examining whether older people might differ from younger people in their views. It is interesting, in particular, to analyze the control group data by age cohort, grouping individuals roughly by the dimensions suggested by Senator Boxer's impression of the public's change over time—that is, individuals ages sixty years or older, who were socialized before the 1960s, versus those who are younger—to see if there are big differences in their views on female candidates.

The candidates in my scenario are running for the U.S. Senate, and on the core measures relevant for such a race (including favorability and likely effectiveness in the Senate) I do not find evidence that older people penalize women candidates disproportionately. However, I do find suggestive evidence that older people penalize female candidates on likely effectiveness in the presidency ten years down the road (they rate women .7 lower than they rate men, $p = .06$), whereas younger people rate male and female candidates the same on this dimension. Furthermore, "ability to handle an international crisis" (which is a factor that should be more critical at the executive than at legislative levels) appears to be a contributing factor to this result: again, younger people do not differ in their assessments on that measure on the basis of candidate gender, but older people rate women candidates .8 lower than men candidates ($p = .04$). Older people are a relatively small portion of the public (they constitute 21 percent of the sample) so the penalty they assess is not enough to penalize women candidates in a manner that results in a significant difference for the public overall at this juncture; however, it may help to explain why women have had trouble breaking into the presidency in past decades and provides a sense that generational replacement may possibly allow female candidates to have a much better chance at the presidency moving forward.

Drilling down further into the data, however, it becomes clear that there is an interesting option for women presidential candidates to do

[12] Boxer 1994, 75.

well even with older voters: they can act in a tough manner. Although older people are less likely at the outset to believe that women are tough enough to be effective as president or to handle an international crisis, this assessment changes dramatically—indeed, it flips—once they are provided with information that a female candidate is tough. Specifically, older people go from rating control group women candidates as significantly lower than male candidates on likely presidential effectiveness (3.2 vs. 3.9) to rating tough women candidates significantly *higher* than tough men candidates on the same measure (4.5 vs. 3.8). Similarly, on ability to handle an international crisis, older people flip from thinking the control group male candidate would handle it better than the comparable female candidate (4.3 vs. 3.5) to thinking that the tough woman candidate would be better than the tough man candidate (4.4 vs. 4.0); again, younger people do not rate the tough male and female candidates significantly differently. In other words, older people—but not their younger counterparts—are less likely to believe that women are not tough enough to handle an international crisis and be a successful president, but once provided with information that a female candidate is tough, the candidate exceeds the low expectations of older individuals and is rewarded for it disproportionately.[13]

These findings regarding age and the presidency do not extend to other candidate behaviors. And, again, these age findings are reserved to the presidential role and not to likely effectiveness in the Senate or favorability. Despite coming of political age amid rampant sexism throughout society, older individuals, at least today, seem to be open to many forms of female leadership and do not appear to hold women to higher standards of behavior. But these results provide some suggestive evidence that older generations may possibly have been contributing to the lack of female presidential leadership to date, perhaps until fairly recently. Considered from the perspective of generational replacement, these findings suggest that the future of public support for women at the presidential level may naturally become progressively more promising over time.

Looking Forward

The percentage of women in politics today is nowhere near parity, but it cannot be forgotten that dramatic changes have occurred over just a cou-

---

[13] These findings are consistent with a theory from psychology called expectancy violations theory, which predicts that people who act in a more favorable manner than expected based on a descriptive stereotype will be rewarded with higher evaluations by others as compared to people who were expected to act in a favorable manner. Jussim, Coleman, and Lerch 1987 and Jackson, Sullivan, and Hodge 1993.

ple of decades. And the 2012 election—which resulted in several milestones for female representation, including the most gender-balanced Congress in the history of the United States, and the first time that one state (New Hampshire) will have an all-female congressional delegation—suggests that women candidates are continuing to make gains. The growing presence of female leaders in politics is likely to inspire, encourage, and energize potential female political leaders. That, in its own right, is cause for optimism.

Writing the day after the 2012 election, journalist Hanna Rosin argued that gains for women candidates were possible precisely because the public does not tend to view women leaders as being unusual anymore: "The larger narrative is a nation becoming gradually acclimated to female power. We are starting to see women in commend as less of a novelty, less of a curious phenomenon to be dissected in all of tis fascinating manifestations – Will she cry? Can she wage wars? Can she bake cookies and wage wars at the same time? – and more as a normal part of our political landscape."[14] The results of my study support that view.

Will it be easy for women to win their campaigns? Make no mistake: it will not be. It is very hard for *any* candidate, man or woman, to win a race, especially a race for national or statewide office. The public has challenging expectations for any candidate. The public tends to want candidates who seem caring *and* tough, who seem empathetic *and* able to make hard decisions, and who seem able to generate change *and* able to keep policies that the public likes in place. We saw throughout this book that some fairly common slip-ups can cost candidates dearly in public support, regardless of whether the candidate is male or female. Winning in politics is a tough business, regardless of gender.

For offices where substantial electoral advantages accrue to incumbents, open seats tend to be rare, and unseating an incumbent can be a Herculean task. There is usually no room for error in a race against an incumbent, and even a perfectly run race by a challenger is very likely to be lost anyway, especially in a congressional race. But over time, incumbents (still predominantly male) will retire, thus creating critical open-seat opportunities for politically confident and ambitious women to try to grab. And through this slow and painstaking process of incumbent attrition, the parity problem can potentially be further reduced over time, but only if more women start making the decision to run for office. Trying to improve the willingness of women to run by correcting misperceptions of how the public will view them is one important step in that direction.

It should be noted that the fact that the parity problem still exists should not take away from the fact that considerable progress has been

---

[14] Hanna Rosin, "A Triumph for Women," *Slate*, Wednesday, November 7, 2012.

made in recent years. On the eve of her swearing-in ceremony as Speaker of the House, Nancy Pelosi's eight-year-old granddaughter, Madeline, gave a short speech at a tea in honor of Ann Richards, the late governor of Texas, and other former women politicians. She said, "My Mimi is going to be the first woman Speaker of the House. Because Mimi got this job, I think more women will get jobs like hers, which is *great*."[15]

I agree with little Madeline. Pelosi's ascendancy to the highest position in the U.S. House, however brief her time as Speaker was, may well have helped create a more-level playing field for female candidates. That effect may already be reflected in the findings presented in this book. The presence of women in senior political positions helps the public envision women as powerful leaders and allows political women to separate themselves from the gender stereotypes that come along with womanhood but which may be at odds with leadership. It helps all of our daughters and granddaughters, current and future, to aspire to leadership and may encourage young women with leadership potential to run for office and to more generally recognize that they should reach high and work hard to turn their dreams into reality.

The same is true for the countless women who ran for a wide range of different offices before, and during, Pelosi's time in national office, and she regularly acknowledges that fact: Ann Richards, Pat Schroeder, Bella Abzug, and Geraldine Ferraro. Dianne Feinstein, Barbara Boxer, Olympia Snowe, Kay Bailey Hutchinson, Elizabeth Dole, Patty Murray, Christine Todd Whitman, and Madeleine Kunin. And, of course, Hillary Clinton and Sarah Palin. All of those women and countless others have helped to create a world in which womanhood is ceasing to be a liability to overcome vis-à-vis the public for leadership positions as it once may have been. Each leader brought her own individual strengths and weaknesses to the table, along with her own gender stereotype-consistent and stereotype-inconsistent personal traits and behaviors. Most of these women stumbled and fell at different points in their careers, and got back up, and tried again and again to make a difference in politics, and they all succeeded in a variety of different ways. Over time, each helped to overcome the token status of women politicians, becoming part of a larger and much more powerful sisterhood. In the process, it seems that candidate gender has become yet another characteristic that brings diverse ideas to the political arena rather than the all-important road block on the campaign trail that it was once believed to be.

[15] Pelosi 2008, 167.

Author's note: Only the "Karen Bailey" versions are shown here; the "Kevin Bailey" versions involve only name and pronoun changes.

CONDITION 1: HIGH EXPERIENCE

Karen Bailey feels ready to be a senator after 10 years in U.S. House, state government

Starts fundraising for open seat

Karen Bailey is considering a bid for the U.S. Senate seat that will be open in 2010 due to a retire-1nent. She has already started attending fundraisers in an effort to raise money for the campaign. Congresswoman Bailey has six years of experience in the U.S. House, four years as a state assemblywoman, and has also owned and operated a chain of eight dry cleaning stores located across the state during that time. She claims that, "As a businesswoman and as a parent, I know the challenges that people face. And as someone who has spent a long time on Capitol Hill passing legislation, I have the kind of experience that is needed to make important changes there."

"Interesting ideas and a great deal of experience," says nonpartisan expert

In a visit to a local community center today, Congresswoman Bailey said, "The message from this state is clear: you want leaders who will fight for pragmatic policies that improve your lives. As your senator, I promise you that I will do that every day I am in office."

Known to be a charismatic speaker, Congresswoman Bailey brought the crowd to its feet with applause at several points during the speech.

With a strong preference for moderate policies, "Karen Bailey is a person who is in the sensible center—someone who is interested in finding bipartisan solutions to the country's problems," says Martin Druckman of the nonpartisan Wilson Institute of American Politics. "Congresswoman Bailey has a great deal of experience in politics and has a number of interesting ideas for policy improvements in Washington."

CONDITION 3: LACK OF EXPERIENCE

Karen Bailey feels ready to be a senator despite lack of political experience

Starts fundraising for open seat

"Karen Bailey is considering a bid for the U.S. Senate seat that will be open in 2010 due to a retirement. She has already started attending fundraisers in an effort to raise 1noney for the campaign. Mrs. Bailey has not held elected office previously, but she has owned and operated a chain of eight dry cleaning stores located across the state for the past 10 years. She claims that, "As a businesswoman and as a parent, I know the challenges that people face and I have the kind of experience that is needed to make important changes on Capitol Hill."

"No background in politics but interesting ideas," says nonpartisan expert

In a visit to a local community center today, Mrs. Bailey said, "The message from this state is clear: you want leaders who will fight for pragmatic policies that improve your lives. As your senator, I promise you that I will do that every day I am in office." Known to be a charismatic speaker, Mrs. Bailey brought the crowd to its feet with applause at several points during the speech.

With a strong preference for moderate policies, "Karen Bailey is a person who is in the sensible center—someone who is interested in finding bipartisan solutions to the country's problems," says Martin Druckman of the non-partisan Wilson Institute of A1nerican Politics. "While Mrs. Bailey does not have a background in politics, she has a number of interesting ideas for policy inprovements."

CONDITION 5: ANGER

Congresswoman Karen Bailey erupts at colleague, reporter

Calls colleague "obstinate S.O.B."

Congresswoman Karen Bailey recently announced she will be seeking a U.S. Senate seat that will be vacated in 2010 due to a retirement. The announcement has been overshadowed by other events, however. In an incident earlier this week, the congresswoman yelled at a committee chair who was trying to block her bill from coming to the House floor, calling him an "obstinate S.O.B." Journalists reporting on the committee hearings caught the representative's outburst on tape.

In a different incident last month, reporters cornered the congresswoman outside of a Washington, D.C., restaurant to ask for her comments on a recent bill she had sponsored. When reporters persisted in their questioning and continued to follow her down the street, the congresswoman shoved one of the reporters out of the way and yelled, "I said I was through taking questions tonight, and I meant it." "She could have made the same point without pushing me and yelling," commented the reporter after Representative Bailey left the scene.

> "She could have made the same point without pushing me and yelling," says reporter

The congresswoman's office declined to comment on the incidents.

Congresswoman Bailey is expected to be a major contender in the Senate race due to her strong appeal to voters from both political parties. "I am a solutions candidate," Bailey says, "with a focus on bringing the parties together to solve challenges for our state and for our country." With a preference for moderate policies, she is "one of the few remaining politicians in the sensible center— someone who tries to find bipartisan solutions to the country's problems," says Martin Druckman of the nonpartisan Wilson Institute of American Politics.

With one full term under her belt and now several months into her second term, Congresswoman Bailey has experienced many legislative successes as well as some legislative challenges. On the success front, the state now has one of the highest per capita levels of road improvement spending in the country and has dramatically increased its total number of small businesses with the help of federal business improvement grants. Congresswoman Bailey has been less successful as the coauthor of two bills to increase spending on safety equipment for soldiers in Iraq and Afghanistan and to make federal bureaucracies more cost-efficient, both of which failed to pass in the House earlier this year.

CONDITION 7: CRYING

Congresswoman Karen Bailey has a teary week

Cries over campaign rigors, legislative challenges

Congresswoman Karen Bailey recently announced she will be seeking a U .S. Senate seat that will be vacated in 2010 due to a retirement. The announcement has been overshadowed by other events, however. In an incident earlier this week, the congresswoman cried during a speech she was giving while discussing the rigors of campaigning in her last election. During another recent press conference, Representative Bailey cried while being questioned by reporters who were pressing her repeatedly to comment on the failure of a recent bill to which she had devoted a great deal of time. With tears in her eyes, Representative Bailey cut the press confer-ence short and said only "I really can't talk about this right now." The congresswoman's office declined to comment on the incidents.

"I really can't talk about this right now," with tears in her eyes

Congresswoman Bailey is expected to be a major contender in the Senate race due to her strong appeal to voters from both political parties. "I am a solutions candidate," Bailey says, "with a focus on bringing the parties together to solve challenges for our state and for our country." With a preference for moderate policies, she is "one of the few remaining politicians in the sensible center— someone who tries to find bipartisan solutions to the country's problems," says Martin Druckman of the non-partisan Wilson Institute of American Politics.

With one full term under her belt and now several months into her second term, Congresswoman Bailey has experienced many legislative successes as well as some legislative challenges. On the success front, the state now has one of the highest per capita levels of road improvement spending in the country and has dramatically increased its total number of small businesses with the help of federal business improvement grants. Congresswoman Bailey has been less successful as the coauthor of two bills to increase spending on safety equipment for soldiers in Iraq and Afghanistan and to make federal bureaucracies more cost-efficient, both of which failed to pass in the House earlier this year.

CONDITION 9: TOUGH

Congresswoman Karen Bailey threatens to hold up bills

"I will be heard,"
Bailey says.

Congresswoman Karen Bailey recently announced she will be seeking a U.S. Senate seat that will be vacated in 2010 due to a retirement. The announcement has been overshadowed by other events, however. In an incident earlier this week, the congresswoman refused to yield time she had remaining on the House floor to a colleague and is seen on a video clip calmly but very firmly stating, "You've had your turn, and now it's my turn. I will not yield the floor until I have said what I need to say," prior to finishing the full length of her speech. And to House leaders who refused to let the congresswoman add provisions to a bill, she said "I don't take 'no' for an answer, and I won't let anyone stand in my way. I will be heard."

Additionally, in an e-mail that was anonymously provided to the media, Representative Bailey threatened to hold up the House leaders' favored bills in committee unless they agreed to hold hearings to consider the provisions she was demanding. The congresswoman's office declined to comment on the incidents.

"I won't let anyone stand in my way"

Congresswoman Bailey is expected to be a major contender in the Senate race due to her strong appeal to voters from both political parties. "I am a solutions candidate," Bailey says, "with a focus on bringing the parties together to solve challenges for our state and for our country." With a preference for moderate policies, she is "one of the few remaining politicians in the sensible center - someone who tries to find bi-

partisan solutions to the country's problems," says Martin Druckman of the non-partisan Wilson Institute of American Politics.

With one full term under her belt and now several months into her second term, Congresswoman Bailey has experienced many legislative successes as well as some legislative challenges. On the success front, the state now has one of the highest per capita levels of road improvement spending in the country and has dramatically increased its total number of small businesses with the help of federal business improvement grants. Congresswoman Bailey has been less successful as the coauthor of two bills to increase spending on safety equipment for soldiers in Iraq and Afghanistan and to make federal bureaucracies more cost-efficient, both of which failed to pass in the House earlier this year.

CONDITION 11: LACK OF EMPATHY

Congresswoman Karen Bailey is curt with constituents in recent encounters

Cuts off parent of a disabled child: "Is there a question here?"

Congresswoman Karen Bailey recently announced she will be seeking a U.S. Senate seat that will be vacated in 2010 due to a retirement. The announcement has been overshadowed by other events, however. In an incident earlier this week, the congresswoman appeared unsympathetic to a constituent at a recent event who described the challenges facing parents of developmentally disabled children. Throughout the constituent's story, Representative Bailey repeatedly checked her watch and finally interrupted, "I'm sorry to cut you off—and I don't doubt the extent of your hardships—but is there a question here?" and moved on to the next question.

At a later visit to a small nursing home while accompanied by reporters, Representative Bailey quickly moved through the hallways. When an elderly man approached the congresswoman and asked if she would look at a photo of his family that the man had not seen in over a year, Representative Bailey brushed past him and did not look up from a conversation with an aide. With tears in his eyes, the man told a reporter, "I just wanted to

"I just wanted to know that she cared," says disappointed elderly man

know that she cared." The congresswoman's office declined to comment on the incidents.

Congresswoman Bailey is expected to be a major contender in the Senate race due to her strong appeal to voters from both political parties. "I am a solutions candidate," Bailey says, "with a focus on bringing the parties together to solve challenges for our state and for our country." With a preference for moderate poli-

cies, she is "one of the few remaining politicians in the sensible center— someone who tries to find bipartisan solutions to the country's problems," says Martin Druckman of the nonpartisan Wilson Institute of American Politics.

With one full term under her belt and now several months into her second term, Congresswoman Bailey has experienced many legislative successes as well as some legislative challenges. On the success front, the state now has one of the highest per capita levels of road improvement spending in the country and has dramatically increased its total number of small businesses with the help of federal business improvement grants. Congresswoman Bailey has been less successful as the coauthor of two bills to increase spending on safety equipment for soldiers in Iraq and Afghanistan and to make federal bureaucracies more cost-efficient, both of which failed to pass in the House earlier this year.

CONDITION 13: KNOWLEDGE GAFFE

Congresswoman Karen Bailey short on facts

*Wrong on leaders'
names, veto
procedure*

Congresswoman Karen Bailey recently announced she will be seeking a U.S. Senate seat that will be vacated in 2010 due to a retirement. The announcement has been overshadowed by other events, however. In an incident earlier this week, Congresswoman Bailey gave a speech in which she misstated the names of the leaders of both Pakistan and Germany. She was still unable to identify the correct leaders when questioned by journalists after the speech.

This occurred on the heels of another situation in which Representative Bailey incorrectly stated that presidential vetoes can be overturned by a three-fifths majority of both the House and the Senate when speaking to a sixth grade class. Representative Bailey appeared flustered when one

of the students pointed out that a veto can be overturned by a two-thirds vote. The teacher confirmed that the sixth grader was correct and tried—unsuccessfully—to quiet the giggling students. "I guess I should have known that," Representative Bailey admitted.

"I guess I should have known that," admits Bailey

The congresswoman's office declined to comment further on the incidents.

Congresswoman Bailey is expected to be a major contender in the Senate race due to her strong appeal to voters from both political parties. "I am a solutions candidate," Bailey says, "with a focus on bringing the parties together to solve challenges for our state and for our country." With a preference for moderate policies, she is "one of the few remammg politicians in

the sensible center—someone who tries to find bipartisan solutions to the country's problems," says Martin Druckman of the nonpartisan Wilson Institute of American Politics.

With one full term under her belt and now several months into her second term, Congresswoman Bailey has experienced many legislative successes as well as some legislative challenges. On the success front, the state now has one of the highest per capita levels of road improvement spending in the country and has dramatically increased its total number of small businesses with the help of federal business improvement grants. Congresswoman Bailey has been less successful as the coauthor of two bills to increase spending on safety equipment for soldiers in Iraq and Afghanistan and to make federal bureaucracies more cost-efficient, both of which failed to pass in the House earlier this year.

CONDITION 15: CONTOL GROUP

Congresswoman Karen Bailey announces Senate bid

Congresswoman Karen Bailey recently announced she will be seeking a U.S. Senate seat that will be vacated in 2010 due to a retirement.

Congresswoman Bailey is expected to be a major contender in the Senate race due to her strong appeal to voters from both political parties. "I am a solutions candidate," Bailey says, "with a focus on bringing the parties together to solve challenges for our state and for our country." With a preference for moderate poli-cies, she is "one of the few remaining politicians in the sensible center—someone who tries to find bipartisan solutions to the country's problems," says Martin Druckman of the nonpartisan Wilson Institute of American Politics.

With one full term under her belt and now several months into her second term, Congresswoman Bailey has experienced many legislative successes as well as some legislative challenges. On the success front, the state now has one of the high-est per capita levels of road improvement spending in the country and has dramatically increased its total number of small businesses with the help of federal business improvement grants. Congresswoman Bailey has been less successful as the coauthor of two bills to increase spending on safety equipment for soldiers in Iraq and Afghanistan and to make federal bureaucracies more cost-efficient, both of which failed to pass in the House earlier this year.

Respondents viewed the following questions in a format very common for online surveys: anchored scales from 1 to 7, displayed horizontally, with equal distances between the numbers. It is not possible to replicate the exact appearance of the questionnaire and response scales here; however, screen shots of the questionnaire are available from the author upon request:

1. [FAVORABILITY] How favorable or unfavorable do you feel toward the candidate?

Extremely   *Extremely*
Unfavorable   *Favorable*

1   2   3   4   5   6   7

2. How good of a job do you think that the candidate would probably do with the following?

A Poor Job   *An Excellent Job*

1   2   3   4   5   6   7

Q: [SENATE EFFECTIVENESS] Be an effective U.S. Senator.
Q: [PRESIDENTIAL EFFECTIVENESS] Be an effective U.S. President about 10 years from now.
Q: [DOMESTIC ISSUES] Strengthen programs like Social Security and Medicare.
Q: [ECONOMY] Help to make America strong economically.
Q: [INTERNATIONAL CRISIS] Effectively handle an international crisis.

3. How well do you think the following words or phrases describe the candidate?

Not Well   *Extremely*
at All   *Well*

1   2   3   4   5   6   7

Q: [HONEST] Honest.
Q: [KNOWLEDGEABLE] Knowledgeable.
Q: [INTELLIGENT] Intelligent.

Q: [STRONG LEADER] Provides strong leadership.
Q: [GETS THINGS DONE] Gets things done.
Q: [CARES ABOUT PEOPLE LIKE YOU] Really cares about people like you.
Q: [COMPASSIONATE] Compassionate.
Q: [IMPORTANT PERSON] An important person.
Q: [WOULD ENJOY TALKING TO] Someone you would probably enjoy talking to.
Q: [WILL IMPROVE WASHINGTON] Will improve things in Washington. *[Asked of CONTROL GROUP + EXPERIENCE conditions only]*

4. Please rate the candidate on the following characteristics:

[The following items were included for CONTROL GROUP + CRYING + ANGRY + TOUGH + LACK OF EMPATHY conditions only]

Emotional						*Unemotional*
1	2	3	4	5	6	7

Angry						*Calm*
1	2	3	4	5	6	7

Unassertive						*Assertive*
1	2	3	4	5	6	7

Uncaring						*Caring*
1	2	3	4	5	6	7

Weak						*Strong*
1	2	3	4	5	6	7

Acts Inappropriately						*Acts Appropriately*
1	2	3	4	5	6	7

5. Please rate the candidate on the following characteristics:

[The following items were included for CONTROL GROUP + KNOWLEDGE GAFFE + EXPERIENCE conditions only]

Incompetent   *Competent*

1   2   3   4   5   6   7

Inexperienced   *Experienced*

1   2   3   4   5   6   7

6. [SITUATIONAL ATTRIBUTION] I think the behavior of the candidate in the article can probably best be explained by:

[The following items were included for all EXCEPT the Control Group and the Experience groups]

Personal characteristics   *The difficulty*
of the candidate   *of the situation*

1   2   3   4   5   6   7

APPENDIX 3. HOW THE PUBLIC RESPONDS TO EACH BEHAVIOR (NOT CONSIDERING CANDIDATE GENDER)

Consequences of Behavior (averaging responses for male and female candidates)	CONTROL GROUP mean	CRY			ANGER			TOUGH			LACK OF EMPATHY			KNOWLEDGE GAFFE		
		Mean	Sig diff?	p-value	Mean	Sig diff?	p-value	Mean	Sig diff?	p-value	Mean	Sig diff?	p-value	Mean	Sig diff?	p-value
Favorability	4.5	4.3	**	p=.04	3.7	***	p=.00	4.4		p=.36	2.8	***	p=.00	3.4	***	p=.00
Senate Effectiveness	4.5	4.3	***	p=.00	3.9	***	p=.00	4.6		p=.84	3.4	***	p=.00	3.4	***	p=.00
Pres Effectiveness	3.8	3.4	***	p=.00	3.0	***	p=.00	3.8		p=.74	2.4	***	p=.00	2.6	***	p=.00
Domestic Issues	4.2	4.1		p=.39	3.8	***	p=.00	4.2		p=.56	2.7	***	p=.00	3.3	***	p=.00
Economy	4.4	4.1	**	p=.02	3.7	***	p=.00	4.3		p=.20	3.4	***	p=.00	3.3	***	p=.00
International Crisis	4.0	3.4	***	p=.00	3.2	***	p=.00	4.0		p=.85	3.0	***	p=.00	2.7	***	p=.00
Honest	4.5	4.8	***	p=.00	4.1	***	p=.00	4.5		p=.43	3.2	***	p=.00	3.9	***	p=.00
Knowledgeable	4.6	4.5		p=.74	4.2	***	p=.00	4.6		p=.64	3.5	***	p=.00	2.6	***	p=.00
Intelligent	4.8	4.6		p=.20	4.0	***	p=.00	4.7		p=.36	3.5	***	p=.00	3.2	***	p=.00
Strong Leadership	4.5	3.8	***	p=.00	3.7	***	p=.00	4.7	*	p=.02	3.2	***	p=.00	3.2	***	p=.00
Gets things done	4.5	4.2	***	p=.00	4.1	***	p=.00	4.7	***	p=.07	3.6	***	p=.00	3.5	***	p=.00
Cares about people like you	4.3	4.6	***	p=.01	3.4	***	p=.00	4.2		p=.33	2.0	***	p=.00	3.5	***	p=.00

Compassionate	4.4	5.0 ***	p=.00	3.2 ***	p=.00	4.1 **	p=.03	2.0 ***	p=.00	3.6 ***	p=.00
Important Person	4.2	4.2	p=.81	3.5 ***	p=.00	4.1	p=.59	3.0 ***	p=.00	3.3 ***	p=.00
Would Enjoy Talking to	4.3	4.3	p=.89	3.3 ***	p=.00	4.1 *	p=.08	2.2 ***	p=.00	3.3 ***	p=.00
Improve Things in Washington										
Unemotional (vs. Emotional)	3.9	2.0 ***	p=.00	2.7 ***	p=.00	3.4 ***	p=.00	5.7 ***	p=.00	
Calm (vs. Angry)	4.4	4.1 ***	p=.00	2.6 ***	p=.00	3.5 ***	p=.00	4.1 ***	p=.00	
Assertive (vs. Unassertive)	4.5	4.1 ***	p=.00	5.2 ***	p=.00	5.5 ***	p=.00	4.5	p=.95	
Caring (vs. Uncaring)	4.6	5.3 ***	p=.00	3.7 ***	p=.00	4.5 *	p=.07	2.2 ***	p=.00	
Acts Appropriately (vs. Acts Inappropriately)	4.5	3.8 ***	p=.00	2.9 ***	p=.00	4.2 ***	p=.00	2.9 ***	p=.00	
Strong (vs. Weak)	4.4	3.6 ***	p=.00	4.3	p=.16	4.9 ***	p=.00	3.7 ***	p=.00	
Competent (vs. Incompetent)	4.4									4.0 ***	p=.00
Experienced (vs. Inexperienced)	4.3									3.4 ***	p=.00

*** p < .01, ** p < .05, * p<.10

Note: These results are from the two-way ANOVA models in which candidate gender and each behavior are interacted. The tables in following appendixes show the interaction effects between candidate gender and behavior; this table shows only the significance of the main effect for behavior, holding candidate gender constant by averaging the scores for male and female candidates

APPENDIX 4: HOW THE PUBLIC RESPONDS TO CANDIDATE EXPERIENCE(NOT CONSIDERING CANDIDATE GENDER)

	EXPERIENCE			
	HIGH EXPERIENCE mean	LOW EXPERIENCE mean	Sig diff?	p-value
Favorability	4.4	4.4		p=.79
Senate Effectiveness	4.4	4.2	*	p=.06
Pres Effectiveness	3.8	3.7		p=.14
Domestic Issues	4.0	4.0		p=.91
Economy	4.1	4.2		p=.35
International Crisis	3.7	3.5	**	p=.02
Honest	4.2	4.6	***	p=.00
Knowledgeable	4.5	3.9	***	p=.00
Intelligent	4.6	4.8		p=.11
Strong Leadership	4.3	4.4		p=.28
Gets things done	4.3	4.4		p=.45
Cares about people like you	4.2	4.6	***	p=.00
Compassionate	4.2	4.5	***	p=.01
Important Person	4.1	4.0		p=.58
Would Enjoy Talking to	4.2	4.5	***	p=.01
Improve Things in Washington	3.9	4.0		p=.24
Competent (vs. Incompetent)	4.2	4.4		p=.23
Experienced (vs. Inexperienced)	4.8	3.2	***	p=.00

*** p < .01, ** p < .05, * p<.10

Note: These results are pulled from the two-way ANOVA model in which candidate gender and experience are interacting. The tables in following appendixes show the interaction effect; while this table shows only the significance of the main effect of experience, holding candidate gender constant by averaging the scores for male and female candidates.

APPENDIX 5: RESULTS FOR CANDIDATE EXPERIENCE * CANDIDATE GENDER

EXPERIENCE	LOW Experience candidates only				HIGH Experience candidates only				Candidate gender * Experience
	MALE candidates	FEMALE candidates	p-value for F-test of gender	% difference	MALE candidates	FEMALE candidates	p-value for F-test of gender	% difference	p-value for F-test of gender * experience
Favorability	4.3	4.4	p=.59		4.4	4.3	p=.48		p=.38
Senate Effectiveness	4.1	4.3	p=.11		4.4	4.4	p=.92		p=.21
Pres Effectiveness	3.6	3.7	p=.51		3.9	3.7	p=.15		p=.15
Domestic Issues	3.9	4.1	p=.13		4.0	4.0	p=.94		p=.24
Economy	4.1	4.4	* p=.10		4.1	4.1	p=1.0		p=.23
International Crisis	3.4	3.6	p=.15		3.8	3.6	p=.13		** p=.04
Honest	4.5	4.8	** p=.03	5%	4.2	4.3	p=.38		p=.30
Knowledgeable	3.7	4.1	*** p=.01	6%	4.6	4.4	p=.34		*** p=.01

	Low Experience					High Experience			Two-way	
Intelligent	4.6	4.9	**	p=.02	5%	4.6	4.6	p=.59		p=.16
Strong Leadership	4.2	4.5	**	p=.05	4%	4.3	4.2	p=.79	*	p=.10
Gets things done	4.3	4.6	**	p=.05	4%	4.4	4.3	p=.82		p=.11
Cares about people like you	4.5	4.8	**	p=.04	5%	4.2	4.2	p=.83		p=.18
Compassionate	4.3	4.7	**	p=.02	5%	4.2	4.3	p=.40		p=.24
Important Person	3.8	4.2	***	p=.01	6%	4.1	4.0	p=.33	***	p=.01
Would Enjoy Talking to	4.3	4.6	*	p=.08	4%	4.2	4.2	p=.73		p=.30
Improve Things in Washington	3.8	4.3	**	p=.02	6%	3.9	3.9	p=.90	*	p=.06
Competent (vs. Incompetent)	4.4	4.4		p=.88		4.3	4.2	p=.79		p=.77
Experienced (vs. Inexperienced)	3.1	3.3		p=.14		4.8	4.9	p=.54		p=.47

*** p < .01, ** p < .05, * p<.10

Note: The first set of columns ("Low Experience candidates only) represents the results of a series of one-way ANOVA models for candidate gender conducted just on respondents exposed to the low-experience article (appendix 1). A significant p-value for the relevant F-test indicates that candidate gender significantly predicts the dependent variable in question (shown in the far left column) for low-experience candidates.

The second set of columns ("High Experience candidates only) represents the results of a series of one-way ANOVA models for candidate gender conducted just on respondents exposed to the high experience article. A significant p-value for the relevant F-test indicates that candidate gender significantly predicts the dependent variable in question (shown in the far left column) for high experience candidates.

The third set of columns represents a series of two-way ANOVA models in which candidate gender and experience are interacted. The p-value for the relevant F-test indicates whether the interaction is significant for each dependent variable; in other words, whether the effect of candidate experience depends upon candidate gender (which also can be thought of as whether the effect of candidate gender depends upon candidate experience).

APPENDIX 6: RESULTS FOR CANDIDATE GENDER (CONTROL GROUP ONLY)

	CONTROL GROUP			
	MALE candidates	FEMALE candidates		p- value for gender diffs (ANOVA)
Favorability	4.5	4.5		p=.66
Senate Effectiveness	4.5	4.6		p=.77
Pres Effectiveness	3.9	3.7		p=.27
Domestic Issues	4.2	4.3		p=.58
Economy	4.4	4.4		p=.93
International Crisis	4.1	3.9		p=.21
Honest	4.4	4.5		p=.31
Knowledgeable	4.5	4.6		p=.29
Intelligent	4.6	4.9	**	p=.05
Strong Leadership	4.4	4.5		p=.55
Gets things done	4.5	4.6		p=.45
Cares about people like you	4.2	4.3		p=.59
Compassionate	4.3	4.4		p=.34
Important Person	4.1	4.3		p=.38
Would Enjoy Talking to	4.2	4.3		p=.55
Improve Things in Washington	4.2	4.3		p=.60
Unemotional (vs. Emotional)	3.9	4.0		p=.60
Calm (vs. Angry)	4.4	4.4		p=.59
Assertive (vs. Unassertive)	4.5	4.6		p=.34
Caring (vs. Uncaring)	4.6	4.7		p=.61
Acts Appropriately (vs. Acts Inappropriately)	4.5	4.5		p=.84
Strong (vs. Weak)	4.4	4.4		p=.78
Competent (vs. Incompetent)	4.5	4.4		p=.71
Experienced (vs. Inexperienced)	4.3	4.3		p=.90

*** p < .01, ** p < .05, * p<.10
Note: This table represents the results of a series of one-way ANOVA models for candidate gender conducted just on respondents exposed to the control group articles. A significant p-value for the F-test indicates that candidate gender significantly affects responses regarding the trait/issue in question among control group respondents.

APPENDIX 7: RESULTS FOR CRYING *
CANDIDATE GENDER

	Control Group		CRYING		p- value for F-test of gender * behavior	
	MALE candidates	FEMALE candidates	MALE candidates	FEMALE candidates		
Favorability	4.5	4.5	4.4	4.2		p=.60
Senate Effectiveness	4.5	4.6	4.3	4.2		p=.69
Pres Effectiveness	3.9	3.7	3.5	3.2		p=.72
Domestic Issues	4.2	4.3	4.1	4.1		p=78
Economy	4.4	4.4	4.2	4.1		p=.84
International Crisis	4.1	3.9	3.6	3.3		p=.58
Honest	4.4	4.5	4.7	4.8		p=.87
Knowledgeable	4.5	4.6	4.6	4.5		p=.23
Intelligent	4.6	4.9	4.6	4.6		p=.13
Strong Leadership	4.4	4.5	3.9	3.8		p=.30
Gets things done	4.5	4.6	4.2	4.1		p=.26
Cares about people like you	4.2	4.3	4.6	4.6		p=.62
Compassionate	4.3	4.4	5.0	5.0		p=.45
Important Person	4.1	4.3	4.2	4.2		p=.63
Would Enjoy Talking to	4.2	4.3	4.3	4.3		p=.47
Unemotional (vs. Emotional)	3.9	4.0	2.1	1.9	*	p=.07
Calm (vs. Angry)	4.4	4.4	4.2	4.0		p=.13
Assertive (vs. Unassertive)	4.5	4.6	4.0	4.1		p=.88
Caring (vs. Uncaring)	4.6	4.7	5.2	5.4		p=.68
Strong (vs. Weak)	4.4	4.4	3.6	3.5		p=.48
Acts Appropriately (vs. Acts Inappropriately)	4.5	4.5	3.7	3.8		p=.92
Situational Attribution (vs. Personal Attribution)	NA	NA	3.5	3.6		p=.35

*** p < .01, ** p < .05, * p<.10
Note: For all but the final measure ("Situational Attribution"), results are based on 2-way ANOVA in which significance of the interaction (candidate gender * behavior) is the focus of the analysis. The p-value indicates the significance of the associated F-test for the interaction. For the "Situational Attribution" measure, the p-value indicates the significance of the F-test for gender alone, because the question was not asked of the control group.

APPENDIX 8 . RESULTS FOR ANGER *
CANDIDATE GENDER

	Control Group		ANGRY		p- value for F-test of gender * behavior	
	MALE candidates	FEMALE candidates	MALE candidates	FEMALE candidates		
Favorability	4.5	4.5	**3.8**	**3.6**		p=.54
Senate Effectiveness	4.5	4.6	**3.9**	**3.9**		p=.75
Pres Effectiveness	3.9	3.7	**3.1**	**2.9**		p=.81
Domestic Issues	4.2	4.3	**3.7**	**3.8**		p=.80
Economy	4.4	4.4	**3.8**	**3.7**		p=.62
International Crisis	4.1	3.9	**3.3**	**3.1**		p=.95
Honest	4.4	4.5	**3.9**	**4.2**		p=.42
Knowledgeable	4.5	4.6	**4.2**	**4.3**		p=.86
Intelligent	4.6	4.9	**4.1**	**4.0**		p=.15
Strong Leadership	4.4	4.5	**3.8**	**3.6**		p=.29
Gets things done	4.5	4.6	**4.1**	**4.2**		p=.92
Cares about people like you	4.2	4.3	**3.4**	**3.4**		p=.75
Compassionate	4.3	4.4	**3.1**	**3.2**		p=92
Important Person	4.1	4.3	**3.5**	**3.5**		p=.52
Would Enjoy Talking to	4.2	4.3	**3.2**	**3.3**		p=.82
Unemotional (vs. Emotional)	3.9	4.0	**2.9**	**2.5**	**	p=.03
Calm (vs. Angry)	4.4	4.4	**2.7**	**2.5**		p=.24
Assertive (vs. Unassertive)	4.5	4.6	**5.0**	**5.5**	*	p=.09
Caring (vs. Uncaring)	4.6	4.7	**3.7**	**3.8**		p=.80
Strong (vs. Weak)	4.4	4.4	**4.3**	**4.3**		p=.80
Acts Appropriately (vs. Acts Inappropriately)	4.5	4.5	**3.1**	**2.7**	*	p=.06
Situational Attribution (vs. Personal Attribution)	NA	NA	**3.5**	**3.3**		p=.18

*** p < .01, ** p < .05, * p<.10
Note: For all but the final measure ("Situational Attribution"), results are based on a 2-way ANOVA model in which significance of the interaction (candidate gender * behavior) is the focus of the analysis. The p-value indicates the significance of the associated F-test for the interaction. For the "Situational Attribution" measure, the p-value indicates the significance of the F-test for gender alone, because the question was not asked of the control group.

APPENDIX 9: RESULTS FOR TOUGHNESS * CANDIDATE GENDER

	Control Group		TOUGH		p- value for F-test of gender * behavior	
	MALE candidates	**FEMALE** candidates	**MALE** candidates	**FEMALE** candidates		
Favorability	4.5	4.5	**4.3**	**4.5**	*	p=.08
Senate Effectiveness	4.5	4.6	**4.5**	**4.7**		p=.34
Pres Effectiveness	3.9	3.7	**3.6**	**3.9**	**	p=.03
Domestic Issues	4.2	4.3	**4.1**	**4.2**		p=.66
Economy	4.4	4.4	**4.2**	**4.3**		p=.51
International Crisis	4.1	3.9	**3.9**	**4.0**		p=.25
Honest	4.4	4.5	**4.4**	**4.7**		p=.29
Knowledgeable	4.5	4.6	**4.5**	**4.7**		p=.83
Intelligent	4.6	4.9	**4.6**	**4.8**		p=.57
Strong Leadership	4.4	4.5	**4.6**	**4.9**		p=.39
Gets things done	4.5	4.6	**4.6**	**4.8**		p=.66
Cares about people like you	4.2	4.3	**4.1**	**4.3**		p=.68
Compassionate	4.3	4.4	**4.0**	**4.3**		p=.56
Important Person	4.1	4.3	**4.0**	**4.2**		p=.60
Would Enjoy Talking to	4.2	4.3	**3.9**	**4.3**		p=.19
Unemotional (vs. Emotional)	3.9	4.0	**3.4**	**3.4**		p=.77
Calm (vs. Angry)	4.4	4.4	**3.5**	**3.5**		p=.67
Assertive (vs. Unassertive)	4.5	4.6	**5.5**	**5.5**		p=.91
Caring (vs. Uncaring)	4.6	4.7	**4.3**	**4.6**		p=.47
Strong (vs. Weak)	4.4	4.4	**4.7**	**5.1**	*	p=.07
Acts Appropriately (vs. Acts Inappropriately)	4.5	4.5	**4.1**	**4.3**		p=.27
Situational Attribution (vs. Personal Attribution)	NA	NA	**3.4**	**3.8**	**	p=.03

*** p < .01, ** p < .05, * p<.10

Note: For all but the final measure ("Situational Attribution"), results are based on a 2-way ANOVA model in which significance of the interaction (candidate gender * behavior) is the focus of the analysis. The p-value indicates the significance of the associated F-test for the interaction. For the "Situational Attribution"" measure, the p-value indicates the significance of the F-test for gender alone, because the question was not asked of the control group.

APPENDIX 10. RESULTS FOR LACK OF EMPATHY * CANDIDATE GENDER

	Control Group		LACK OF EMPATHY			p- value for F-test of gender * behavior
	MALE candidates	**FEMALE** candidates	**MALE** candidates	**FEMALE** candidates		
Favorability	4.5	4.5	2.7	2.8		p=.46
Senate Effectiveness	4.5	4.6	3.5	3.3		p=.23
Pres Effectiveness	3.9	3.7	2.5	2.3		p=.59
Domestic Issues	4.2	4.3	2.7	2.7		p=.73
Economy	4.4	4.4	3.4	3.3		p=.49
International Crisis	4.1	3.9	3.1	2.8		p=.37
Honest	4.4	4.5	3.2	3.1		p=.34
Knowledgeable	4.5	4.6	3.7	3.4	**	p=.05
Intelligent	4.6	4.9	3.5	3.4	**	p=.04
Strong Leadership	4.4	4.5	3.2	3.2		p=.69
Gets things done	4.5	4.6	3.6	3.6		p=.60
Cares about people like you	4.2	4.3	2.0	2.0		p=.82
Compassionate	4.3	4.4	1.9	2.0		p=.96
Important Person	4.1	4.3	3.0	2.9		p=.40
Would Enjoy Talking to	4.2	4.3	2.1	2.2		p=.78
Unemotional (vs. Emotional)	3.9	4.0	5.6	5.7		p=.86
Calm (vs. Angry)	4.4	4.4	4.0	4.1		p=.72
Assertive (vs. Unassertive)	4.5	4.6	4.5	4.6		p=.97
Caring (vs. Uncaring)	4.6	4.7	2.1	2.2		p=.85
Strong (vs. Weak)	4.4	4.4	3.6	3.9		p=.32
Acts Appropriately (vs. Acts Inappropriately)	4.5	4.5	3.0	2.9		p=.67
Situational Attribution (vs. Personal Attribution)	NA	NA	2.5	2.7		p=.24

*** p < .01, ** p < .05, * p<.10
Note: For all but the final measure ("Situational Attribution"), results are based on a 2-way ANOVA model in which significance of the interaction (candidate gender * behavior) is the focus of the analysis. The p-value indicates the significance of the associated F-test for the interaction. For the "Situational Attribution" measure, the p-value indicates the significance of the F-test for gender alone, because the question was not asked of the control group.

APPENDIX 11: RESULTS FOR KNOWLEDGE
GAFFE * CANDIDATE GENDER

	Control Group		KNOWLEDGE GAFFES		p- value for F-test of gender * behavior
	MALE candidates	FEMALE candidates	MALE candidates	FEMALE candidates	
Favorability	4.5	4.5	3.3	3.5	p=.13
Senate Effectiveness	4.5	4.6	3.3	3.5	p=.62
Pres Effectiveness	3.9	3.7	2.6	2.6	p=.74
Domestic Issues	4.2	4.3	3.2	3.4	p=.78
Economy	4.4	4.4	3.3	3.4	p=.53
International Crisis	4.1	3.9	2.8	2.7	p=.63
Honest	4.4	4.5	3.8	4.1	p=.41
Knowledgeable	4.5	4.6	2.5	2.7	p=.95
Intelligent	4.6	4.9	3.1	3.2	p=.32
Strong Leadership	4.4	4.5	3.2	3.2	p=.79
Gets things done	4.5	4.6	3.5	3.6	p=.85
Cares about people like you	4.2	4.3	3.5	3.5	p=.76
Compassionate	4.3	4.4	3.5	3.8	p=.61
Important Person	4.1	4.3	3.2	3.4	p=.80
Would Enjoy Talking to	4.2	4.3	3.2	3.3	p=.80
Competent (vs. Incompetent)	4.5	4.4	3.9	4.0	p=.42
Experienced (vs. Inexperienced)	4.3	4.3	3.4	3.5	p=.71
Situational Attribution (vs. Personal Attribution)	NA	NA	3.3	3.2	p=.92

*** p < .01, ** p < .05, * p<.10

Note: For all but the final measure ("Situational Attribution"), results are based on a 2-way ANOVA model in which significance of the interaction (candidate gender * behavior) is the focus of the analysis. The p-value indicates the significance of the associated F-test for the interaction. For the "Situational Attribution" measure, the p-value indicates the significance of the F-test for gender alone, because the question was not asked of the control group.

REFERENCES

Adams, B. E., and R. Schreiber. 2011. "Gender, Campaign Finance, and Electoral Success in Municipal Elections." *Journal of Urban Affairs* 33(1): 83–97.

Alexander, Deborah, and Kristi Andersen. 1993. "Gender as a Factor in the Attribution of Leadership Traits." *Political Research Quarterly* 46: 527–45.

Anderson, Mary, Christopher Lewis, and Charlie Baird. 2011. "Punishment or Reward? An Experiment on the Effects of Sex and Gender Issues on Candidate Choice." *Journal of Women, Politics, & Policy* 32(2): 136–57.

Antonakis, J., and L. Atwater. 2002. "Leader Distance: A Review and a Proposed Theory." *Leadership Quarterly* 13(6): 673–704.

Anzia, Sarah F., and Christopher R. Berry. 2011. "The Jackie (and Jill) Robinson Effect: Why Do Congresswomen Outperform Congressmen?" *American Journal of Political Science* 55(3): 478–93.

Archer, John. 2004. "Sex Differences in Aggression in Real-World Settings: A Meta-Analytic Review." *Review of General Psychology* 8(4): 291–322.

Asher, Herbert. 2012. *Polling and the Public: What Every Citizen Should Know.* 8th ed. Washington, DC: Sage Press.

Atkeson, Lonna Rae. 2003. "Not all Cues Are Created Equal: The Conditional Impact of Female Candidates on Political Engagement." *Journal of Politics* 65(4): 1040–61.

Atkeson, Lonna Rae, and Nancy Carrillo. 2007. "More Is Better: The Influence of Collective Female Descriptive Representation on External Efficacy." *Politics & Gender* 3(1): 79–101.

Atkeson, Lonna Rae, and T. B. Krebs. 2008. "Press Coverage of Mayoral Candidates: The Role of Gender in News Reporting and Campaign Issue Speech." *Political Research Quarterly* 61(2): 239–52.

Averill, James R. 1997. "The Emotions: An Integrative Approach." In R. Hogan, J. A. Johnson, and S. R. Briggs (Eds.), *Handbook of Personality Psychology* (pp. 513–41). San Diego, CA: Academic Press.

Babcock, Linda, and Sara Laschever. 2003. *Women Don't Ask: Negotiation and the Gender Divide.* Princeton, NJ: Princeton University Press.

Banwart, Mary Christine. 2010. "Gender and Candidate Communication: Effects of Stereotypes in the 2008 Election." *American Behavioral Scientist* 54(3): 265–83.

Banwart, Mary Christine, Dianne G. Bystrom, and Terry Robertson. 2003. "From the Primary to the General Election: A Comparative Analysis of Candidate Mixed-Gender 2000 Races for Governor and U.S. Senate." *American Behavioral Scientist* 46: 658–74.

Barrett, Lisa Feldman, and Eliza Bliss-Moreau. 2009. "She's Emotional. He's Having a Bad Day: Attributional Explanations for Emotion Stereotypes." *Emotion* 9(5): 649–58.

Berrens, Robert P., Alok K. Bohara, Hank Jenkins-Smith, Carol Silva, and David L. Weimer. 2003. "The Advent of Internet Surveys for Political Research: A Comparison of Telephone and Internet Samples." *Political Analysis* 11(1): 1–22.

Bindra, Dalbir. 1972. Weeping. *Bulletin of the British Psychological Society* 25: 281–84.

Boxer, Barbara. 1994. *Strangers in the Senate: Politics and the New Revolution of Women in America*. Bethesda, MD: National Press Books.

Brescoll, Victoria L., and Eric Luis Uhlmann. 2008. "Can an Angry Woman Get Ahead? Status Conferral, Gender, and Expression of Emotion in the Workplace." *Psychological Science* 19(3): 268–75.

Brooks, Deborah Jordan. 2006. "The Resilient Voter: Moving toward Closure in the Debate over Negative Campaigning and Turnout." *Journal of Politics* 68(3): 684–96.

———. 2011. "Testing the Double Standard for Candidate Emotionality: Voter Reactions to the Tears and Anger of Male and Female Politicians." *Journal of Politics* 73(2): 597–615.

Burgess, Diana, and Eugene Borgida. 1999. "Who Women Are, Who Women Should Be: Descriptive and Prescriptive Gender Stereotyping in Sex Discrimination." *Psychology, Public Policy, and Law* 5(3): 665–92.

Burrell, Barbara C. 1996. *A Woman's Place Is in the House: Campaigning for Congress in the Feminist Era*. Ann Arbor: University of Michigan Press.

———. 2005. "Campaign Financing: Women's Experience in the Modern Era." In Sue Thomas and Clyde Wilcox (Eds.), *Women and Elective Office: Past, Present, and Future* (pp. 26–40). New York: Oxford University Press.

Bystrom, Dianne G., Mary Christine Banward, Lynda Lee Kaid, and Terry A. Robertson. 2004. *Gender and Candidate Communication*. New York: Routledge.

Bystrom, Dianne G., T. Robertson, and M. Banwart. 2001. "Framing the Fight: An Analysis of Media Coverage of Female and Male Candidates in Primary Races for Governor and US Senate in 2000." *American Behavioral Scientist* 44(12): 1999–2013.

Caizza, Amy. 2004. "Does Women's Representation in Elected Office Lead to Women-Friendly Policy? Analysis of State-Level Data." *Women and Politics* 26(1): 35–70.

Campbell, David E., and Christina Wolbrecht. 2006. "See Jane Run: Women Politicians as Role Models for Adolescents." *Journal of Politics* 68: 233–47.

Carli, Linda L. 2001. "Gender and Social Influence." *Journal of Social Issues* 57: 725–41.

Carroll, Susan J. 1994. *Women and Candidates in American Politics*. Bloomington: Indiana University Press.

Carroll, Susan J., and Kelly Dittmar. 2010. "The 2008 Candidacies of Hillary Clinton and Sarah Palin: Cracking the 'Highest, Hardest Glass Ceiling.'" In Susan J. Carroll and Richard L. Fox (Eds.), *Gender and Elections: Shaping the Future of American Politics* (2nd ed., pp. 44–77). New York: Cambridge University Press.

Carroll, Susan J., and Richard L. Fox (Eds.). 2010. *Gender and Elections: Shaping the Future of American Politics* (2nd ed.). New York: Cambridge University Press.

Catalyst Report. 2007. "The Double-Bind Dilemma for Women in Leadership: Damned if You Do, Doomed if you Don't." http://www.catalyst.org/publication/83/the-double-bind-dilemma-for-women-in-leadership-damned-if-you-do-doomed-if-you-dont.

Chang, Chingching, and Jacqueline C. Bush Hitchon. 2004. "When Does Gender Count? Further Insights into Gender Schematic Processing of Female Candidates' Political Advertisements." *Sex Roles* 51(3–4): 197–208.

Cialdini, Robert B., and Melanie R. Trost. 1998. "Social influence: Social Norms, Conformity, and Compliance." In D. T. Gilrt, S. T. Fiske, and G. Lindzey (Eds.), *The Handbook of Social Psychology* (4th ed., Vol. 2, pp. 151–92). Boston: McGraw-Hill.

Clift, Eleanor, and Tom Brazaitis. 2000. *Madam President: Shattering the Last Glass Ceiling*. New York: Scribner.

Cohen, Geoffrey L., and Julio Garcia. 2005. "'I Am Us': Negative Stereotypes as Collective Threats." *Journal of Personality and Social Psychology* 89(4): 566–82.

Costrich, Norma, Joan Feinstein, Louise Kidder, Jeanne Marecek, and Linda Pascal. 1975. "When Stereotypes Hurt: Three Studies of Penalties for Sex-Role Reversals." *Journal of Experimental Social Psychology* 11: 520–30.

Crespin, M. H., and J. L. Deitz. 2010. "If You Can't Join 'em, Beat 'em: The Gender Gap in Individual Donations to Congressional Candidates." *Political Research Quarterly* 63(3): 581–93.

Darcy, R., Susan Welch, and Janet Clark. 1994. *Women, Elections, and Representation*. Lincoln: University of Nebraska Press.

Davidson, Heather K., and Michael J. Burke. 2000. "Sex Discrimination in Simulated Employment Contexts: A Meta-Analytic Investigation." *Journal of Vocational Behavior* 56: 225–48.

Deaux, Kay, and Tim Emswiller. 1974. "Explanations for Successful Performance on Sex-Linked Tasks: What Is Skill for the Male Is Luck for the Female." *Journal of Personality and Social Psychology* 29: 80–85.

Deaux, Kay, and Marianne LaFrance. 1998. "Gender." In D. T. Gilbert, S. T. Fiske, and G. Lindzey (Eds.), *The Handbook of Social Psychology* (4th ed., pp. 788–827). Boston: McGraw-Hill.

Devitt, J. 2002. "Framing Gender on the Campaign Trail: Female Gubernatorial Candidates and the Press." *Journalism & Mass Communication Quarterly* 79(2): 445–63.

Dolan, Julie, Melissa Deckman, and Michele Swers. 2011. *Women and Politics.* Boston: Pearson Education.

Dolan, Kathleen. 1997. "Gender Differences in Support for Women Candidates: Is There a Glass Ceiling in American Politics?" *Women & Politics* 17: 27–41.

———. 2004. *Voting for Women: How the Public Evaluates Women Candidates.* Boulder, CO: Westview Press.

———. 2008a. "Women as Candidates in American Politics: The Continuing Impact of Sex and Gender." In Christina Wolbrecht, Karen Beckwith, and Lisa Baldez (Eds.), *Political Women and American Democracy* (pp. 110–27). New York: Cambridge University Press.

———. 2008b. "Is There a 'Gender Affinity Effect' in American Politics? Information, Affect, and Candidate Sex in U.S. House Elections." *Political Research Quarterly* 61(1): 79–89.

———. 2010. "The Impact of Gender Stereotyped Evaluations on Support for Women Candidates." *Political Behavior* 32: 69–88.

Dolan, Kathleen, and Kira Sanbonmatsu. 2009. "Gender Stereotypes and Attitudes toward Gender Balance in Government." *American Politics Research* 27(3): 409–28.

Eagly, Alice H., and Linda L. Carli. 2007. *Through the Labyrinth.* Boston: Harvard University Press.

Eagly, Alice H., and Steven J. Karau. 2002. "Role Congruity Theory of Prejudice toward Female Leaders." *Psychological Review* 109: 573–98.

Eagly, Alice H., Steven J. Karau, and Mona Makhijani. 1995. "Gender and the Effectiveness of Leadership Styles of Women and Men." *Psychological Bulletin* 117: 125–45.

Eagly, Alice H., Mona Makhijani, and Bruce G. Klonsky. 1992. "Gender and the Evaluation of Leaders: A Meta-analysis." *Psychological Bulletin* 111(1): 3–22.

Eagly, Alice H., and Valerie J. Steffen. 1986. "Gender and Aggressive Behavior: A Meta-Analytic Review of the Social Psychological Literature." *Psychological Bulletin* 100(3): 309–30.

Eagly, Alice H., Wendy Wood, and Amanda B. Diekman. 2000. "Social Role Theory of Sex Differences and Similarities: A Current Appraisal." In H. M. Trautner and T. Eckes (Eds.), *The Developmental Social Psychology of Gender* (pp. 123–74). Mahwah, NJ: Lawrence Erlbaum Associates.

Elkstrand, Laurie E., and William A. Eckert. 1981. "The Impact of Candidate's Sex on Voter Choice." *Western Political Quarterly* 34(1): 78–87.

Ely, Robin J. 1994. "The Effects of Organizational Demographics and Social Identity on Relationships among Professional Women." *Administrative Science Quarterly* 39(2): 203–38.

———. 1995. "The Power of Demography: Women's Social Constructions of Identity at Work." *Academy of Management Journal* 38(3): 589–634.

Fabes, Richard A., and Carol L. Martin. 1991. "Gender and Age Stereotypes of Emotionality." *Personality and Social Psychology Bulletin* 17: 532–40.

Falk, Erika. 2010. *Women for President: Media Bias in Nine Campaigns*. Urbana: University of Illinois Press.

Falk, Erika, and Kate Kenski. 2006. "Issue Saliency and Gender Stereotypes: Support for Women as Presidents in Times of War and Terrorism." *Social Science Quarterly* 87(1): 1–18.

Ferraro, Geraldine A. 1985. *Ferraro: My Story*. New York: Bantam Books.

Flannery, Kathleen A., and Rena Walles. 2003. "How Does Schema Theory Apply to Real versus Virtual Memories." *CyberPsychology & Behavior* 6(2): 151–59.

Fowler, Linda L., and Jennifer L. Lawless. 2009. "Looking for Sex in All the Wrong Places: Press Coverage and the Electoral Fortunes of Gubernatorial Candidates." *Perspectives on Politics* 7(3): 519–36.

Fox, Richard L. 1997. *Gender Dynamics in Congressional Elections*. Thousand Oaks, CA: Sage.

———. 2000. "Gender and Congressional Elections" In Sue Tolleson-Rinehart and Jyl J. Josephson (Ed.), *Gender and American Politics: Women, Men, and the Political Process* (pp. 227–56). Armonk, NY: M. E. Sharpe.

———. 2010. "Congressional Elections: Women's Candidacies and the Road to Gender Parity." In Susan J. Carroll and Richard L. Fox (Eds.), *Gender and Elections: Shaping the Future of American Politics* (2nd ed., pp. 187–209). New York: Cambridge University Press.

Fox, Richard L. and Jennifer L. Lawless. 2011. "Gendered Perceptions and Political Candidacies: A Central Barrier to Women's Equality in Electoral Politics." *American Journal of Political Science* 55(1): 59–73.

Fox, Richard L., and Zoe M. Oxley. 2003. "Gender Stereotyping in State Executive Elections: Candidate Selection and Success." *Journal of Politics* 65(3): 833–50.

Fox, Richard L., and Eric Smith. 1998. "The Role of Candidate Sex in Voter Decision-Making." *Political Psychology* 19(2): 405–19.

Fridkin, Kim L., and Patrick J. Kenney. 2009. "The Role of Gender Stereotypes in U.S. Senate Campaigns." *Politics & Gender* 5: 301–24.

Fridkin, Kim L., Patrick J. Kenney, and Gina Serignese Woodall. 2009. "Bad for Men, Better for Women: The Impact of Stereotypes During Negative Campaigns." *Political Behavior* 31: 53–77.

Funk, Carolyn L. 1999. "Bringing the Candidate into Models of Candidate Evaluation." *Journal of Politics* 61: 700–720.

Gerrity, Jessica C., Tracy Osborn, and Jeanette Morehouse. 2007. "Women and Representation: A Different View of the District?" *Politics & Gender* 3(2): 179–200.

Gillespie, Diane, and Cassia Spohn. 1987. "Adolescents' Attitudes toward Women in Politics: The Effect of Gender and Race." *Gender and Society* 1(2): 208–18.

Glaser, Jack, and Peter Salovey. 1998. "Affect in Electoral Politics." *Personality and Social Psychology Review* 2: 156–72.

Goldberg, Philip. 1968. "Are Women Prejudiced against Women?" *Transaction* 5: 316–22.

Grossman, Michele, and Wendy Wood. 1993. "Sex Differences in Intensity of Emotional Experience: A Social Role Interpretation." *Journal of Personality and Social Psychology* 65: 1010–22.

Hamilton, David L., and Tina K. Trolier. 1986. "Stereotypes and Stereotyping: An Overview of the Cognitive Approach." In John Eovidio and Samuel L. Gaertner (Eds.), *Prejudice, Discrimination, and Racism* (pp. 127–263). Orlando, FL: Academic Press.

Hansen, Susan B., and Laura Wills Otero. 2006. "A Woman for U.S. President? Gender and Leadership Traits before and after 9-11." *Journal of Women, Politics & Policy* 28(1): 35–60.

Hayes, Danny. 2011. "When Gender and Party Collide: Stereotyping in Candidate Trait Attribution." *Politics & Gender* 7(2): 133–65.

Heilman, Madeline E. 1983. "Sex Bias in Work Settings: The Lack of Fit Model." In L. L. Cummings and B. M. Straw (Eds.), *Research in Organizational Behavior* (Vol. 5, pp. 269–98). Greenwich, CT: JAI.

———. 2001. "Description and Prescription: How Gender Stereotypes Prevent Women's Ascent Up the Organizational Ladder." *Journal of Social Issues* 57(4): 657–74.

Heilman, Madeline E., Aaron S. Wallen, Daniella Fuchs, and Melinda M. Tamkins. 2004. "Penalties for Success: Reactions to Women Who Succeed at Male Gender-Typed Tasks." *Journal of Applied Psychology* 89: 416–27.

Heldman, Caroline, Susan J. Carroll, and Stephanie Olson. 2005. "'She brought only a skirt': Print Media Coverage of Elizabeth Dole's Bid for the Republican Presidential Nomination." *Political Communication* 22(3): 315–35.

Herrnson, Paul S., J. Celeste Lay, and Atiya Kai Stokes. 2003. "Women Running 'as Women': Candidate Gender, Campaign Issues, and Voter-Targeting Strategies." *Journal of Politics* 65(1): 244–55.

Herrick, Rebekah, Jeanette Mendez, Sue Thomas, and Amanda Wilkerson. 2012. "Gender and Perceptions of Candidate Competency." *Journal of Women, Politics, & Policy* 33(2): 126–50.

Hess, Ursula, Reginald B. Adams, and Robert E. Kleck. 2005. "Who May Frown and Who Should Smile? Dominance, Affiliation, and Displays of Happiness and Anger." *Cognition and Emotion* 19(4): 515–36.

High-Pippert, Angela, and John Comer. 1998. "Female Empowerment: The

Influence of Women Representing Women." *Women and Politics* 19(4): 53–65.

Hitchon, Jacqueline C., Chingching Chang, and Rhonda Harris. 1997. "Should Women Emote? Perceptual Bias and Opinion Change in Response to Political Ads for Candidates of Different Genders." *Political Communication and Persuasion* 14: 49–69.

Huddy, Leonie, and Theresa Capelos. 2002. "Gender Stereotyping and Candidate Evaluation: Good News and Bad News for Women Politicians." In Victor C. Ottati, R. Scott Tindale, John Edwards, Fred B. Bryant, Linda Heath, Daniel C. O'Connell, Yolanda Suarez-Balcazar, and Emil J. Posavac (Eds.), *The Social Psychology of Politics* (pp. 29–53). New York: Kluwer Academic/Plenum Publishers.

Huddy, Leonie, and Nayda Terkildsen. 1993a. "The Consequences of Gender Stereotypes for Women Candidates at Different Levels and Types of Office." *Political Research Quarterly* 46(3): 503–25.

———. 1993b. "Gender Stereotypes and the Perception of Male and Female Candidates." *American Journal of Political Science* 37(1): 119–47.

Ilgen, D. R., and Youtz, M. A. 1986. "Factors Affecting the Evaluation and Development of Minorities in Organizations." In K. Rowland and G. Ferris (Eds.), *Research in Personnel and Human Resource Management: A Research Manual* (pp. 307–37). Greenwich, CT: JAI Press.

Irmen, Lisa. 2006. "Automatic Activation and Use of Gender Stereotypes." *Sex Roles* 55: 435–44.

Jackson, Linda. A., Linda A. Sullivan, and Carole N. Hodge. 1993. "Stereotype Effects on Attributions, Predictions, and Evaluations: No Two Social Judgments Are Quite Alike." *Journal of Personality and Social Psychology* 65: 69–84.

Jalalzai, F. 2006. "Women Candidates and the Media: 1992–2000 Elections." *Politics & Policy* 34(3): 606–33.

Jamieson, Kathleen Hall. 1995. *Beyond the Double Bind: Women and Leadership*. New York: Oxford University Press.

Johnson, Stefanie K., Susan E. Murphy, Selamawit Zewdie, and Rebecca J. Reichard. 2008. "The Strong, Sensitive Type: Effects of Gender Stereotypes and Leadership Prototypes on the Evaluation of Male and Female Leaders." *Organizational Behavior and Human Decision Processes* 106: 39–60.

Jost, John T., and Aaron Kay. 2005. "Exposure to Benevolent Sexism and Complementary Gender Stereotypes: Consequences for Specific and Diffuse Forms of System Justification." *Journal of Personality and Social Psychology* 88(3): 498–509.

Jussim, Lee, Lerita M. Coleman, and Lauren Lerch. 1987. "The Nature of Stereotypes: Comparison and Integration of Three Theories." *Journal of Personality and Social Psychology* 52(3): 536–46.

Kahn, Kim Fridkin. 1992. "Does Being Male Help? An Investigation of the Effects of Candidate Gender and Campaign Coverage on Evaluations of U.S. Senate Candidates." *Journal of Politics* 54: 497–517.

———. 1994. "Does Gender Make a Difference? An Experimental Examination of Sex Stereotypes and Press Patterns in Statewide Campaigns." *American Journal of Political Science* 38(1): 162–95.

———. 1996. *The Political Consequences of Being a Woman: How Stereotypes Influence the Conduct and Consequences of Political Campaigns.* New York: Columbia University Press.

Kahn, Kim Fridkin, and E. N. Goldenberg. 1991. "Women Candidates in the News: An Examination of Gender Differences in U.S. Senate Campaign Coverage." *Public Opinion Quarterly* 55(2): 180–99.

Kanter, Rosabeth Moss. 1977a. *Men and Women of the Corporation.* New York: Basic Books.

———. 1977b. "Some Effects of Proportions on Group Life: Skewed Sex Ratios and Responses to Token Women." *American Journal of Sociology* 82: 965–90.

Kelly, Janice, and Sarah L. Hutson-Corneux. 2000. "The Appropriateness of Emotional Expression in Women and Men: The Double-Bind of Emotion." *Journal of Social Behavior and Personality* 15(4): 515–28.

Kenski, Kate, and Erika Falk. 2004. "Of What Is that Glass Ceiling Made?" *Women & Politics* 26(2): 57–80.

Kinder, Donald R. 1986. "Presidential Character Revisited." In Richard R. Lau and David O. Sears (Eds.), *Political Cognition* (pp. 233–56). Hillsdale, NJ: Lawrence Erlbaum Associates.

King, David C., and Richard E. Matland. 2003. "Sex and the Grand Old Party: An Experimental Investigation of the Effect of Candidate Sex on Support for a Republican Candidate." *American Politics Research* 31: 595–612.

Knight, George P., Ivanna K. Guthrie, et al. 2002. "Emotional Arousal and Gender Differences in Aggression: A Meta-Analysis." *Aggressive Behavior* 28: 366–93.

Koch, Jeffrey W. 2000. "Do Citizens Apply Gender Stereotypes to Infer Candidates' Ideological Orientations?" *Journal of Politics* 62(2): 414–29.

———. 2002. "Gender Stereotypes and Citizens' Impressions of House Candidates' Ideological Orientations." *American Journal of Political Science* 46(2): 453–62.

Koenig, Anne M., Alice H. Eagly, Abigail A. Mitchell, and Tiina Ristikary. 2011. "Are Leader Stereotypes Masculine? A Meta-Analysis of Three Research Paradigms." *Psychological Bulletin* 127(4): 616–42.

Kornblut, Anne E. 2009. *Notes from the Cracked Ceiling: Hillary Clinton, Sarah Palin, and What It Will Take for a Woman to Win.* New York: Crown.

Kousser, Thad. 2005. *Term Limits and the Dismantling of State Legislative Professionalism.* New York: Cambridge University Press.

Kunda, Ziva. 1999. *Social Cognition: Making Sense of People*. Cambridge, MA: MIT Press.

Kunda, Ziva, and Kathryn C. Oleson. 1995. "Maintaining Stereotypes in the Face of Disconfirmation: Constructing Grounds for Subtyping Deviants." *Journal of Personality and Social Psychology* 68(4): 565–79.

Kunda, Ziva, and Bonnie Sherman-Williams. 1993. "Stereotypes and the Construal of Individuating Information." *Personality and Social Psychology Bulletin* 19: 90–99.

Kunda, Ziva, and Paul Thagard. 1996. "Forming Impression from Stereotypes, Traits, and Behaviors: A Parallel-Constraint-Satisfaction Theory." *Psychological Review* 103(2): 284–308.

Kunin, Madeleine. 1994. *Living a Political Life: One of America's First Woman Governors Tells Her Story*. New York: Random House.

———. 2008. *Pearls, Politics, and Power: How Women Can Win and Lead*. White River Junction, VT: Chelsea Green.

LaFrance, Marianne, and Marvin Hecht. 1999. "Option or Obligation to Smile: The Effects of Power and Gender on Facial Expression." In P. Phillipot, R. S. Feldman, and E. J. Coats (Eds.), *The Social Context of Nonverbal Behavior* (pp. 45–70). Cambridge: Cambridge University Press.

———. 2000. "Gender and Smiling: A Meta-Analysis." In Agneta M. Fischer (Ed.), *Gender and Emotion: Social Psychological Perspectives* (pp. 118–42). New York: Cambridge University Press.

Lawless, Jennifer. 2004. "Women, War, and Winning Elections: Gender Stereotyping in the Post-September 11th Era." *Political Research Quarterly* 57: 479–90.

———. 2012. *Becoming a Candidate: Political Ambition and the Decision to Run for Office*. New York: Cambridge University Press.

Lawless, Jennifer L., and Richard L. Fox. 2010. *It Still Takes a Candidate: Why Women Don't Run for Office*. New York: Cambridge University Press.

Lawless, Jennifer L., and Kathryn Pearson. 2008. "The Primary Reason for Women's Under-Representation: Re-evaluating the Conventional Wisdom." *Journal of Politics* 70(1): 67–82.

Lawrence, Regina G., and Melody Rose. 2010. *Hillary Clinton's Race for the White House: Gender Politics & the Media on the Campaign Trail*. Boulder, CO: Lynne Rienner.

Leeper, Mark. 1991. "The Impact of Prejudice on Female Candidates: An Experimental Look at Voter Inference." *American Politics Quarterly* 19: 248–61.

Lewis, Kathryn E., and Margaret Bierly. 1990. "Toward a Profile of the Female Voter: Sex Differences in Perceived Physical Attractiveness and Competence of Political Candidates." *Sex Roles* 22(1–2): 1–12.

Lewis, Kristi M. 2000. "When Leaders Display Emotion." *Journal of Organizational Behavior* 21: 221–34.

Lippa, Richard A. 2005. *Gender, Nature, and Nurture.* Mahwah, NJ: Lawrence Erlbaum Associates.

Locksley, Anne, Eugene Borgida, Nancy Brekke, and Christine Hepburn. 1980. "Sex Stereotypes and Social Judgment." *Journal of Experimental Social Psychology* 18: 23–42.

Locksley, Anne, Christine Hepburn, and Vilma Ortiz. 1982. "Social Stereotypes and Judgments of Individuals. *Journal of Experimental Social Psychology* 18(1): 23–42.

Lombardo, William K., Gary A. Cretser, Barbara Lombardo, and Sharon L. Mathis. 1983. "Fer Cryin' Out Loud - There Is a Sex Difference." *Sex Roles* 9: 987–95.

Lombardo, William K., Gary. A. Cretser, and Scott C. Roesch. 2001. "For Crying Out Loud: The Differences Persist into the '90s." *Sex Roles* 45(7–8): 529–47.

Mandel, Ruth. 2007. "She's the Candidate! A Woman for President." In Barbara Kellerman and Deborah L. Rhode (Eds.), *Women and Leadership: The State of Play and Strategies for Change* (pp. 283–307). San Francisco: John Wiley & Sons.

Marques, J. M., and D. Paez. 1994. "The 'Black Sheep Effect.'" In W. Stroebe and M. Hewstone (Eds.), *European Review of Social Psychology* (Vol. 5, pp. 37–68). West Sussex, England: Wiley.

McDermott, Monika L. 1997. "Voting Cues in Low-Information Elections: Candidate Gender as a Social Information Variable in Contemporary United States Elections." *American Journal of Political Science* 41(1): 270–83.

———. 1998. "Race and Gender Cues in Low-Information Elections." *Political Research Quarterly* 51(4): 895–918.

McGinley, Ann. 2009. "Hillary Clinton, Sarah Palin, and Michelle Obama: Performing Gender, Race, and Class on the Campaign Trail." *Denver University Law Review* 86: 709–25.

McGraw, Kathleen M. 2003. "Political Impressions: Formation and Management." In David O. Sears, Leonie Huddy, and Robert Jervis (Eds.), *Oxford Handbook of Political Psychology* (pp. 394–432). New York: Oxford University Press.

Milyo, J., and S. Schosberg. 2000. "Gender Bias and Selection Bias in House Elections." *Public Choice* 105(1–2): 41–59.

Miller, Arthur H., Martin P. Wattenberg, and O. Malunchuk. 1986. "Schematic Assessments of Presidential Candidates." *American Political Science Review* 80(2): 521–40.

Miller, Melissa K., Jeffrey S. Peake, and Brittany Anne Boulton. 2010. "Testing the Saturday Night Live Hypothesis: Fairness and Bias in Newspaper Coverage of Hillary Clinton's Presidential Campaign." *Politics & Gender* 6: 169–98.

Murray, Rainbow. 2010. *Cracking the Highest Glass Ceiling: A Global Comparison of Women's Campaigns for Executive Office*. Santa Barbara, CA: Praeger.

Mutz, Diana. 2011. *Population-Based Survey Experiments*. Princeton, NJ: Princeton University Press.

Myers, Dee Dee. 2008. "What Hillary Means for Women." *Vanity Fair*, February 26.

Neufeld, Derrick J., Zeying Wan, and Yulin Fang. 2010. "Remote Leadership, Communication Effectiveness, and Leader Performance." *Group Decision and Negotiation* 19(3): 227–46.

Niven, David, and Jeremy Zilber. 2001. "How Does She Have Time for Kids and Congress?" Views on Gender and Media Coverage from House Offices." *Women & Politics* 23(1): 147–65.

Nieva, Veronica F., and Barbara A. Gutek. 1980. "Sex Effects on Evaluation." *Academy of Management Journal* 5: 267–76.

Norton, Noelle H. 1999. "Uncovering the Dimensionality of Gender Voting in Congress." *Legislative Studies Quarterly* 24(1): 101–21.

O'Connor, Karen (Ed.). 2001. *Women and Congress: Running, Winning, and Ruling*. New York: Haworth Press.

Ogletree, Shirley Matile, Mary C. Coffee, and Shyla A. May. 1992. "Perceptions of Female/Male Presidential Candidates: Familial and Personal Situations." *Psychology of Women Quarterly* 16: 201–8.

O'Leary, Virginia E., and Ranald D. Hansen. 1984. "Sex as an Attributional Fact." In D. Levine (Ed.), *Nebraska Symposium on Motivation* (pp. 133–77). Lincoln: University of Nebraska.

Palmer, Barbara, and Dennis Simon. 2001. "The Political Glass Ceiling: Gender, Strategy, and Incumbency in U.S. House Elections, 1978–1998." In Karen O'Connor (Ed.), *Women and Congress: Running, Winning, and Ruling*. New York: Haworth Press.

Paul, David, and Jessi L. Smith. 2008. "Subtle Sexism? Examining Vote Preferences When Women Run against Men for the Presidency." *Journal of Women, Politics & Policy* 29(4): 451–76.

Pearson, Kathryn. 2010. "Demographic Change and the Future of Congress." *PS: Politcal Science and Politics* 43: 235–38.

Pearson, Kathryn, and Logan Dancey. 2011. "Speaking for the Underrepresented in the House of Representatives: Voicing Women's Interests in a Partisan Era." *Politics & Gender* 7: 493–519.

Peffley, Mark, and John Hurwitz. 1997. "Perceptions of Race and Crime: The Role of Racial Stereotypes." *American Journal of Political Science* 41(2): 375–401.

Pelosi, Nancy. 2008. *Know Your Power: A Message to America's Daughters*. New York: Doubleday.

Plant, E. Ashby, Janet Shibley Hyde, Dacher Keltner, and Patricia G. Devine. 2000. "The Gender Stereotyping of Emotions." *Psychology of Women Quarterly* 24: 81–92.

Prentice, Deborah A., and Erica Carranza. 2002. "What Women and Men Should Be, Shouldn't Be, Are Allowed to Be, and Don't Have to Be: The Contents of Prescriptive Gender Stereotypes." *Psychology of Women Quarterly* 26: 269–81.

———. 2003. "Sustaining Cultural Beliefs in the Face of Their Violation: The Case of Gender Stereotypes." In Mark Schaller, Christian S. Crandall, and Lucian Gideon Conway (Eds.), *The Psychological Foundations of Culture* (pp. 259–80). Mahwah, NJ: Lawrence Erlbaum Associates.

Reingold, Beth (Ed.). 2008. *Legislative Women: Getting Elected, Getting Ahead.* Boulder, CO: Lynne Rienner.

Riggle, Ellen D. B., Penny M. Miller, Todd G. Shields, and Mitzi M. S. Johnson. 1997. Gender Stereotypes and Decision Context in the Evaluation of Political Candidates. *Women & Politics* 17(3): 69–88.

Rivers, Douglas. 2006. "Sample Matching: Representative Sampling from Internet Panels." http://www.polimetrix.com/documents/Polimetrix_Whitepaper_Sample_Matching.pdf.

Rojahn, Krystyna, and Thomas F. Pettigrew. 1992. "Memory for Schema-Relevant Information: A Meta-Analytic Resolution." *British Journal of Social Psychology* 31: 81–109.

Rosenthal, Cindy Simon. 1995. "The Role of Gender in Descriptive Representation." *Political Research Quarterly* 48(3): 599–611.

Rosenwasser, Shirley M., and Norma G. Dean. 1989. "Gender Role and Political Office: Effects of Perceived Masculinity/Femininity of Candidate and Political Office." *Psychology of Women Quarterly* 13: 77–85.

Rosenwasser, Shirley M., Robyn R. Rogers, Sheila Fling, Kayla Silvers-Pickens, and John Butemeyer. 1987. "Attitudes toward Women and Men in Politics: Perceived Male and Female Candidate Competencies and Participant Personality Characteristics." *Political Psychology* 8(2): 191–200.

Rosenwasser, Shirley M., and Jana Seale. 1988. "Attitudes toward a Hypothetical Male or Female Presidential Candidate: A Research Note." *Political Psychology* 9(4): 591–98.

Rudman, Laurie A. 1998. "Self-Promotion as a Risk Factor for Women: The Costs and Benefits of Counterstereotypical Impression Management." *Journal of Personality and Social Psychology* 74: 629–45.

Rudman, Laurie A., and Peter Glick. 1999. "Feminized Management and Backlash toward Agentic Women: The Hidden Costs to Women of a Kinder, Gentler Image of Middle Managers." *Journal of Personality and Social Psychology* 77: 1004–10.

———. 2001. "Prescriptive Gender Stereotypes and Backlash toward Agentic Women." *Journal of Social Issues* 57(4): 743–62.

Rudman, Laurie A., and Julie E. Phelan. 2008. "Backlash Effects for Disconfirming Gender Stereotypes in Organizations." *Research in Organizational Behavior* 28: 61–79.

Rutherford, Andrew. 2001. *Introducing ANOVA and ANCOVA: A GLM Approach*. London: Sage.

Sanbonmatsu, Kira. 2002. "Gender Stereotypes and Vote Choice." *American Journal of Political Science* 46(1): 20–34.

———. 2006. *Where Women Run: Gender & Party in the American States*. Ann Arbor: University of Michigan Press.

Sanbonmatsu, Kira, and Kathleen Dolan. 2009. "Do Gender Stereotypes Transcend Party?" *Political Research Quarterly* 62(3): 485–94.

Sanders, David, Harold D. Clarke, Marianne C. Stewart, and Paul Whiteley. 2007. "Does Mode Matter for Modeling Political Choice? Evidence from the 2005 British Election Study." *Political Analysis* 15(3): 257–85.

Sapiro, Virginia. 1981–82. "If U.S. Senator Baker Were a Woman: An Experimental Study of Candidate Images." *Political Psychology* 3(1–2): 61–83.

Schroedel, Jean Reith, and Marcia L. Godwin. 2005. "Prospects for Cracking the Political Glass Ceiling: The Future of Women Officeholders in the Twenty-first Century." In Sue Thomas and Clyde Wilcox (Eds.), *Women and Elective Office: Past Present, and Future* (pp. 264–80). Oxford: Oxford University Press.

Seltzer, Richard A., Jody Newman, and Melissa Voorhees Leighton. 1997. *Sex as a Political Variable: Women as Candidates and Voters in U.S. Elections*. Boulder, CO: Lynne Rienner.

Shamir, Boas. 1995. "Social Distance and Charisma: Theoretical Notes and Exploratory Study." *Leadership Quarterly* 6: 19–47.

Shields, Stephanie A., and Kathleen A. MacDowell. 1987. " 'Appropriate' Emotion in Politics: Judgments of a Televised Debate." *Journal of Communication* 37(2): 78–89.

Sigelman, Carol C., Dan B. Thomas, Lee Sigelman, and Fredrick D. Ribich. 1986. "Gender, Physical Attractiveness and Electability." *Social Psychology Quarterly* 45: 263–69.

Sigelman, Lee, Carol Sigelman, and Christopher Fowler. 1987. "A Bird of a Different Feather? An Experimental Investigation of Physical Attractiveness and the Electability of Female Candidates." *Social Psychology Quarterly* 50: 32–43.

Sinclair, Lisa, and Ziva Kunda. 2000. "Motivated Stereotyping of Women: She's Fine if She Praised but Incompetent if She Criticized Me." *Personality and Social Psychology Bulletin* 26: 1329–42.

Slaughter, Anne-Marie. 2012. "Why Women Still Can't Have It All." *The Atlantic*, July–August.

Smith, Elizabeth S., Ashleigh Smith Powers, and Gustavo A. Suarez. 2005. "If

Bill Clinton Were a Woman: The Effectiveness of Male and Female Politicians' Account Strategies Following Alleged Transgressions." *Political Psychology* 26: 115–34.

Smith, Eric R. A. N., and Richard L. Fox. 2001. "The Electoral Fortunes of Women Candidates for Congress." *Political Research Quarterly* 54(1): 205–21.

Smith, Jessi L., David Paul, and Rachel Paul. 2007. "No Place for a Woman: Evidence for Gender Bias in Evaluations of Presidential Candidates." *Basic and Applied Social Psychology* 29(3): 225–33.

Smith, Kevin B. 1997. "When All's Fair: Signs of Parity in Media Coverage of Female Candidates." *Political Communication* 14(1): 71–82.

Spence, Janet Taylor, and Robert L. Helmreich. 1978. *Masculinity and Femininity: Their Psychological Dimensions, Correlates, and Antecedents.* Austin: University of Texas Press.

Stalsburg, Brittany L. 2010. "Voting for Mom: The Political Consequences of Being a Parent for Male and Female Candidates." *Politics & Gender* 6: 373–404.

Steele, Claude. M., and Joshua Aronson. 1995. "Stereotype Threat and the Intellectual Test Performance of African Americans." *Journal of Personality and Social Psychology* 69: 797–811.

Streb, Matthew, Barbara Burrell, Brian Frederick, and Michael Genovese. 2008. "Social Desirability Effects and Support for a Female American President." *Public Opinion Quarterly* 72(1): 76–89.

Swers, Michele L. 1998. "Are Women More Likely to Vote for Women's Issues Bills Than Their Male Colleagues?" *Legislative Studies Quarterly* 23(3): 435–48.

Swiss, Deborah J. 1996. *Women Breaking Through: Overcoming the Final 10 Obstacles at Work.* Princeton, NJ: Peterson/Pacesetter Books.

Tepper, Bennett J., Sheryl J. Brown, and Marilyn D. Hunt. 1993. "Strength of Subordinates upward Influence Tactics and Gender Congruency Effects." *Journal of Applied Social Psychology* 23: 1903–19.

Thomas, Sue. 1991. "The Impact of Women on State Legislative Policies." *Journal of Politics* 53(4): 958–76.

———. 1994. *How Women Legislate.* New York: Oxford University Press.

Thomas, Sue, and Clyde Wilcox. 2005. *Women and Elective Office: Past, Present, and Future.* New York: Oxford University Press.

Thompson, Seth, and Janie Steckenrider. 1997. "The Relative Irrelevance of Candidate Sex." *Women & Politics* 17(4): 71–92.

Tolleson-Rinehart, Sue, and Jyl J. Josephson (Ed.). 2000. *Gender and American Politics: Women, Men, and the Political Process.* Armonk, NY: M. E. Sharpe.

Traister, Rebecca. 2010. *Big Girls Don't Cry: The Election That Changed Everything for American Women.* New York: Free Press.

Tyler, James M., and Jennifer Dane McCullough. 2009. "Violating Prescriptive

Stereotypes on Resumes: A Self-Presentational Perspective." *Management Communication Quarterly* 23(2): 272–82.

Uhlaner, C., and Kay Lehman Schlozman. 1986. "Candidate Gender and Congressional Campaign Receipts." *Journal of Politics* 48(1): 30–50.

Verba, Sidney, Kay Lehman Schlozman, and Henry E. Brady. 1995. *Voice and Equality: Civic Volunteerism in American Politics*. Cambridge, MA: Harvard University Press.

Watson, Robert P., and Anne Gordon. 2003. *Anticipating Madam President*. Boulder, CO: Lynne Rienner.

Webber, R., and J. Crocker. 1983. "Cognitive Processes in the Revision of Stereotypical Beliefs." *Journal of Personality and Social Psychology* 45: 961–77.

Weikart, Lynne A., Greg Chen, Daniel W. Williams, and Haris Hromic. 2007. "The Democratic Sex: Gender Differences and the Exercise of Power." *Journal of Women, Politics, & Policy* 28(1): 119–40.

Werner, B. 1997. "Financing the Campaigns of Women Candidates and Their Opponents: Evidence from Three States, 1982–1990." *Women & Politics* 18(1): 81–97.

The White House Project. 2002. "Barriers and Opportunities: Results and Strategic Recommendations from Dial Groups." http://www.thewhitehouseproject.org/culture/researchandpolls/Barriers.php.

Whitney, Catherine, et al. 2001. *Nine and Counting: The Women of the Senate*. New York: HarperCollins.

Williams, John E., and Deborah L. Best. 1982. *Measuring Sex Stereotypes: A Thirty-National Study*. Beverly Hills, CA: Sage.

Winter, Nicholas. 2010. "Masculine Republicans and Feminine Democrats: Gender and Americans' Explicit and Implicit Images of Political Parties." *Political Behavior* 32: 587–618.

Witt, Linda, Karen M. Paget, and Glenna Matthews. 1995. *Running as a Woman: Gender and Power in American Politics*. New York: Free Press.

Yarkin, Kerry L., Jerri P. Town, and Barbara Strudler Wallston. 1982. "Blacks and Women Must Try Harder." *Personality and Social Psychology Bulletin* 8: 21–24.

INDEX

The letter *n* following a page number indicates a note on that page. The figure following the *n* indicates the number of the note if there is more than one on the page. Page numbers in italic type indicate a figure, map, or table on that page.